D0238368

LEEDS BE

Leeds Metropolitan University

17 0353973 3

# THE UNINVITED GUEST

# THE UNINVITED GUEST

Emerging from Narcissism
towards Marriage

*James V. Fisher*

*Foreword by*
Alberto Hahn

London
KARNAC BOOKS

First published in 1999 by
H. Karnac (Books) Ltd.
58 Gloucester Road
London SW7 4QY

© 1999 James V. Fisher and the Tavistock Institute of Medical Psychology

The rights of James V. Fisher to be identified as the author of this work have been asserted in accordance with §§ 77 and 78 of the Copyright Design and Patents Act 1988.

Extracts from *Complete Poems and Plays of T.S. Eliot* reproduced by permission of Faber & Faber Ltd.

Extracts from *Marriage: Studies in Emotional Conflict and Growth*, edited by Lily Pincus, reproduced by permission of the Tavistock Marital Studies Institute, London.

Cover illustration, *Baco*, by Enrique Torrijos, reproduced by kind permission of Enate Vineyard, Sala Bajas, Spain.

All rights reserved. No part of this publication may be reproduced, stored in a retrieval system, or transmitted, in any form or by any means, electronic, mechanical, photocopying, recording, or otherwise, without the prior written permission of the publisher.

**British Library Cataloguing in Publication Data**

A C.I.P for this book is available from the British Library

ISBN 1 85575 196 8

10 9 8 7 6 5 4 3 2 1

Edited, designed, and produced by Communication Crafts

Printed in Great Britain by Polestar Wheatons Ltd, Exeter

LEEDS METROPOLITAN
UNIVERSITY
LEARNING CENTRE
1703554
CC-31818
155.645 FIS

For that gracious couple whom I have and have not lost

Esther Chapman Fisher, my mother

and in memory of

George Clinton Fisher, my father

*O, alas!*
*I lost a couple, that 'twixt heaven and earth*
*Might thus have stood, begetting wonder, as*
*You, gracious couple, do.*

Shakespeare, *The Winter's Tale*, V.i.130-133

JAMES FISHER takes his title from the mysterious psychiatric figure of T. S. Eliot's play, *The Cocktail Party*. He identifies himself with this theatrical representation of a "marital therapist" in order to conduct his own review of what he convincingly tells us is Eliot's internal account of his first marriage, to Vivienne Haigh-Wood. It forms the centre-piece of his book. He does it from the vantage point of a distinguished marital psychoanalytic psychotherapist who is as willing to delve into English literature as he is into the psychoanalytic literature. The reader of this book will get the benefit of his considerable knowledge and enthusiasm for both.

He begins with Shakespeare's· *The Winter's Tale* and ends with *Othello* in an account of the vicissitudes of marriage to illuminate his central thesis, which is that in intimate relationships there is a struggle and oscillation: "*narcissism ↔ marriage*". In-between, in addition to the chapters on *The Cocktail Party*, he reviews published pioneering marital work in order to throw light on his current practice and his view of marital disturbance. Both in the literary and clinical contexts, these are troubled waters, and James Fisher is not one to dangle his toes in them—he plunges in and invites us to plunge in after him. He manages to expound his and various analytic writers' ideas on human relationships in a clear and scholarly way whilst keeping the reader in touch with the passion, suffering, and horror that is its raw material. Literature carefully analysed suits this purpose admirably. Whilst outlining his thesis of the eternal tension between narcissism and object love in marriage, he reminds us that the ultimate possessive act is murder, as celebrated in a poem by T. S. Eliot, *The Love Song of St. Sebastian*.

*Ronald Britton*
*Training and Supervising Analyst,*
*British Psycho-Analytical Society*

\* \* \*

THIS IS a fascinating, complex, and imaginative book. James Fisher brings together a deep thoughtfulness about the insights of psycho-analysis and its application to work with troubled couples with an original and closely argued reading of some classic plays about marriage. Shakespeare's *The Winter's Tale* and Eliot's *The Cocktail Party* both concern the reunion of a husband and a lost wife. These marriages have been damaged, Fisher argues, as a consequence of narcissistic withdrawal from engagement with the "otherness" of the other. Marriage is hauntingly described as the "inheritor of the tension and the intimacy of the Oedipal drama", and it is this fact that makes the marital relationship such a potent place for therapeutic inter-vention, as well as for exploration in the drama. The history of psycho-analytic work with couples in the Tavistock Marital Studies Institute and its precursors sets the scene for this *tour de force* of clinical and theoretical thinking. The book will give pleasure and much food for thought to readers interested in psychoanalysis and literature. It should enrich both clinical practice and our experience of theatre.

*Margaret Rustin*
*Consultant Child Psychotherapist,*
*Dean of Postgraduate Studies, Tavistock & Portman Clinics*

\* \* \*

JAMES FISHER is a gifted and imaginative thinker and teacher. His writing is soundly rooted in a profound love of the clinical work and is a reflection of his honest and sometimes relentless search after the truth. His fascination for the darker dynamics of the couple relation-ship—envy, jealousy, betrayal, and abandonment—and the corre-sponding challenge to the "self" of the therapist is a thread through all his work.

In contemporary society, with its changing pattern of marriage, the subject is of profound interest and importance. The psychic centrality of "marriage" is irrefutable; we are endlessly fascinated by it and its vicissitudes. This book is timely in reflecting the present preoccupa-tion with the question of what it really means to move into marriage, to encounter the other and the self in the other.

Fisher's use of "the play" and "the story" as vehicles for this ex-ploration captures the imagination in a way that standard textbooks cannot do and makes reflection and reverie on the subject irresistible.

This is a profound yet accessible book of interest to clinicians and non-clinicians alike. Marital therapists will find it a welcome addition to their libraries.

Gillian Walton
Director of Training and Clinical Services,
London Marriage Guidance

* * *

FROM THE very first paragraph, I felt like an invited guest at a wonderfully exciting dinner-party given by Fisher. He invites the reader to join literary figures—Shakespeare and Eliot—and psychoanalysts—Freud, Klein, Bion, and Meltzer, to name just a few—in thinking with him. The book is very creative in style, and I doubt that there is another volume like it. The use of *The Winter's Tale*, *The Cocktail Party*, and *Othello* as vehicles towards understanding narcissism, marriage, and the role of the couples therapist reminds me of Tom Stoppard's use of a story within a story to make the experience both intellectually and emotionally meaningful. Like marriage itself, Fisher brings readers to new places and at the same times reminds them of old, familiar scenes.

*The Uninvited Guest* is wonderful to read at many levels. I found the book enjoyable and useful from the very first chapter on for working with individuals as well as couples. I particularly like the stretching of the mind to think about psychoanalytic theory, playwrights, literature, and couples, integrating them as a couple therapist has to integrate the couples' histories, their stories, and the here-and-now of what is going on in a session. I look forward to using it in teaching couples therapists.

Joyce Lowenstein
Vice Chair,
Psychoanalytic Object Relations Family & Couple
Psychotherapy Training Program,
Washington School of Psychiatry, Washington DC

# CONTENTS

# ACKNOWLEDGEMENTS

This book has had a long gestation, as those who have awaited its delivery know all too well. During that time, it has taken on a life and mind of its own—or so it feels to me. As if trying to keep track of that process, I have written a "preface" numerous times, the first one soon after I completed a sample chapter as a proposal to potential publishers. This impulse to shape and reshape a "pre-face" has now run its course. The book has the face that it has. And the time has arrived for me to let go of it, and, what is more difficult, to insist that it let go of me. It is a time when I can acknowledge publicly those people who have been important in the various stages of its complex evolution, thanking them, but without a Leontean imputation of parentage to them. That is, it is time to let it go, but without disowning it.

Of the many transformations in the shape of the book, the final form only emerged as we entered 1998 when the idea of opening with *The Winter's Tale* began to be irresistible. This play had been on my mind increasingly as a consequence of my renewed interest in the writings of the American philosopher Stanley Cavell, a teacher whose lectures had fascinated me as a graduate student. His ideas

xi

only began to take hold of my imagination, however, as I read several of his more recent books in the high hills of the Garfagnana in north Tuscany during the previous summer.

Having already decided to conclude the book by using Shakespeare's *Othello* to explore thoughts about termination in psychoanalytic therapy with couples, I found that Cavell's unusual reading of *The Winter's Tale*, linked with his similarly provocative reading of *Othello*, began to illuminate for me the dynamic tensions between narcissism and intimate relationships in a new way. The use of these two plays complemented, indeed seemed a natural outgrowth of, my exploration of T. S. Eliot's play *The Cocktail Party*, which already formed the central chapters of the book. For the record, Eliot's play had caught my attention when I came across R. D. Laing's intriguing reference to it while looking at research he did on couple relationships in conjunction with the Family Discussion Bureau (FDB) at the Tavistock back in the 1950s (Laing, Phillipson, & Lee, 1966). Had I not had the good fortune subsequently to become acquainted with Lyndall Gordon's two-volume biography (1977, 1988) of Eliot, however, I do not think this little-appreciated play would have come alive in my mind as a picture of the couple and their "therapist", their "uninvited guest". T. S. Eliot's writings have been critical for the illustration of many of the ideas in this book, and I hope that reading it might take the reader back to this poet with a new interest in the human being who reveals himself more than he disguises himself in his work, especially his plays and early poems.

Some years ago, my wife, Mary, drew me into her fascination with writing and writers, introducing me to, among other things, that remarkable collection of interviews in the volumes of *Writers at Work: The Paris Review Interviews* (Plimpton, 1963). It is interesting to me how so many writers talk about being a vehicle, an amanuensis, recording what comes through, not from, them. Classically the picture has been of the Muses, the goddesses of memory and poetic inspiration, as the source of what one writes. I find it an uncanny experience now to be reflecting on the process of my own writing, in particular writing something that seems continually to break free of the leash of (conscious) intention. Usually, in my experience, a paper or a lecture is tightly constrained by a subject and/or an occasion. Perhaps a book is not so easily held to task. At least, this book has not been held to the task as I had envisaged it. Without trying to evade responsibility for what I have written, it nevertheless feels in some ways as if this book has written itself. Looking back, I can find no point at which I imagined that it would have the form that it now has.

For example, I am no longer sure whether this is a book about marriage, or narcissism, or psychoanalysis, or therapy with couples—and perhaps in the end it is not for me to say what it is about. Leontes agonizes, "is whispering nothing?" I think I have begun at last to give up trying to respond to those whispering internal voices challenging me: what are you doing? Intention is not nothing, that is true. But more and more it seems painfully clear to me with regard to writing, and with many other areas of life as well, that intention, conscious intention, is not the everything we might wish, or fear, it to be.

* * *

The approach described in this book is rooted in a long tradition in the Tavistock Marital Studies Institute (TMSI) of the application of psychoanalysis to thinking about and working therapeutically with the adult intimate couple relationship. Founded over half a century ago as the Family Discussion Bureau, this institution has played an important part in the development of a psychoanalytic interest in couples. Its history is traced and discussed by Stanley Ruszczynski in *Psychotherapy with Couples: Theory and Practice at the Tavistock Institute of Marital Studies* (Ruszczynski, 1993).

My book, however, is not about the TMSI, nor does it pretend in any way to speak for the Institute, although I am pleased that it is included in the Karnac series of TMSI publications. Even now I vividly recall the moment at the beginning of 1993 when, as a TMSI staff member, I decided to write a systematic account of contemporary psychoanalytic psychotherapy with couples. It was a rather audacious ambition, and sensibly therefore I approached another TMSI staff member, Diana Daniell, to persuade her to join me in this project. She was the first Organising Tutor of the Institute's intensive training in psychoanalytic psychotherapy with couples, and I was able to gain much from her experience as a teacher and supervisor. We were already working together then as co-therapists and began regular weekly discussions specifically aimed at developing the ideas and collecting the material for the book. Her enthusiasm for the project never flagged, even when the book began to depart from our detailed outline and her relation to the book changed. She has carefully read all the chapters as they emerged, and her challenging and incisive comments have been important to me. I am grateful to her for the many ways in which she has contributed to this book.

For three of those years of work together towards the book, Diana and I had direct financial and institutional support from TMSI. For this "seedbed" I want to thank the Institute and especially Christopher Clulow, its Director, and Stanley Ruszczynski, who at that time was Deputy Director. In addition I want to acknowledge the encouragement and friendship of all my other TMSI colleagues who have helped me understand something of the dynamics of relationships. A list of names does not seem adequate to convey my indebtedness to each of them for the specific ways in which they have been important to me. I hope the book itself will be taken as an expression of my gratitude to them for the different ways in which they have contributed to its evolution.

Four TMSI colleagues, Christopher Clulow, Francis Grier, Dorothy Judd, and Mary Morgan, read early versions of some chapters and took time to make helpful comments. Both the comments and the encouragement were very important to me. Also Noel Hess, an old friend and colleague, read the literary chapters and his knowledgeable criticisms helped to clarify my own thinking.

I would also like to thank the internal and external students at TMSI who allowed me to learn from and with them. Many of them now form the core of the Society of Psychoanalytical Marital Psychotherapists (SPMP), working imaginatively to strengthen this relatively undeveloped area of psychoanalytic psychotherapy. To be quite candid, they were one of the most vivid audiences in my mind as I wrote this book, always raising the difficult questions, insisting on clarification, wanting to see the links with what goes on in the consulting-room. Others from whom I have learned much include those child psychotherapists who were in my marital therapy seminars as part of the post-qualification training for psychotherapy with adults at the Tavistock Clinic. They were among the first to read some of these chapters, and their insightful comments encouraged me to develop my thinking further.

Other material in this book had its origin in various public presentations, and I want to acknowledge my gratitude for those opportunities. For example, much of the discussion in chapter seven was originally presented at a TMSI Autumn Conference. Material from chapters two and twelve was presented at an Annual Study Day of the SPMP. Other material now scattered through the book was originally presented at occasions in Washington, DC, organized by the Washington School of Psychiatry and by the International Institute for Object Relations Therapy. It has been a special pleasure to be able to work with a number of these Washington friends here in London as well, and I want especially to acknowledge the many thought-provoking exchanges with Carolyn Ericson, Joyce Lowenstein, Kent Ravenscroft, David and Jill Scharff, Pamela Sorenson, Robert Winer, and John Zinner, to name but a few.

The ideas in the chapters on the "Webbs" and the chapters on *The Cocktail Party* I have discussed in workshops over several years at the London Marriage Guidance (LMG), and I want to acknowledge the friendly and productive links with Gillian Walton and Judy Cunnington. I was also able to develop my thoughts on *The Cocktail Party* in a lively workshop discussion sponsored by the West Kent Pastoral Association. And I have benefited from clinical discussions over a couple of years now with the psychotherapy workshop organized by Clara Lew in Cambridge at the Addenbrookes Hospital. For all of those occasions, I would like to thank not only the organizers but also the participants, who may recognize some of their own ideas transmuted in my voice in the pages that follow.

It gives me particular pleasure to acknowledge the enthusiasm of two counsellors at LMG, Jane Seymour and Neville Jason, both of whom are also experienced professionals in the theatre world. They made possible an unusual combination of a play reading of *The Cocktail Party* and a dramatized conversation with T. S. Eliot using some of his early poetry. Jane was production manager organizing the event, and Neville both directed and acted in it, having first directed this Eliot play professionally some time previously. Neville was also responsible for gathering a cast of fellow professional actors, who delighted the full house at the Tavistock Centre in June 1998 with a remarkably gripping performance: David Timson, Max Wilson, Daisy Donovan, Benjamin Soames, and Karen Archer. I was tempted to try to find a way to include a recording of their performance with this book, but I will have to be satisfied with thanking all those involved for bringing Eliot's play to life in a way that would, I am sure, have delighted TSE himself.

I also want to note with pleasure and gratitude two readers who have followed the emergence of each chapter with careful scrutiny and thoughtful comments, suggestions, and criticisms. As readers they have been more important than I think they realize, especially since I was not always in a good mood when told that something was obscure or unnecessary. However, in other ways I am sure Barbara Swinyard and Molly Beswick know how much I treasure their continuing encouragement and enthusiasm for the book.

Also among those people who have been important personally to me in the evolution of this book, I want to mention Professor Carol Black of the Royal Free Hospital. It was when I was a guest (not uninvited) on one of her wards that the idea of this book was conceived. And it is largely through her care, along with members of her team at the Free, including Dr Christopher Denton and many others, that I have missed only a few days of work since that day in December 1990 when, as a stranger, she introduced me, in the most kind and gentle way, to the realities of a new stage of my life. This book is one way of saying "thank you" to her and her colleagues.

* * *

With particular delight I want to acknowledge the kind generosity of Señor Louis Geinaerdt of Enate, a firm that both produces Spanish wine and also commissions work by contemporary artists. Through his efforts, we were able to use the painting *Baco* by Enrique Torrijos on the cover of the book. The artist was reported to have said that it represents Bacchus and an amphora of wine, smiling because it contains the finest wine in the world. It was Mary's idea to approach Enate to try to get permission to use it on the cover, and it is a painting that continues to give us endless delight in picturing the complex ambiguities of the "container–contained" relationship. Who is holding what for whom, or what is holding whom?

Again it is a pleasure to acknowledge my gratitude to Eric and Klara King, whose facility and care in the task of copy editing and whose unfailing patience with a fretful author expedited the last stages of the book. I also want to acknowledge the skill and ingenuity of Malcolm Smith in creating the cover design. Above all, I want to express my gratitude to Cesare Sacerdoti and Graham Sleight of Karnac Books for their faith in this book from first proposal, throughout its prolonged evolution and many changes, to its rapid and timely appearance once the manuscript was approved.

\* \* \*

For me, the people most critical in the writing of the book are those whose thinking has been resonating irresistibly in my mind. In terms of the genesis of the ideas in this book, I have already mentioned Stanley Cavell whose provocative writings on a wide variety of topics from marriage to scepticism to psychoanalysis have taken a hold on my imagination. They seem to link, in a way that I do not fully understand, with the writings of the other thinker who more than any other person shapes my thinking, and not just in this writing project. To my mind, Donald Meltzer has taken forward the development of psychoanalysis, in a succession he traces from Freud to Abraham to Klein to Bion, in ways that are only beginning to be appreciated. I do not want to try here to assess that contribution, only to mark my appreciation for the work of Donald Meltzer, someone from whom I learn something new on each encounter with his creative thinking and clinical acumen. The reader will see throughout the book how much I value his ideas and particularly his sensibilities.

It has been helpful for me that I have been able for a long time to discuss these ideas, in the context of my own personal struggles, with someone on whose thoughtfulness, clarity, and good sense I have come to depend. I am especially pleased that Alberto Hahn agreed to write the Foreword to this book, since I am grateful to him for what grounding in the discipline of psychoanalysis I have, as well as, I would want to add, for much of the grounding in my life.

This most intriguing of conversations, as Donald Meltzer once characterized it, was preceded many years ago by one that extended over several years with Mrs Sadie Gillespie. I would wish her to know of my appreciation for the way she attended to my early, faltering steps towards an understanding of psychoanalysis, and through it towards an understanding of myself.

\* \* \*

Left to last is a person who has been intimately involved in the evolution of these ideas and in the details of their formulation. If writing
has intense reverberations with what is most personal and private,
writing about narcissism, marriage, and psychoanalysis creates particularly intense reverberations. As in psychoanalytic therapy with
individuals or couples, it opens one to new dimensions of "taking
part", of being a *part-ner*. This is even more the case where the thinking is shared at the intersection of the personal and the professional,
where the discussions are with one who is both colleague and
spouse, a *partner* in both senses.

Mary, my wife, has made this, in so many ways, more the book
I wanted it to be. Her detailed editing and creative suggestions are
in evidence on virtually every page—and in the excised pages and
chapters you will not see. In an important sense, the book is a tran-
scription of a dialogue in my mind with the many people I have
mentioned, a dialogue that became an actual dialogue between Mary
and me. I want to acknowledge how much this has been a shared
project from beginning to end, but not, as Eliot would have it, as
lovers "Who think the same thoughts without need of speech / And
babble the same speech without need of meaning" (Eliot, 1969). No,
it has been more that her ideas grafted onto my voice, or my ideas
grafted on to hers, are like Perdita's gillyvors. I do not share Leontes'
anxiety that it (he meant the child and I mean this book) has too
much of her in it. Nor do I think the ideas "bastards", in their having
more than one parent. (The first chapter on *The Winter's Tale* will, I
trust, help make sense of these obscure allusions.)

\* \* \*

I have not yet mentioned a group of people who were vital to this
project, the couples and individuals I have seen in psychoanalytic
therapy. The clinical material in this book has been disguised in
ways that are intended to protect the confidentiality of the work and
the anonymity of all those involved, with, of course, one obvious
exception. I want here to express my gratitude to those who have
shared with me some of the most intimate moments that are possible
to us as human beings. There is little I can say that feels adequate
except "thank you".

If you do read this book, those of you who have shared the experiences of therapy with me, I hope you will read it neither as person-

ally addressed to you, nor in fact about you in particular. You will understand, I trust, on the basis of the relationship we have had, that if I make reference in this book to experiences that you shared with me in the privacy of therapy, that I do so in the same spirit in which I take those experiences to my colleagues, supervisors, and analyst for their help in thinking and understanding. I have used these experiences in an effort to help myself and others in the shared quest for understanding. And that is also in part why I have not asked your permission to use those experiences in this book, why I have chosen not to impose on you what I believe is my work and responsibility. What is most truly private between you and me I cannot, and will not, speak of—intimacies for which there are no adequate words, feelings that lie restlessly at the core of our souls and in our shared memories.

* * *

It must be obvious that none of the people I have mentioned should be held responsible for the final content of this book. In spite of helpful comments from many readers, there remain, I am all too aware, suggestions not accepted, questions left unclarified, hobbyhorses not abandoned. But I have gone on revising right up to the last moment of copy editing, and I can see it is time to let go.

Finally, I would like to share something of the mood in which I (wish to) have written this book. I am thinking of an image to which I referred in a recent paper to be published by Karnac Books as a *Festschrift* to Donald Meltzer on his seventy-fifth birthday. In it, I described that enchanting scene

> . . . in the film version of Michael Ondaatje's *The English Patient* when the nurse Hana, who has been tenderly nursing the English patient for whom she feels something indefinably like love, steps out into the night. There she finds a candle, then another at some distance, and another, and another, innumerable lights in the dark of the garden, following them, almost dancing in rising expectation until she comes to where Kip, the Sikh sapper, waits. Then on his motor bike to the church in town where in the dark shadows of the cavernous space he hoists her on a sling at the end of a rope coming from the distant dark ceiling. Then the torch in her hand as she is swung from wall to wall, each approach illuminating details of a medieval mural, then swinging away to another wall.

That was an invitation. It is so engaging that we might overlook the intensity of Kip's experience as he anticipates, but cannot know, how Hana will respond. The intercourse is a constant back and forth in the reciprocity of giver and receiver. There are no doubt moments in which each can identify with the other, an acceptance of the invitation to visit in imagination the mind of the other. But it is *in imagination*, not in the certainty of identification. The underlying mood is freedom, the freedom of coming together and moving apart.

Does this suggest that, in some sense, one must *love* the psychoanalytic method, as Hana seems already to love Kip and thus is receptive to the candles he lights? Perhaps so. She must, at least, be curious enough to follow his candles far enough to find out what she feels. In any case, this is to my mind a picture of the way I would invite you, the reader, lighting a candle, and another, and another, hoping you will follow my invitation. It is only an invitation, not to an identification with me or my perspective, but to an intercourse with my thoughts, my observations.

Or, in the words of the quotation that Stanley Cavell uses on the title page of his book *The Claim of Reason*,

"Truly speaking, it is not instruction, but provocation, that I can receive from another soul." — Ralph Waldo Emerson, 1838

You will have to decide for yourself whether what follows is a provocation, or an inviting candle, or both, or neither. My hope is that some of the ideas in this book might "mate" with those in your mind, and the result might be ideas that are not the same as mine, nor the same as those with which you began. Although those ideas will not be identical with those that gave rise to them, I can hope some family resemblance may be seen.

*James V. Fisher*
March 1999

# FOREWORD

## Alberto Hahn
British Psycho-Analytical Society

If, as Bion suggests, the acceptance of truth in psychic reality is an indispensable requirement for growth and for the development of intimate relationships, we know all too well from our analytic work that in narcissism, and other developmental failures, obstacles are thrown up that mar our analytic enquiry and the possibility of progress. For this reason, these obstacles deserve our detailed attention, and, from an object-related point of view, we need to focus on the way in which internal object-relations are organized and structured, and on how they appear in the external world. The harvest of examples from the arts, case histories, and personal experiences show, as they do in this book, how inroads can be made into the investigation of truth avoidance and hence into the poverty of development.

Clearly, psychic reality deals with intrapsychic facts, and these may or may not match facts in external reality: drawing an *a priori* distinction between internal and external is meant to allow us as analysts not to be swayed or influenced by the same confusion that afflicts our patients. This confusion, a sign of projective identification which often leads to fanatic states of mind—something that James

Fisher clearly shows us in the characters of Leontes and Othello—
carries the seeds of the relentless destructiveness of the personality
and, ultimately, of life itself.

These and other issues are addressed here in a manner that extracts, from the multi-layered complexity of the "couple as patient",
those points that are relevant to the discovery of psychic reality in
the presence of an analytic figure. The context is the marital situation, which suggests a relationship in which both members feel that
something of value, worthwhile preserving and protecting, is generated by this association. The nature and meaning of this association,
the kind of enrichment created by "being in a couple", and the protection or not of these values—children, home, affects—cover the
whole area of internal object relations and lead us very naturally into
an understanding of the individual character and of the importance
of destructive impulses towards primary internal objects.

In his comprehensive discussion of the conditions for the observation of marital interaction, Fisher not only emphasizes the importance of the analytic availability to unconscious phenomena on the
part of the therapist, but also implies the desirability of retaining
both "memory and desire" in order to concentrate on a particular
(marital) focus, to recreate a historical pattern of development, and
to produce formulations as working hypotheses. These tasks, which
are not very different from those used by practitioners of individual
focal psychotherapy with the aim of carrying the process forward,
probably mark the one big difference between psychoanalytic work
with couples and that done with individuals. Psychotherapeutic interventions in psychoanalysis are geared towards a search for truth
that is of interest to both analyst and patient, even when they may
have different individual motives for this pursuit. This paradoxical
"truth with an agenda" and the application of psychoanalytic concepts provide signposts that help further this enquiry.

The natural history of the process described in this book starts
with the question of what brings couples to therapy, and it does not
end until the establishment of mourning in the denouement of the
analytic process. It is within this range that we might think further
about the nature of the transference and introjective processes, both
in the heat of a full-blown individual transference (which gets analysed and is worked through over a period of time at a pre-genital

and later whole-object level) and in the process that arises in the complex interaction of a threesome or a foursome.

These issues were actively discussed in the Marital Unit of the Adult Department of the Tavistock Clinic to which I belonged in the late 1960s and 1970s. It was composed mainly of enthusiastic psychoanalysts, candidates, senior social workers, and clinical assistants who followed the exacting psychoanalytic standards of its chairman, Dr Pierre Turquet. These were stimulating and inspiring times, when marital therapy was still considered the ugly duckling of the psychotherapeutic world. The clinical and theoretical discussions and cross-reference with the Family Discussion Bureau (now the Tavistock Marital Studies Institute) developed an area of investigation and clinical work which proved to be very fertile. The period under Dr Henry Dicks' chairmanship, followed by that of Dr Turquet, saw the heyday of the Marital Unit, and it is indeed surprising that so little written work came out of it, a situation that persists to this day.

Therefore, one cannot stress enough the value of the book you are about to read. In it, various marriages of ideas, observations, and comments are woven with substance and credibility into the fabric of a truly Kleinian psychoanalytic nosology for marital work. The text moves gracefully between psychoanalytic interpretations of literary texts and clinical experience, opening up for us rich and unexpected vistas of familiar landscapes.

# THE UNINVITED GUEST

# CHAPTER ONE

# The Winter's Tale:
# marriage and re-marriage

Let's begin with a tale, a tale of hateful jealousy and suspicion, as well as, one might say, a tale of remarriage. But why begin there? Not all of the couples who seek therapy by any means suffer the kind of jealousy and doubts that plague Leontes in Shakespeare's *The Winter's Tale*. Nor would I suggest that the experience of couples in therapy can always be described as a process of "emerging from narcissism towards marriage", to reiterate the subtitle of this book. Juxtaposing these states, *narcissism* and *marriage*, in polar opposition may seem puzzling. And yet that is just what I mean to do throughout this book, to set in opposition *narcissism* and *marriage*, in ways perhaps familiar and unfamiliar. Adapting Bion's notation, we could then picture "*narcissism* ↔ *marriage*" as a fundamental human tension.

By *marriage*, I mean to emphasize the passion for and dependence on the intimate other. By *narcissism*, on the other hand, I do not mean a preoccupation with the self, a kind of self-love. Rather, I mean to point to a kind of object relating in which there is an intolerance for the reality, the independent existence of the other. Narcissism in this sense is in fact a longing for an other, but a longing for an other who

1

is perfectly attuned and responsive, and thus not a genuine other at all.

But why then a tale of re-marriage? Couples seeking therapy are not usually literally exploring the issue of remarriage—although a number of couples I have in mind do describe their therapy as a quest to discover whether re-marriage is desirable, even possible. In that, I think they make explicit what I believe can in a sense be said of all couples who engage in the psychoanalytic process *as a couple*. That is, "re-marriage" is the issue. And this is true whether or not the couple is married in the eyes of the state, engaged to be married, or separated after many years. And it is true even when the aim is to separate. There is no good divorce that is not at the same time a marriage in the sense of a relationship that is not completely distorted by the narcissism of each partner, especially when there are children.

But, finally, why the telling of a *tale*? Because—and this is perhaps the most important observation about the book that you have in your hands—it is not meant as an explanation, either of marriage or of therapy, even though it may sometimes, despite my best efforts, sound as if it were. Even if it were possible, I think there would be no value in trying to reduce the complexities of the painful conflicts and dilemmas that couples bring to therapy to some formula. Rather, my intent is to offer a point of view, an understanding of narcissism, defined not as a preoccupation and investment in the self as opposed to others, but as states of mind in which the reality of the other is attacked, undermined, and denied. I have chosen *The Winter's Tale* as a beginning because it is a tale of narcissistic rage and jealousy. At least that is one way of reading Shakespeare's play—just as it can, plausibly I think, be read as a romance of remarriage. At the end, a husband and a wife are reunited (as are two childhood friends alienated by jealousy) by the "falling-in-love-towards-marriage" of just those two children who at times occasioned their respective fathers' jealous rage and rejection.

In this opening chapter, I want briefly to recount Shakespeare's *Winter's Tale*. Perhaps because its chilling narcissistic rage reminded me of so many sessions with so many couples trapped in something they felt they could neither comprehend, nor escape, nor endure. Recounting this tale will allow me to introduce this theme of emergence from narcissism towards "re-marriage". Hopefully it will become clearer in subsequent chapters why I view the enterprise of psychoanalytic therapy with couples as an exploration of the possibility of remarriage, even, as I said, when the couple seek and hope finally to separate in the end. Separation and marriage are, paradoxically, inseparable.

Interestingly, although it was not in my mind when I selected T. S. Eliot's play *The Cocktail Party* as the illustrative story for the central portion of this book, it too is a tale of "re-marriage". Not only does this theme resonate autobiographically throughout the play, it is also the case, as Eliot himself suggested, that *The Cocktail Party* was based on Euripides' play *Alcestis*, a drama that turns on the reunion of the king Admetus with Alcestis his wife after she had been brought back from the dead by Heracles. It only consciously dawned on me long after having written my commentaries on the Eliot and Shakespeare plays that this theme of the reunion of a husband and his lost wife— call it *re-marriage*—is central to both plays.

Finally, these opening comments would not be complete without a brief remark about the *uninvited guest* of the title of the book. When we turn to Eliot's play *The Cocktail Party* in chapter eight, the source of this image will come more clearly into view. Even in *The Winter's Tale* there is a role for someone who is both an ambiguous player in the drama, and yet stands in a unique position as one who is neither entirely welcome nor invited. This equivocal "insider" appears to choreograph what happens, making it possible for the other participants to see what they might otherwise never see. The unidentified guest, Sir Henry Harcourt-Reilly, at the eponymous cocktail party of Eliot's play is indeed a "therapist" (of some sort). Paulina, Hermione's lady-in-waiting in *The Winter's Tale*, who progressively takes centre stage as the one who facilitates Leontes' facing the consequences of his narcissistic rage, is not, on any plausible reading of the play, a therapist. Nor am I saying that these plays are in any straightforward sense pictures of the analytic process. I am only, as I tried to say in the Acknowledgements, lighting a candle or two in the hope that they might lead to some illumination of a profoundly complex, dare I say, even mystical, process in our therapy with couples.

But now to our tale. What I hope to do in recounting this tale is to invite you to listen to it with a different accent. My retelling is not meant to be taken as a literary or a psychoanalytic analysis of this play. Those interested in psychoanalytic literary interpretations will find no shortage of interesting, and surprisingly varied expositions. (e.g. Williams & Waddell, 1991; and, for selective but helpful references, Adelman, 1992)

It would be my hope that this telling of *The Winter's Tale* might lead you back to the play itself. You might even want to go back to Robert Greene's prose romance *Pandosto*, published in 1588, which was the story Shakespeare transformed into *The Winter's Tale*. In that respect these literary sources have an advantage over the stories that I will tell from my experience with couples in therapy. For the fragmentary clinical accounts that I will share with you, you will just have to rely on my version, as any earlier version is now inaccessible. In some sense, I suppose I remain the "uninvited guest", interposing myself in the retelling of the stories of Shakespeare and T. S. Eliot—as well as the story of a couple seen by a previous generation of therapists and, of course, stories from couples I have seen. But I hope not always an unwelcome third.

## Is whispering nothing?

We begin in Act II, as Hermione, Leontes' very pregnant queen, turns her attention back to her young son, Mamillius, from whatever had been distracting her—her husband's dark mood or, perhaps, the baby moving inside ready to emerge. She somewhat teasingly invites the boy to tell her a tale at a time that we, the audience, already know of the threatening jealous rage of a father who cannot believe that his children are his own:

*Her.*                Come, sir, now
I am for you again: 'pray you, sit by us,
And tell 's a tale.

*Mam.*                Merry, or sad, shall't be?

*Her.*    As merry as you will.

*Mam.* A sad tale's best for winter: I have one
Of sprites and goblins.

*Her.*                Let's have that, good sir.
Come on, sit down, come on, and do your best
To fright me with your sprites: you're powerful at it

*Mam.* There was a man—

*Her.*                    Nay, come sit down: then on.

*Mam.* Dwelt by a churchyard: I will tell it softly,
Yond crickets shall not hear it.

*Her.*                    Come on then,
And giv't me in mine ear.

[Shakespeare, *The Winter's Tale*, II.i.21–32]

Shakespeare alerts us to the fact that this tale for winter, whispered by a precocious lad into his mother's ear, is to be a sad tale. Is that because this son Hermione invites to "fright her" is himself soon to die, or should we be anxious for her baby? It brings to mind Donald Meltzer's comment about the sense of "hostage-holding" in the world of the claustrum, where in the last resort the hostages turn out to be the children (Meltzer, 1992, p. 95). Although it is not a theme that I will explore in this book, it is all-too-often literally the case that it is the children who are hostage to the destructive narcissism of their parents. It hovers in the background of our work with many couples.

Here at the beginning of Act II, we the audience already know what Hermione does not yet know, that she has reason to be frightened, that Leontes, her husband is disturbed by something; perhaps it is that he is convinced that she has been unfaithful to him with Polixenes, their present guest and his closest childhood friend. Their world appears suddenly about to collapse as Leontes gradually gives voice to the only feeling he can identify, the feeling that he has been betrayed. He becomes quickly certain that his friend, whom he calls his brother and who has visited with them for the past nine months, is the true father of the child his wife is about to deliver. Early in the opening scene we had already heard rumblings of suspicion as Leontes repeatedly questions, in what appears less light-hearted and humorous with each repetition, whether his young son Mamillius, on whom he appears to dote, is really his. Well, how can any father really know? What is proof enough?

I want to call attention to the fact that Shakespeare positions the scene of Mamillius whispering his winter's tale in mother's ear immediately following the end of the scene dominated by the shock of the sudden viciousness of the father's suspicion of the mother. Why? On the face of it, there is no question whom he suspects of betrayal. Is there something about Leontes' feeling betrayed, some unconscious resonance with dread, which makes it inevitable that we too feel some unease, that perhaps the father has indeed been betrayed? We must, I think, feel its weight, what makes it feel like truth. And yet there is also something about it that makes it clearly incredible, that makes us feel that it is mad to believe there has been such a betrayal. Shakespeare creates a mood of apprehension for which the clear sense of betrayal is almost a relief to this husband.

We are not surprised when, as with the rest of Leontes' Court, Camillo, his loyal confidant, finds these slanders unbelievable and challenges the King. Nor do we feel surprised that Camillo is met with a barrage of abuse from the King which makes us feel just how hopeless it is to try to reason with him. He is a man whose world is falling apart, a man who "knows" all he needs to know of his wife's unfaithfulness:

> Is whispering nothing?
> Is leaning cheek to cheek? Is meeting noses?
> Kissing with inside lip? Stopping the career
> Of laughter with a sigh (a note infallible
> Of breaking honesty)? Horsing foot on foot?
> . . .
> Is this nothing?
> Why then the world, and all that's in't, is nothing,
> The covering sky is nothing, Bohemia nothing,
> My wife is nothing, nor nothing have these nothings,
> If this be nothing.
>
> [I.ii.284–288, 292–296]

Were I listening to this in my consulting-room—and who has not endured similar barrages of certainties posing as questions from outraged wives and husbands—I would find myself wondering about the sequence of things. Why immediately after this outburst do I find myself listening to a description of the *son's* whisperings, leaning cheek to cheek with *mother*. Is the teller of this tale of horror trying to let us know that the betrayal is real, but, because quite unbearable, it has been re-located? These questions are reinforced when in this latter scene we see Mamillius playing the seductive young lord, quite capable in his, or even in his father's, unconscious imagination to be a plausible rival. When one of his mother's ladies-in-waiting asks if *she* should be the son's play-fellow, he responds: "No, I'll none of *you."* When asked why, he says: "You'll kiss me hard, and speak to me *as if / I were a baby still."* He then engages in a spirited, precocious repartee with the other lady-in-waiting about women's make-up. "Who taught' this!" she replies in mock horror.

Rejecting anyone but mother, the young prince is teased by the Queen's ladies-in-waiting that as his mother "rounds apace", there is soon to be a "fine new prince". Again, in a bit of repartee we encounter the pain of triangular tensions as the first lady-in-waiting torments the young prince: "and then you'd wanton with us / If we would have you." Mamillius seems to do his best to ignore this suggestion of what could be seen as an invitation to an identification with his jealous father.

This is no straightforward story of a husband's horror believing that his wife has been seduced by his best friend—is there ever a "straightforward" story! We shall take a closer look at it in a moment. However, there is no doubt as to the consequences. The son dies as his imprisoned mother gives birth to her second child, a daughter, who herself is saved from certain death only by a father's relenting, ordering instead that she be abandoned in some remote place. Shades of Oedipus—but here the motive of this father seems quite different from that of the father in that tragedy. Is this a different story, or is it the same story, but told from another's perspective, perhaps another generation's point of view? One thing is clear in both stories: all this leads to the death of the mother/wife. Leontes' world has indeed fallen apart, a tragic tale, would we say, of hubris of some kind which manifests itself as the hubris of jealous rage?

What we the audience do not know until the very last scene is that this is also a romantic tale of re-marriage. We are led to believe with Leontes that his imprisoned wife died in shock at the news that, not only had her baby daughter been exiled to almost certain death, but now her young son has died, apparently of grief. Leontes attributes the son's grief to his shame at his mother's betrayal, but it is grief that we the audience are more likely to feel comes in the wake of his father's disloyal accusations and loss of faith in his wife's love. In the last scene, presented as under Paulina's direction, Hermione is portrayed as a stone statue who slowly comes to life. It is a scene of reunion, a wife with her repentant husband, a mother with her lost daughter, a young couple who thought their union doomed, an old friend with his oldest friend—even the two whose faithfulness sustains the possibility of this re-union, Paulina and Camillo, are (re-) united. As the curtain falls they all depart to what Stanley Cavell convincingly pictures as a celebration of *re-marriage* (Cavell, 1987, pp. 193–221).

## Marriage and re-marriage

Alerted by Cavell to this theme of remarriage in *The Winter's Tale*, I want to use this play to introduce the image of *re-marriage* as a way of picturing the process of psychoanalytic therapy with couples. It will be obvious that what I have in mind is not some socio–legal notion of marriage, but rather I am inviting the thought that couples who engage in the psychoanalytic process *as couples* are in the nature of things in some important *psychological* sense married. In that sense what they seek in therapy is to find out whether re-marriage is possible, or even desirable, and what it might entail.

In the picture I am portraying of the centrality of marriage, I mean to suggest that marriage, in the sense of a capacity for what we in our psychoanalytic language term *object relating*, is not a once-and-for-all achievement. As with Bion's description of the oscillation between the paranoid–schizoid and depressive positions, which he images as *Ps ↔ D*, can we imagine a similar oscillation between *narcissistic* and *object-relating* states of mind? I want to invite you throughout this book to entertain a picture of it as an oscillating tension between *narcissism* and *marriage*. More than states of mind, these are alternating states of self.

I hasten to make clear that in this emphasis on marriage I am not suggesting that the aim of psychoanalytic marital psychotherapy is literally the re-marriage of the couples who come to therapy. It is more subtle and complex than that. I am trying to characterize a process in which there is the possibility of emergence from narcissism towards a genuine relating in the therapy relationship. Throughout this book I hope to show why this focus on the emergence from narcissism means that the transference relationship is at the heart of the analytic process. Conversely one might say that the focus on the analytic *relationship* in contemporary psychoanalysis means that the tension between forms of narcissistic object relating and genuine object relating cannot help but be at the forefront of the transference and countertransference experience.

Related to this emphasis on the emergence from narcissism is the realization that marriage is the intimate dyadic adult relationship that is most importantly shaped by the influence of the internal object known as the "internal parental couple" or the "combined object". That is to say, the idea of a couple coming together to produce a child, whether or not any given couple has children or not, is central to the dynamics of the relationship. Throughout this chapter, and indeed throughout the book, we shall return repeatedly to Oedipal issues in the *development towards marriage* in the mood of Ronald Britton's particularly apt description:

> "Marriage", whether celebrated or uncelebrated, socially con-
> tracted or uncontracted, or simply conspicuous by its absence, re-
> mains at the centre of "family life". I think it does so because the
> idea of a couple coming together to produce a child is central in
> our psychic life, whether we aspire to it, object to it, realize we are
> produced by it, deny it, relish it, or hate it. [Britton, 1995, p. xi]

We do of course encounter "marriages" that feign to recreate the illusion of a *pre-Oedipal couple*, acknowledging nothing of a genuine third or the reality of the potential to become a parental couple. It is a kind of sibling fantasy which we shall see in the next section por-trayed as "twinn'd lambs" in an eternal bliss in which the only change is "innocence for innocence". Shakespeare presents us in *The Winter's Tale* with Leontes' vision of what he experiences as an attack on this illusion, the terrifying possibility not that these children are *not* his, but that they *are his*.

At the heart of what challenges this illusion of eternal oneness, this twinned sameness, is the image of the pregnant mother, might we say the unbearably beautiful image. Donald Meltzer has intro-duced the idea that it is just this beauty of the object which over-whelms, and which therefore cannot be acknowledged (Meltzer & Williams, 1988). Perhaps the version we see here portrays the capac-ity to acknowledge the beauty of the object as the capacity of the father to acknowledge his participation in the mystery of the preg-nancy of the mother. If so, acknowledging the child as one's own may be, for the father, a moment intense—perhaps too intense—with emotion. As an attack on the narcissistic illusion of the eternal twin relationship, it is felt to be one that must be met by a vigorous and resolute counterattack: acknowledgement countered by rejection. *These children cannot be, are not, mine. I have been betrayed.* We might imagine that commonly in marriage there is an oscillation between the excitement of the twinned dyad united in sameness, on the one hand, and the 'consequent fear of fusion. The narcissism is clearly unstable and tends to end in a sense of betrayal, with the attendant feelings of hatred and revenge. It is a theme that we will trace not only through *The Winter's Tale*, but throughout the book.

At one level, we can regard *marriage*, the married couple, as the inheritor of the tension and the intimacy of the Oedipal (I will want to say the "Leontean") drama. Couples come to us for therapy because, to some extent, there is a "missing link"—call it a dead or exiled child. In this Oedipal drama considered from the child's point of view, as we are accustomed to do in psychoanalysis, the child's primal experience of the links with each parent, and the confrontation with the link between them, has faced it with a potentially overwhelming emotional conflict. This emotional conflict re-emerges in the Leontean drama, where, from the point of view of one who is, or who may become, the parent, the experience of these same triangular links revives a similar sense of being overwhelmed.

This conflict is never completely resolved, neither in its Oedipal nor its Leontean form. But when and if the primitive emotions of love and hate for the beloved objects can be tolerated in the child's *and the parents'* minds, we find, in Britton's phrase, "the prototype for an object relationship of a third kind". There is a third position from which object relationships can be observed. Given this, we can also envisage *being* observed. This provides us with a capacity for seeing ourselves in interaction with others and for entertaining another point of view while retaining our own, a capacity for reflecting on ourselves while being ourselves, what Britton called a "triangular space", creating ". . . the possibility of being a participant in a relationship and observed by a third person as well as being an observer of a relationship between two people" (Britton, 1989, pp. 86–87).

This third position, or rather the encounter with those whose existence represents it, is what Leontes experiences as an attack, a betrayal. And it is what he in turn attacks. It is in this sense that Leontes' intuition that he has been betrayed represents a kind of truth for him, and one that we do well not to ignore. The fact that the "Oedipal" drama is seen here from the perspective of the father rather than that of the son is important for our understanding of the dilemma of *narcissism* ↔ *marriage*. The murderous attack here is directed not at the father whom the son would displace, but against the child (both son and daughter) who threaten to displace the father. I think, therefore, that it makes some sense to speak of a "Leontean" drama, of which the Oedipal is a version. Deciding which way round it is depends, I imagine, on how one reads the Genesis myth. But here we stumble into gender-inflected complexities which will have to wait another occasion.

At another level, we can regard *marriage* as another, and perhaps the most complex and difficult, encounter with the beauty of the object. It is an encounter shaped by that original encounter of the baby with its incomparably beautiful mother and of the mother with her incomparably beautiful baby. One might say that around the dilemma of *re-marriage* hover the tensions of the impact of beauty in the passionate intimacy with another human being. As we consider what we might think of as struggles towards re-marriage marked with such brutal coldness as we see in *The Winter's Tale*, we shall find throughout this book what Meltzer has so clearly described:

> It is necessary for our understanding of our patients, for a sympathetic view of the hardness, coldness and brutality that repeatedly bursts through in the transference and countertransference, to recognize that conflict about the *present* object is prior in significance to the host of anxieties over the *absent* object. [Meltzer & Williams, 1988, p. 29]

## Leontes' jealousy: boyhood friends forever

It would be tempting to go through this play of Shakespeare in detail since there is much that is relevant to our theme in almost every scene. This could distract us, however, from my intention to take *The Winter's Tale* as an introduction to the rest of the book. My aim here, rather, is to sketch the development of the theme of what I am calling Leontean jealousy and murderous rage as an expression of narcissism and then to consider how Leontes can be seen to emerge from this state towards the possibility of *re*-marriage.

We have already become aware of some of the complications in making sense of the precipitous appearance of Leontes' suspicion of his wife. While the initial joking exchanges between this couple and Leontes' childhood friend Polixenes seem to be expressions of a close, enduring friendship, triangular tensions emerge at every turn. Again, we are alerted by Shakespeare to the theme of an intimate couple and the shadow of a third—the couple in the first instance not being Leontes and Hermione as husband and wife, but Leontes and Polixenes as two young kings, one of Sicilia, the other of Bohemia. The picture could hardly be clearer in the brief prose dialogue that opens the play, between Camillo, minister to Leontes, and Archidamus, minister to Polixenes. Responding to the effusive thanks of the Bohemian lord for the Sicilian hospitality and his invitation for a return visit, Camillo describes the intimacy of the two kings:

> They were trained together in their childhood, and there
> rooted betwixt them then such an affection which cannot
> choose but branch now. Since their more mature dignities and
> royal necessities made separation of their society, their en-
> counters, though not personal, have been royally attorneyed
> with interchange of gifts, letters, loving embassies, that they
> have seemed to be together, though absent; shook hands, as
> over a vast; and embraced, as it were, from the ends of op-
> posed winds. The heavens continue their loves!
>
> [I.i.21–32]

Even if we discount the effusive court language, this offers a vivid portrait of a separation treated as an illusion, one in which the two *seemed to be together, though absent*. The theatre audience cannot help but feel the chill of a shadow coming over this scene when Archidamus responds: "I think there is not in the world either malice or matter to alter it." Irresistibly we wonder what malice, to what matter, ought we be alert. And without pause or breath the Bohemian minister goes on: "You have an unspeakable comfort of your young prince Mamillius: it is a gentleman of greatest promise that ever came into my note."

A less subtle author here might have dropped hints pointing towards a relationship between Hermione and Polixenes, the ostensible cause of Leontes' jealousy. But why juxtapose this hint of "malice or matter", which could threaten the intimate link between these boyhood friends, with Leontes' young prince—especially the "unspeakable comfort" of this son? Both kings have healthy young male heirs who are said to be a delight to their fathers, and thus Shakespeare seems to prompt us to wonder why the existence of this son should be a threat to the relationship of the two kings.

In fact, we are given a rather exaggerated portrait of a young prince said to be so precious that subjects of the kingdom long to survive to see him grown to manhood. Time, personified as a chorus, has an important role in *The Winter's Tale,* suggesting Shakespeare's focus on the wishes *and* anxieties of the displacement of one generation by the next. Early in the play, we see Leontes picturing his son *as himself as a lad.* It is as if any evidence of the reality of next generation refocuses attention on one's own mortality and ultimate absence. Sons may be a joy to their fathers, but they can also be painful reminders that their own time for leaving is closer.

Separation, or at least leaving, is the explicit theme that opens the play, as Polixenes insists that it is time he return to Bohemia. Leontes, for reasons we immediately suspect, demands that he remain longer with them. Unable to convince his brother king, Leontes turns to Hermione, who, when she succeeds in persuading their guest, only really succeeds in providing evidence to Leontes of the relationship he suspects between them. Polixenes would stay for her, but not for him. Interestingly, what persuades Polixenes is not some rational argument that all is well at home. In fact, Hermione playfully suggests that had Polixenes pleaded that he wanted to leave to see his own young son, she would have "thwacked" him for his delay in leaving. No, what seems to be the point at which the guest relents and agrees to stay comes when his hostess, seductively perhaps, announces that he has no choice, that he *will* stay—stay as her guest or as her prisoner. "Your guest then, madam."

Leaving, separation, is impossible! Immediately Shakespeare takes us back to the childhood of the two kings, as Hermione teasingly asks about their "tricks" as boys and Polixenes replies:

> We were, fair queen,
> Two lads that thought there was no more behind,
> But such a day to-morrow as to-day,
> And to be boy eternal.
> . . .

> We were as twinn'd lambs that did frisk i' th' sun,
> And bleat the one at th' other: what we chang'd
> Was innocence for innocence: we knew not
> The doctrine of ill-doing, nor dream'd
> That any did. . . .

[I.ii.62–65, 67–71]

This boyhood friendship is pictured as eternal and innocent because, as Polixenes puts it to Hermione, "Your precious self had then not cross'd the eyes / Of my young play-fellow." Although Hermione playfully refers to herself and Polixenes's queen as "devils" with whom these two young friends "slipp'd", we have the uneasy sense that the shadow of an *other*, and the desire for that other, suggests a threat to the idyllic innocence of the two youths. Is this a hint that the "pleasure principle" of Freud's fable, which I will discuss in the next chapter, is about to disturb and confuse what seems uncomplicated in relationships? Or is this the emerging awareness of the over-whelming beauty of an other that is experienced as a threat to the "innocent" ignorance of this narcissistic twinship?

The most obvious version of this threat is, in terms of "time's arrow", what might be described as horizontal, the threat of the other within that same generation. Leontes speaks of Hermione's having persuaded Polixenes to stay for another week as her having never spoken to better purpose—"never but once"! In response to her puzzlement, he refers bitterly to his desperate wooing her before she would say "I am yours for ever", a phrase we will hear again in this book, towards the end of the last chapter, on the lips of Iago as he says it to Othello. We have no doubt of Leontes' capacity to imagine his friend as more successful than he with the woman he loves, or his wife more attracted to another man. This triangle, with Leontes' consequent jealous rage, is presented as the first apparent pivot point to the action of the play.

Beyond the drama of a husband's jealousy—what we might describe as an *intra*-generational drama focused on husband, wife, and alleged lover—there rumbles an *inter*-generational tension that echoes the earlier loss of the idyllic primary dyad of mother and child. The acknowledgement that mother is not mine, not my posses-sion or an extension of myself, is hard won and easily undermined by the father's experience of the repetition of the Oedipal drama. For the child, this hard-won acknowledgement entails a recognition that mother belongs to another generation, and thus to an *other* whose status as an adult is not open to it. The omnipotent refusal to acknowledge this reality leaves one open to an equally unbearable dilemma when, as a father, one is then faced with evidence of exclusion from another idyllic primary dyad, the mother–child dyad. "Is whispering nothing!" Faced with a young son who is a picture of his own young self, Leontes is also faced with the unbearable exclusion once again.

At this point, I want to acknowledge a remarkable essay by Stanley Cavell which sparked my interest in *The Winter's Tale*. In his characteristically modest way he notes how Shakespeare casts the Oedipal drama in an intriguingly unfamiliar, yet all-too-familiar, way:

> While evidently I expect considerable agreement that in Leontes' intrusion we have an Oedipal conflict put before us, I am not assuming that we thereupon know how to work our way through the conflict. Freud, I guess like Sophocles, seems to look at the conflict as initiated by the son's wish to remove or replace the father, whereas in *The Winter's Tale* the conflict, on the contrary, seems primarily generated by the father's wish to replace or remove the son. Perhaps this speaks of a difference between tragedy and romance—hence of their inner union—but in any case I do not wish to prejudge such a matter. [Cavell, 1987, p. 199]

The more he can acknowledge the evidence that Mamillius is indeed his own son, his calf, the more Leontes is drawn into the triangle that seems to threaten his omnipotent insistence on an exclusive relationship with the woman who is both his [wife] and the boy's [mother]. Leontes' apparent emotional solution is to split the child into a son, whom he can (with many reservations) acknowledge, and the child his wife is about to deliver, whom he rejects as not-his. Murdering this *child-of-unfaithfulness*, or at least abandoning it to die, and executing his unfaithful wife rids him of this source of unbearable jealousy. What is the explicit ostensible motive? In Leontes' view, it is justified jealousy of an unquestionably unfaithful woman.

We might say, although Leontes cannot openly face this since it would make procreation impossible, that Hermione has been unfaithful precisely in her becoming the mother to his child. It is the logic, should we say the psychotic logic, of narcissism: reproduction is possible only as a *re-producing* of oneself. It is represented in this play as the "twinn'd lambs that did frisk i' th' sun" who only changed "innocence for innocence" in an Eden before the fall. Just as Leontes and Polixenes as adult friends echo their innocent twinning, Leontes and Mamillius as father and son can be twinned, "as like as eggs". But even in this idyllic picture Leontes is plagued by the sexuality that makes him father, not twin to this boy, a sexuality that repeats that sexuality of the parental couple from which as a boy he was excluded. A sexuality that once more lands him on the outside of the couple's intimacy.

> Looking on the lines
> Of my boy's face, methoughts I did recoil
> Twenty-three years, and saw myself unbreech'd,
> In my green velvet coat; my dagger muzzl'd
> Lest it should bite its master, and so prove,
> As ornaments oft do, too dangerous;
> How like, methought, I then was to this kernel,
> This squash, this gentleman.

> [I.ii.153–160]

Even as Leontes banters with his childhood friend about their fondness for their respective sons, he is wary of the sexuality, the unmuzzled dagger. In the child's version of adult maleness, this phallus is a weapon, an essential "ornament" marking power, while this child/man has discovered sexual desire too dangerous. After all, his Queen Hermione has already joked that she and Polixenes' Queen were "devils" with whom the boys sinned, losing the innocence of their "unfledg'd days".

## Evasion of the truth in delusional jealousy

At the heart of the story of Leontes' delusional jealousy, in this picture I am attempting to draw, is his refusal to acknowledge his offspring as his. What does it mean to picture this version of narcissism as revolving around the father's doubt of his paternity? What does Leontes, or indeed any father, need to know in order to acknowledge his children? What is required for him to believe his wife Hermione when she reaffirms that they are indeed his—or, conversely, why is she so clear that swearing (as in a court of law?) that they are in fact his would add nothing to her simple acknowledgement that he is the father? Might we be tempted to think that this is a situation that might arise differently in our modern era—for example, picturing Leontes insisting on genetic testing to determine whether or not his suspicions are justified, whether or not the child is his?

But is it really different? When Leontes discovers that Polixenes has fled back to Bohemia, having been warned, instead of murdered, by the king's minister Camillo, he orders Hermione imprisoned in preparation for a "trial". But clearly this is not because he doubts her guilt. Even when he instructs a delegation be sent to the Oracle of Apollo ostensibly to determine her guilt or innocence, Leontes makes clear that it is a public gesture towards *objectivity*, which only appears to demonstrate his commitment to the discovery of the truth. The Oracle, we might say, represents what science—for example, in the form of genetic testing—might offer us today, a way offering an *objective* source of truth.

It is a salutary warning, if one is needed, for therapists who undertake therapy with couples. One of the most common dynamics revolves around the pressure on the therapist to function as judge, determining who is right, what the truth of the matter is. Although one may resist more overt forms of this kind of pressure, therapists often experience, nevertheless, a longing to know—and indeed sometimes have a conviction that they do know—who is telling the truth. Did Hermione sleep with Polixenes, or is Leontes' suspicion as implausible as it seems? Every therapist seeing couples will be able to recount session after session filled with arguments in which both partners cannot be right in what they claim, no matter how plausible the accounts might be or the depth of conviction with which each defends the conflicting reports of what happened. There is a fantasy in such situations, frequently an openly proclaimed wish, that an "impartial", "objective" third party will be able to determine the truth.

The *judge* in such a fantasy is an extension of an unconscious scene in which the children, most often siblings, appeal to the adults, most often the parents, who are experienced as the ones who know and thus have the right to pronounce judgements. In the society pictured in *The Winter's Tale*, conflict among human beings could be referred to divine judgement, in specific to the Oracle of Apollo at Delphos. Leontes has sent two of his ministers to the Oracle, not for his benefit, as we have seen, since he is convinced he knows the truth, but to put others' minds at rest:

> Though I am satisfied, and need no more
> Than what I know, yet shall the Oracle
> Give rest to th' minds of others; such as he
> Whose ignorant credulity will not
> Come up to th' truth.

[II.ii.189–193]

In the trial scene, after Leontes has repeated his accusations and Hermione has spoken in defence of her honour, the two ministers return from Delphos with the sealed pronouncement from Apollo. The judgement is as unambiguous and definitive: "Hermione is chaste; Polixenes blameless; Camillo / a true subject; Leontes a jealous tyrant; his innocent babe truly begotten." Ominously the Oracle concludes with a dire warning: "and the king shall live without an heir, if that which is lost be not found"—a chilling warning since at that point the young prince Mamillius is still alive. Leontes' omnipotent belief in his own omniscient conviction is unshaken, nor would we think that any genetic examination would shift it:

> There is no truth at all i' th' Oracle:
> The sessions shall proceed: this is falsehood.

In the Leontean drama, it is not the son's question: was that my father whom I killed? It is the father's question: is this my child whom I am killing? And the judgement of the truth of the matter cannot be made by some external authority, some god, some parental figure to whom the warring children appeal. This seems clear when we see that Leontes is not moved by the Oracle, definitive though it appeared to be. As soon as he utters the lines above, a servant enters with the news that his son, the prince, is gone! Gone? Dead. It is informative to note how Shakespeare alters the story as it appears in his source, Robert Greene's *Pandosto*. There the king's delusional jealousy dissipates when he hears the judgement of the Oracle. Although in *The Winter's Tale* Shakespeare retains the Oracle's judgement almost literally word for word as it was in his source, he portrays Leontes' acknowledgement of the truth as coming not at the moment of hearing the pronouncement of his wife's innocence by the Oracle, but a moment later with the news of the death of his son.

It is a dramatic moment that has echoes of the biblical story in which a parent, in this case a mother, is faced with a question of acknowledging a child as her own. It was brought to mind during supervision with two co-therapists who were describing their work with a couple who often left them in this impossible position of "judge". One of the co-therapists commented on the pressure put on them by the couple that it reminded her of the story of the judgement of Solomon. The more I listened to their account of the pressure to have the "wisdom of Solomon", the more it seemed to me to echo Leontes' story. In the biblical story, two women both claim to be the genuine mother. In a moment of inspired irony, Solomon offered to divide the disputed baby in half. The wisdom of Solomon lay not in being a "third person" with some "objective" knowledge of the truth, but in challenging each woman to face the internal truth of their experience. Each woman was confronted with the reality of what it is to acknowledge a child as one's own. Only the false mother, or the false father, prepared to accede to the death of the child.

In *The Winter's Tale*, Shakespeare presents a picture of a father who is released from the grip of delusional jealousy only as he is faced with the reality of it as an attack on his son resulting in his death. In this version of the Oedipal drama, the third is not the father who threatens the exclusive relationship between mother and baby. Nor in this version does the son unconsciously wish the death of the father in the desire of keeping mother to himself. In the Leontean drama the baby comes as the mark of the impossibility of the husband's wished-for exclusive possession of his wife.

And it is also the mark of the "defilement" of the perfect love object, a version that will only become clear when we turn to *Othello* in the final chapter. Might we say that, just as the son's wished for exclusive possession of his mother unconsciously contains the desire for the death of the father, this desire of the husband for exclusive possession of his wife unconsciously contains the wish for the death, or the non-existence, of the child. The Leontean drama ends in filicide as the Oedipal ends in patricide (Rascovsky & Rascovsky, 1972).

And just as the Oedipal story has a gender counterpoint in the girl's struggle with her wish for exclusive possession of mother, and both boys and girls in their gender-distinct ambivalent feelings towards father, there is a version of the Leontean drama which includes the mother's filicidal impulses. This is a much less explored area, with some notable exceptions such as Estela Welldon's *Mother, Madonna, Whore* (Welldon, 1988). It is a topic in psychoanalytic therapy with couples which deserves a study in its own right, taking up the numerous gender-focused issues both within therapy and within the couple relationship itself.

But for now we must return to our story with its picture of Leontes' evasion of the truth. Having dismissed the external authority of Apollo's Oracle, Leontes begins to confront the truth of what he has done when shocked by the news of the death of his son. How do we understand this transformation? This is a question that belongs, I suggest, with an exploration of Leontes' emergence from the delusional jealousy that marks the narcissism of which it is an integral part.

## Remorse leading to a dream of reparation and reconciliation

How is it that this tragic story of a husband losing all that is precious to him in his intimate relationships turns suddenly into a romance of young love succeeding against the intrusive fury of another father, Polixenes, determined to see his son not marry "beneath him" for love? It can seem on some readings of *The Winter's Tale* that there is too great a shift from the mood of terror in the face of delusional jealousy to the light-hearted delight of a sheep-shearing fertility festival celebrating the joy of a fortunate shepherd and his son. Having discovered a foundling, whom we know to be the abandoned daughter of Leontes', and the treasure of "fairy gold" that accompanied her, this shepherd father is hosting what is in effect a betrothal celebration for this lost, and now found, daughter, Perdita. This "shepherd's" daughter is in love with a young man who unknown to her is the prince Florizel, rebellious son to King Polixenes.

Given my suggestion that *The Winter's Tale* portrays Leontes' emergence from narcissism, it is fair to ask in what way it does. What makes plausible a move from tragedy to romance leading towards an ending in which *re-marriage*, for Leontes and Hermione, becomes possible? It is, if you like, a question about the nature of the hoped-for change in couples trapped in narcissistic patterns of relating. Does Shakespeare throw a beam of light on this process in this play, this question of what leads from narcissistic rage to the possibility of re-marriage? Or, since *narcissism* ↔ *marriage* is a never-resolved dynamic in intimate relationships, what moves that dynamic in the direction of hope?

One answer is that it is a process that begins in remorse. *The Winter's Tale* can be read in a way that makes it appear that remorse simply happens. Leontes seems suddenly to collapse into a penitence that is to last sixteen years, the length of time between the first part of the play and the Bohemian romance of the second part.

We note that, at the moment Leontes hears the words "the prince your son . . . is dead", he has what seems a complete change of heart: "Apollo's angry, and the heavens themselves / Do strike at my injustice." At that point Hermione faints, and Paulina, whose central role in the story is about to become clear, announces that the "news is mortal" to her: "See what death is doing." Leontes dismisses this, insisting that she will recover, that "her heart is but o'char'gd". Remembering that our interest here is not in an exposition of Shakespeare's play, but in this drama as a picture that illustrates some important dynamics in the psychoanalytic process with couples, what do we make of this scene?

It brings to mind a common dynamic that, in my experience, couples more often report than actually demonstrate in the consulting-room. Either partner, although perhaps it is more frequently the woman, will report the harshness, cold cruelty, and aggressiveness of the other, right up to the moment she (or he) is reduced to tears. "He can only love me and be gentle with me when he has reduced me to a snivelling wreck", as one woman put it.

But in the story of Leontes and Hermione, the husband's vengeful attack on his wife only stops when he hears that his *son* is dead. At that point he is brought to face the consequence of his delusional jealousy, the consequence that also faced Othello, but for Leontes not the murderous devastation of his wife with whom he cannot be twinned. No, for Leontes it is the murderous devastation of his son with whom he could still see himself twinned. For this father, an offspring is tolerable, perhaps even welcome, as long as it can be construed as a *twin* to himself (Neely, 1978).

Might we think of a splitting of the child into the child that is "almost as like as eggs" to him (I.ii.130), his son, and the unborn child he rejects as not his. It was very interesting to me that in the 1998–1999 Royal Shakespeare Company production the director, Gregory Doran, cast a young actress both as Mamillius, the young son, and as the daughter we learn later is Perdita. "Perdita" is clearly a play on the Latin *perditus* meaning lost, ruined, abandoned; as "Mamillius" seems to be a play on the Latin *mamilla* meaning breast or teat (Adelman, 1992, p. 357). It suggests a story in itself were we to explore the play further in its own right, a story of what the baby at the breast can say is mine, is me, and not know which until it is lost, slipping out of the mouth and out of sight: send it to perdition, it was none of mine!

In this emotionally powerful RSC production, Doran also had the actress, Emily Bruni, play Mamillius in a (wheel) chair (as though ill with polio?), giving an ironic edge to Leontes' speeches about this son whom he sees as twinned to himself. In this version, the audience cannot escape a feeling that Anthony Sher as Leontes portrays a father shocked that what he is seeing, as he describes his "calf", is not a strong young masculine twin to himself, but a sickly, feminine twin. He is unnerved, desperate to latch on to some explanation for his growing disquiet.

If the child his wife Hermione is now carrying in fact *is his*, might it not be another reflection of something sickly, something feminine in him. We can feel why he cries that this child, he means his son, has too much of his mother in him. His suspicion is fuelled by comments about his son's likeness to him when he says to his wife in jealous rage: "I am glad you did not nurse him: / Though he does bear some signs of me, yet you / Have too much blood in him" (II.i.56–58). But, if the child his wife is now carrying *is not his*, will it be the twin of his brother king Polixenes? And, if so, will the child be the strong, manly twin Leontes wanted to be his reflection, his calf?

As the delusional jealousy takes hold of Leontes, his twinship with his son is also threatened. We in the audience see what Leontes cannot see until the shock of Mamillius' death. What Leontes is resisting is the *Oedipal* reality of his children, that is, that they are the off-spring of two parents, related to both but identical to neither. The child is a third, an individual in its own right, capable of relating to either parent and thus forming a couple with that parent, but belonging to neither.

But here I want to return to Leontes' remorse and his declared repentance for the damage he had caused. Sending Paulina and the other ladies-in-waiting to attend to the wife he believes has merely fainted, he announces his intention to seek pardon and reconciliation from those he has offended. The order of the list is interesting. Asking pardon of Apollo, he says: "I'll reconcile me to Polixenes, / New woo my queen, recall the good Camillo" (III.iii.155–156). The next sixteen lines focus on the minister Camillo, whom he commanded to kill his friend Polixenes. Hermione does not return to his thoughts until Paulina reenters to rehearse what his tyranny and jealousy run mad has done: betrayal of his friend Polixenes, poisoning of Camillo's honour by ordering him to kill a king, casting to the crows his baby daughter. At this point Paulina's central role becomes clear (Sanders, 1978). This lady-in-waiting to Hermione is the only character in the play who can call Leontes to account once he has begun to face the truth of his narcissistic omnipotence. Ironically, in her listing of the victims of Leontes' narcissism, only Mamillius' death, she says, cannot be directly attributed to him. The last, and by implication the most heinous, crime is the death of Hermione his wife.

Leontes is able to hear all this from Paulina because he seems now suddenly to value the seeking and facing of truth. Up to this point, he felt no need to *seek* truth, as he had a certainty that needed no evidence. In the grip of delusional jealousy there was nothing more he needed to know. Paulina is an interesting character, as she moves to centre stage as the one whose role is to speak the truth which Leontes can begin to acknowledge. When she begins to retreat from her role of facing Leontes with the truth of his tyrannical omnipotent jealousy, he responds: "Thou didst speak but well / When most the truth: which I receive much better / Than to be pitied of thee" (III.ii.232–234). This acknowledgement of the truth of the damage he has inflicted leads Leontes towards a state of mind that we might describe, following Melanie Klein, as the depressive position.

Our contemporary understanding of the depressive position leads us to a sharpened awareness of the centrality of the role of mourning for the lost and damaged object, mourning which is possible only when there can be an acknowledgement of the truth (Steiner, 1989). Donald Meltzer further develops the Kleinian understanding by suggesting that there is a sense in which the depressive position represents the struggle to acknowledge—or to use his term, to apprehend—that first, overwhelming beautiful object (Meltzer, 1988). Failing that acknowledgement, the infant has to turn away, attacking and distorting that awareness of truth in a paranoid–schizoid defence.

I am proposing that we entertain for a moment a view of Shakespeare's play as a portrait of the developmental process oscillating between the paranoid–schizoid state of mind, with its aim to possess the other, to the depressive position with its mourning, regretting both the failure to acknowledge the beauty of the other as well as the damage consequently done to it. The remorse and mourning aim at reparation and the giving the object its freedom. From this way of viewing *The Winter's Tale*, we are faced with an interesting question about the second half of the play.

Described as it usually is as a romance, the Bohemia half of *The Winter's Tale* can also be seen, I suggest, as Leontes' *dream* of reconciliation, restitution, and reparation. As a "dream" this romance could be thought of as a picture of what is going on in the internal world of this mourner. The Sicilian half, the first half, of the play ends with Leontes vowing his repentance for the death of his wife and son:

> Once a day I'll visit
> The chapel where they lie, and tears shed there
> Shall be my recreation.
>
> [III.ii.238–240]

The *recreation* here is also his *re-creation*. But what does that mean? How can Leontes emerge from his narcissism? It is as if Shakespeare suggests that this is not a "road to Damascus" experience, but rather a process, a process of transformation in Leontes' internal world, and offers his audience an account, a dream of one version of that process.

It is also a version of Leontes' pledge that he will begin again to woo his queen. In his Bohemian dream, the wooing is done by Polixenes' son Florizel, and the one he woos is a shepherd's daughter. That is, she was not born of a shepherd but was an abandoned foundling infant raised by a shepherd, who represents a genuinely fatherly figure who can accept a child as a gift. He is also "motherly", since Leontes' "dream" requires that the shepherd have no wife—"requires", I think, because one can see him as the father Leontes aspires to be. It might be noted that Polixenes' wife, Florizel's mother, is absent from the play, further tightening the focus on the play's portrayal of a man's desperate struggle to be a father.

The young woman is of course the lost daughter Perdita. And Leontes' Bohemian dream is a picture of a process to recover "that which is lost". It takes place in the internal world, the world of dreaming and unconscious phantasy, a process in which grief and remorse for the damage caused to one's good internal objects becomes reparation and reconciliation. It is to one fascinating picture of this process that I now want to turn.

## A Bohemian dream

This second half of the play is full of life and liveliness as the trickster and fool Autolycus moves the romance forward. It is the story of an intense but forbidden love of a young couple which survives the attempt of the father, here Leontes' "twin" Polixenes, to thwart it. In this it is an interesting, although often ignored, version of the attack on the "parental couple". In the Leontean version of the Oedipal drama, the couple that is attacked is the couple that will form the *next* generation. Perhaps we should say that it is hidden rather than ignored, hidden in the sentimentality of the narcissistic desire for children and grandchildren—profoundly wished for as long as they represent a narcissistic extension of ourselves, but profoundly frustrating when recognized as the next generation, a couple in its own right, no more our possession than was the parental couple with the privacy and exclusivity of its bedroom.

Shakespeare's ambiguous "fool" Autolycus is playfully grandiose as a thief, pickpocket, singer, and rogue. His attacks on the other— for example, the shepherd's rather dim son—are not the expression of a narcissistic grandiosity offended at the otherness of the other, as with Leontes. Instead, he needs and thrives on his "victims", and they, although wounded, are not destroyed by him. In the end, the shepherd and his son embrace him, generously forgiving his irrepressible mischief. We shall see something of this complex dynamic in the next few chapters with a couple in therapy, the "Webbs", when, especially in chapter five, they are able to row openly with each other, a development that feels like relating to each other as real persons rather than what has previously felt more like each attacking a projection of the self.

In fact, Autolycus' skill in getting into the pockets and purses of others is radiant with sexual images, this phallic man who charms the women with his erotic sheets of music so suggestive not of dark destructive sexuality, but of playful procreativity. In this Bohemian dream of Leontes, the focus is on the differences that make true intercourse possible. In *Othello*, the other Shakespeare play we shall explore, it is the difference of race that sharpens the sense of difference. In the romance part of *The Winter's Tale*, it is class that highlights difference, the flower of royalty, the royal son, about to be grafted to the sturdy stock of the peasant shepherd. Or is it the flower of the lusty, procreative peasant world, the beautiful singing and dancing Perdita, about to be grafted onto the solid world of royal wealth and privilege?

This reparative dream, this second part, this romance of *The Winter's Tale*, is an exploration not of how the two become one, *one flesh* in the language of Genesis, but how the one becomes two. The destructive narcissism of Leontes which became delusional jealousy was grounded in the wish that two should be one. But it was not a wish experienced in the ecstasy of love, what T. S. Eliot described as "the breathing in unison / of lovers" (Eliot, 1969). It was a wish contaminated by narcissistic omnipotence. Leontes' remorse at the damage this has led to now takes the form, I suggest, of a dream of how the couple united in love can become genuinely, emotionally, two.

Cavell (1987) pointed out that *The Winter's Tale* explores the paired ideas of participation and parturition, what we might describe as the core picture of marriage. The dilemma is that this coming together results in what can then be experienced as a threat to the "perfect union" of the two, their "twinning". The offspring, like the relationship itself, partakes of each but is identical with neither. It is as if the participation in this intimate union emphasizes, and indeed requires, a parting. In both its Oedipal and its Leontean versions, this is a story of participation and parturition, with separateness and separation being as important as any coming together, any union.

It is interesting that, as Cavell (1987) notes, *The Winter's Tale* "punctuates its language with literal 'part' words, as if words to the wise, words such as depart, parting, departure, apart, party to, partner, and, of course, bearing a part" (p. 200). This playing a part, he suggests, is one reason why the theatre itself is of endless interest for Shakespeare. And this takes us in turn, as Cavell points out, "to that other region of parting, that of separating, dividing, branching, grafting, flowering, shearing, issuing, delivering, breeding: parturition" (p. 207).

The centre point in this Bohemian dream is, I suggest, the lively discussion between Polixenes, the father, and Perdita, the daughter, about "hybrids". She is unsure about her "streak'd gillyvors", hybrid plants produced by grafting one stock onto another, because this results in what she anxiously suggests are "nature's bastards". As she voices her anxiety, the audience cannot fail to notice that this daughter has been depicted in her father's delusional jealousy as herself a "bastard".

Polixenes at this point seems to be the kind of father who not only can tolerate but even values the reality that the offspring has two parents, that it need not be a clone of one—well, that is what he says. However, when it comes to his own son, there is no question of this father permitting his son to marry a shepherd's daughter. Instead, he threatens to disown and disinherit his son to prevent his grafting royal stock onto a peasant one. The scene is marked by the irony that he utters these fine sentiments to the young woman we are already beginning to suspect will bear him grandchildren:

> You see, sweet maid, we marry
> A gentler scion to the wildest stock,
> And make conceive a bark of baser kind
> By bud of nobler race. This is an art
> Which does mend nature—change it rather—but
> The art itself is nature.

Perdita responds simply "so it is", while Polixenes concludes with the lines that echo through the play from the opening scene to the last:

> Then make your garden rich in gillyvors,
> And do not call them bastards.
>
> [IV.iv.92–99]

This Bohemian dream gives a lively account of the frustrating of the (pseudo)-paternal attempts to interfere with the young couple, as we might imagine remorse leading to a dream in which one discovers the futility of one's interference with one's internal creative couples. As the audience, we are drawn irresistibly into a passionate hope for their success as the two young lovers are helped to flee Bohemia by Camillo, now Polixenes' minister as he once was Leontes', and by the scheming rogue Autolycus, neither of whom have the interests of the would-be couple primarily at heart. In the climactic scene, the pursuing, interfering father Polixenes catches up with the lovers just as they seem to have made good their escape in the court of Leontes. Again, all seems lost for them.

It is interesting to note that this resolution at the end of *The Winter's Tale* reveals a version of what Freud called a "family romance". Of course, it is a version of a family romance in the way the Leontean drama is a version of the Oedipal one. In Freud's description, the impulse to imagine parents grander than or in some way superior to the real parents comes from a particular kind of disappointment with the actual parents:

> There are only too many occasions on which a child is slighted, or at least *feels* he has been slighted, on which he feels he is not receiving the whole attention of his parents' love, and, most of all, on which he feels regrets at having to share it with brothers and sisters. His sense that his own affection is not being fully reciprocated then finds a vent in the idea, often consciously recollected later from early childhood, of being a step-child or an adopted child. [Freud, 1909c, pp. 235–236]

Interestingly, Freud observes that this imagining of superior "real" parents tends increasingly to focus more on the father as the child increasingly realizes, as he reminds us, that "'*pater semper incertus est*' while mother is '*certissima*'" (Freud, 1909c, p. 238). The uncertainty of paternity not only leaves scope for a particular form of family romance focused on the question of the *real* father, but it can also lead to a delusory envy of the woman viewing her as having a relationship based on the certainty of in-corporation, the child literally inside her body. While Freud's version of the family romance centres on the child's doubts about its parents, the Leontean version centres on the father's doubt about his *real* offspring.

Freud goes on to suggest that, as the maternal origin cannot be doubted, the version of the family romance that focuses on the mother is one that has to do with her unfaithfulness. Expanding on this theme the following year, and in a context where the editors note that he used the term "Oedipus complex" for the first time in print, Freud observes of the little boy:

> He does not forgive his mother for having granted the favour of sexual intercourse not to himself but to his father, and he regards it as an act of unfaithfulness. . . . As a result of the constant combined operation of the two driving forces, desire and thirst for revenge, phantasies of his mother's unfaithfulness are by far the most pre-ferred [of all the phantasies about mother's sexual activities]; the lover with whom she commits her act of infidelity almost always exhibits the features of the boy's own ego, or more accurately, of his own idealized personality, grown up and so raised to a level with his father. [Freud, 1910h, p. 238]

In the Leontean version, we encounter both the son's and the hus-band's jealous reaction to the very pregnant mother/wife as she "rounds apace", flaunting the evidence of her sexuality. Here the husband's delusional jealousy—after all, we know in the end that it was he himself who made her pregnant—seems to mirror the little boy's unforgiving hatred that mother grants the favour of sexual intercourse not to him but to his father. It is as if the pseudo-mature father cannot believe in what as a boy he thought he longed for. The reality of intercourse, of sexual penetration, ironically seems to con-taminate the dream of the woman who should be his exclusively. It is a disbelief that marks Othello's delusional jealousy fed by his Iago-jaded suspicions, to which we shall return in the last chapter.

When we reach the conclusion of *The Winter's Tale*, we find not only the dynamics I have been discussing, but other echoes of the family romance as well. The shepherd is not only the "good father", he and his son are given a royal welcome into the king's family. In a playful banter between the shepherd and his son (called simply "Clown"), the son responds to his father's claim that he has been "a gentleman born these four hours":

So you have: but I was a gentleman born before my father; for
the king's son took me by the hand, and called me brother;
and then the two kings called my father brother; and then the
prince, my brother, and the princess, my sister, called my
father father; and so we wept; and there was the first gentleman-like tears that ever we shed.

[V.ii.139–145]

But this Bohemian dream, this romance which transforms *The Winter's Tale* from a tragedy into a story where grieving leads to reparation and reconciliation, does not turn on a defensive fantasy of
family romance. Shakespeare simply enjoys this picture of a happy
ending, poking gentle fun at those "gentleman-like" tears. No,
Leontes' tears are accompanied by a transformation in his internal
world pictured as this dream of the child-couple Perdita and Florizel
emerging from the interfering omnipotence of the little-boy–father—
an interference that we will encounter in subsequent chapters described as intrusive (projective) identification with one's internal
objects. Instead of interfering with this couple, a couple who as the
new generation represents the renewed parental couple able now to
become the procreative couple, Leontes now can acknowledge his
loss. He greets Florizel and Perdita, not yet realizing that she is his
daughter:

Your mother was most true to wedlock, prince;
For she did print your royal father off,
Conceiving you. Were I but twenty-one,
Your father's image is so hit in you,
His very air, that I should call you brother,
As I did him, and speak of something wildly
By us perform'd before. Most dearly welcome!
And your fair princess,—goddess!

[V.i.123–130]

But now we come to the climax of the scene, and in a sense the
climax of the play. Out of Leontes' remorse, regret for the lives his
delusional jealousy has destroyed, has come something for which he
could hardly hope. He has lost a wife, destroying one a couple, and
he has lost two children, another couple. Now in his amazement he
sees before him, as in a dream, the couple they might have been. A
couple, a gracious couple, begetting wonder:

> O, alas!
> I lost a couple, that 'twixt heaven and earth
> Might thus have stood, begetting wonder, as
> You, gracious couple, do.
>
> [V.i.130–133]

If *The Winter's Tale* can for a moment be imagined as a picture of the emergence from narcissism towards marriage, then might we imagine that in Leontes' Bohemian dream the (pro-)creative couple have emerged safe despite the attempts of a controlling father to interfere with their coming together in marriage? It mirrors the child's struggle with its infantile wishes to interfere with the internal parental couple, preventing their procreative coming together. In the Leontean version of this developmental struggle, the attack is on the child, and ultimately on the couple that marks the difference between one's own generation and the next. It is true that *The Winter's Tale* seems on the face of it to transfer all hopes to the new generation. However, if we read this as a story of the transformation happening in the dreamer's internal world, this can also be seen as one picture of the process leading towards the possibility of a marriage—or should we say re-marriage—as one becomes two.

## A gracious couple, begetting wonder: the possibility of re-marriage

Throughout the play, we have been given hints that there is something unsettled and unsettling about Hermione's death and thus about the finality of the destructiveness of Leontes' omnipotence. Perhaps believing his wife to be dead is necessary for him to recognize the consequence of the state of mind that exposes him to delusional jealousy. I think Shakespeare paints an intriguing picture of despair and repentance which not only precedes the emergence of hope, but also seems somehow linked with it and with it the possibility, therefore, of the renewal of the marriage.

But what of the wife in this story? Perhaps, by the wildest stretch of the imagination, we can allow the figure of Paulina to resonate with the role of the analytic therapist who is "invited" to help couples seek and face the truth of their relationship. If so, those of us who work with couples might be forgiven for thinking of her as a "therapist" accustomed to working only with individuals. She has been brilliant in her courage in facing Leontes with the truth of his omnipotent rage and jealousy. Ah, but what of Hermione? It is such a temptation to see the stories couples bring us, stories easily as desperate as that of Hermione and Leontes, in terms of who is at fault. Listening to this story, however, with an ear to the mutuality of such dynamics, might we wonder what is going on here in terms of the *couple*?

All therapists will recognize Shakespeare's portrait of Hermione's state—or should we call it his "sculpt" of her state of mind. It is a state of living death. In the last scene Paulina offers to take Leontes to her house so that Perdita—now recognized as the princess she is, the daughter her father can now acknowledge—can view a statue of her mother. But it is not just an ordinary statue. We are told that it has recently been completed by an Italian sculptor who is master of a lifelike image, who

> could put breath into his work, would beguile Nature of
> her custom, so perfectly he is her ape: he so near to Hermione
> hath done Hermione, that they say one would speak to her
> and stand in hope of answer.

> [V.ii.97–101]

When Leontes, in the company of Polixenes and the young couple who now unite them all into one family, stands before the painted statue, there is a mood of puzzled anticipation. In the Doran RSC production of this scene, a scene that could descend to farce, the tension is almost unbearable. Even the moment when Leontes notices that the disturbingly lifelike statue does not appear as Hermione did when she "died" but as she might look now, we are more inclined to cry than to laugh, or at least I was. Cry, I mean, for the shock of those sixteen lost years, years when this repentant husband and this innocent (is she?) wife might have found reconciliation in their shared grief for their two lost children.

When, in the consulting-room, couples begin to emerge from the living death in which they have been trapped, it is a bit like caricatures of human beings coming to life. And often as they begin to emerge into life it can have some quality of humour, as some may see in that final scene when Paulina invites the music to strike and

Hermione "to be stone no more". But the sadness, the pathos, only makes it the kind of humour that is in fact the recognition of truth.

The image of Hermione as being "stone" for those sixteen years reflects a sense that Leontes' remorseless delusional jealousy at the beginning of the play made him as impenetrable and as unmoveable as this statue his wife has become. That side of the picture seems unmistakable, and couple therapists will have many stories come to mind where one partner is in an impenetrable state, and nothing said by the partner or the therapist can be heard. Until the death of his son, Leontes was able to hear nothing that was said by his wife or advisors, or even by Paulina, who after the death of his son was able to be frank, brutally frank, with him.

But what about Hermione? Is it a question we are allowed to ask? I find the question of *her* sixteen years irresistible, years during which, as we come to realize at the conclusion of the play, she has been alive! We have had hints, the most explicit when one of the narrators of the climactic events muses that he had wondered about the house where Paulina's "sculptures" were kept: "I thought she had some great matter there in hand; for she hath privately twice or thrice a day, ever since the death of Hermione, visited that removed house" (V.ii.104–107). What, I wonder, did Paulina and Hermione talk about those sixteen years?

If Leontes in his jealous rage was cut off from his own humanity as well as from that of those around him, what about the stony anger of the woman who must have known of her husband's remorse and repentance? For sixteen years he visited the tomb that he believed held his wife and son, expressing that remorse. And for sixteen years she let him. Is this not the most bitter revenge?

As I write these words, I can think sadly of couples for whom this unbearable picture would be all too familiar. Perhaps we might say that from the point of view of the couple, Shakespeare's tale is ironically a tale of the mutuality of narcissism, not just the one entombed in a world in which the reality of the other is intolerable, but the other whose revenge simply mirrors this narcissistic repudiation of a genuine other.

In his comments on this last scene of The Winter's Tale, Cavell places the emphasis on the centrality of separation in marriage, or shall we say in the ceremony of *re-marriage* to which the last scene seems to lead:

Then let us emphasize that this ceremony of union takes the form of a ceremony of separation, thus declaring that the question of the two becoming one is just half the problem; the other half is how the one becomes two. It is separation that Leontes' participation in parturition grants—that Hermione has, that there is, a life beyond his, and that she can create a life beyond his and hers, and beyond plenitude and nothingness. The final scene of *The Winter's Tale* interprets this creation as their creation by one another. Each awakes, each was stone, it remains who stirs first, who makes the first move back. The first move of revenge it seems easy to determine; the first move to set aside revenge, impossible. [Cavell, 1987, p. 220]

At the close of that final dramatic scene, as mother greets her lost daughter, and husband introduces his wife to her son-in-law, who is "son unto the king" and thus in a sense his lost son, Shakespeare invites us to reflect on the links between union and separation, between having a part and parturition. With Leontes' final lines we end this winter's tale which introduces the stories of the couples in the chapters to follow, stories of being partners, having a part, parting, sometimes forever, and sometimes leading to reunion, remarriage:

> Good Paulina,
> Lead us from hence, where we may leisurely
> Each one demand, and answer to his part
> Perform'd in this wide gap of time, since first
> We were dissevr'd: hastily lead away.
>
> [V.iii.151–155]

# CHAPTER TWO

# The "false-self" couple:
# seeking truth and being true

In *The Winter's Tale* we have a vivid portrayal of how the couple relationship can become, or perhaps inevitably does become, a setting of intense emotions in which truth itself becomes precarious. In the face of Leontes' certainty that Hermione has been false to him, all protestations to the contrary are swept aside, whether from Hermione herself or from Leontes' own courtiers. Indeed, Apollo's oracle too is dismissed by this husband who *knows* he has been betrayed, betrayed by his wife, betrayed by his childhood friend, betrayed by his loyal minister. And Shakespeare presents this perversion of truth as an attack on the newborn child, the mother's baby, as well as an attack on the mother herself.

When questions of truth take centre stage in therapy with couples, one is rightly cautious. We hardly ever encounter these questions in a mood of gentle inquiry. Most often they accost us with an angry, accusatory tone. "Tell me *the truth!*" seldom feels like a genuine invitation to a constructive coming together in a marriage. And, in therapy, seeking the truth can easily be confused with claims to be *in possession of* the truth, which in turn feels contrary to a mood of exploration.

Leontes, for example, was certain of the truth, could "see't and feel't". He only acceded to the formality—the charade, to be more precise—of a trial and only commissioned the consulting of the Oracle for, you might say, appearances' sake. We sometimes meet a similar state of mind in couples who seek out therapy. They consult us as if we were "judges" or "oracles", but only in order to confirm what they already know, not to pursue the truth. In the words of Leontes:

> Though I am satisfied, and need no more
> Than what I know, yet shall the Oracle
> Give rest to th' mind of others; such as he
> Whose ignorant credulity will not
> Come up to th' truth.

> [*The Winter's Tale*, II.ii.189–193]

In his dismissive reference to those whose ignorant credulity will not come up to the truth, Leontes seems to have in mind those people who believe Hermione, those who take her at her word. Why do they fail to see what he sees, feel what he feels? If he sees something, everyone should see it just as he sees it. Anything less is an ignorant, or perhaps wilful, blindness to the truth. Leontes is a familiar figure in our consulting-rooms, encountered daily in his (or her) blustering denigration of those who do not see things the way he (or she) does. Listening to him, however, we are shocked by *his* ignorant credulity, his blind insistence on *her* unfaithfulness. That is, we are shocked only if we expect to hear his adult reflections about his feelings towards his pregnant wife and her relationship with her son and with his best friend. If we are prepared to listen to his infantile outrage, we might find ourselves less shocked and better able to help him reflect on his experience, his wishes and his fears (Adams, 1999).

There is one question, central to our therapeutic work with couples, that I want to explore now at the beginning of our examination of the theory and technique of a psychoanalytic approach to this work: what does it take to be able to "come up to the truth", to seek, rather than claim to possess, the truth? What would it take in this couple, or in any couple, for both partners to enter and to sustain a truthful relationship with us as therapists and with each other, to seek to be true and truthful, rather than each omnipotently asserting exclusive possession of the truth?

Characteristically, claims to possess the truth exist in a world of *either/or*, in a world in which, if one is true, the other must be false. It is her word or his, and those who believe the other partner are therefore committing treason. Experienced couple therapists can feel themselves becoming tense when claims about the truth are made. They know from many painful encounters how difficult it is to be in a position of being a traitor to one or the other in the couple when they seek to drag us into court, so to speak.

In this chapter, I want to follow our exploration of *The Winter's Tale* with an examination of the important issues that cluster around the theme of truth, and particularly in terms of the issues that emerge when we try to think about truth and truthfulness in the couple relationship. I want to suggest that a psychoanalytic understanding both of therapy and of relationships, particularly following the contribution of Wilfred Bion, gives centre place in the developmental process to the capacity to acknowledge and think about the truth, the reality, of one's experience. This insight, however, tends to get lost in the intense conflicts of the couple relationship. And yet I think the quest for truth and the capacity to be true is at the heart of the therapeutic enterprise, as it is of the developmental process.

I want to set this exploration in the context of a discussion of what I am calling the "false-self couple", drawing on a well-known concept of Donald Winnicott, the false self as distinguished from the true self (Winnicott, 1960). Looked at in developmental terms, it will be seen that the notion of the false self is a relational concept. We often hear people citing Winnicott's dictum that there is no such thing as a baby. We could also say that there is no such thing as a false self, only the false-self couple. Or, in the words of Sir Henry Harcourt Reilly in T. S. Eliot's *The Cocktail Party*, to which we shall turn in chapters eight to ten,

> The single patient
> Who is ill by himself, is rather the exception.
>
> [Eliot, 1950, p. 114, Act II, lines 195–196]

In a sense, this chapter will be an exploration of Bion's exposition of the centrality of truth in relationships and in the psychoanalytic enterprise, and his linking of the pursuit of truth with what he called the *container–contained* relationship. He expresses his view in his paper "On Arrogance" in a remarkably clear statement of what is required "to come up to the truth":

> Briefly, it appears that overwhelming emotions are associated with the assumption by the patient or analyst of the *qualities required to pursue the truth,* and in particular a capacity to tolerate stresses associated with the introjection of another person's projective identifications. Put into other terms, *the implicit aim of psycho-analysis to pursue the truth at no matter what cost* is felt to be synonymous with a claim to a capacity for containing the discarded, split-off aspects of other personalities while *retaining a balanced outlook.* This would appear to be the immediate signal for outbreaks of envy and hatred. [Bion, 1967, pp. 88–89, italics added]

What Bion describes here in his characteristically condensed way is, I think, one of his most important contributions to contemporary psychoanalytic understanding of the capacity for intimate relationships. What I want to do at this point is to explore what I think Bion is saying about the qualities required to pursue the truth in the face of primitive projective processes. In fact, the relating through intrusive projective identification, along with the capacity to tolerate the anxieties and stresses of being on the other end of someone's intrusive projections, are themes that we shall explore throughout this book.

This chapter takes us into some theoretical considerations that underlie the approach I have taken with *The Winter's Tale* and will be pursuing in the clinical and literary material to follow. This inevitably involves some discussions of contemporary as well as classical psychoanalytic theory, and some readers may prefer to move on to the more clinical chapters before returning to what may feel rather abstract discussions.

Returning to Bion, it is important to note that he links his discussion of the pursuit of truth with Sophocles' play *Oedipus the King,* suggesting a reading of the myth of Oedipus in which "the central crime is the arrogance of Oedipus in vowing to lay bare the truth at no matter what cost" (Bion, 1967, p. 86). What constitutes the difference between the arrogance of Oedipus to lay bare the truth and our search for truth with our patients in the psychoanalytic enterprise? What distinguishes the husband or wife arrogantly demanding to know the truth from the couple who pursue truth in the spirit of seeking to be true? When does arrogance take over? And why?

Bion's answer is that "in the personality where life instincts predominate, pride becomes self-respect, where death instincts predominate, pride becomes arrogance" (Bion, 1967, p. 86). But that answer leaves us with yet more questions, questions not so much about instincts as about the difference between what is linked with life and what with death, what promotes life and what works against it. It is the difference between a couple coming together in an intercourse that leads to new life, and a couple coming together destructively that leads to the death of new life.

## Does truth matter for the couple?

How important is truth in intimate relationships? Two couples I saw in therapy stand out in my mind when I think about this question, not because they were unique, but because they so vividly illustrated something common to all relationships in one way or another. Both couples were desperate to uncover the truth of what had happened between them and to them in their relationships. Although it is true, as I suggested in the previous chapter, that most couples who seek out therapy are not literally exploring the possibility of re-marriage, I have seen a number of couples who are anxiously exploring whether there is anything in the relationship that would warrant coming together again. This often means coming to terms with their shared history—that is, a history they agree they shared, but not a history of which they could have a shared, or common, account.

The first of these two couples came to therapy prior to getting married, while the other, with grown children, sought out therapy after having formally separated and with divorce proceedings under way. One might have thought in consequence that these two couples would have had little in common. It very soon became clear to me, however, that both couples were similarly engaged in an anxious search to uncover the truth of what had happened between them that had driven them apart after a genuine coming together. They both seemed, perhaps more unconsciously than consciously, to recognize that they could not come (back) together unless and until they could find, or create, an account of their history which could be shared enough for it to feel like a common history. A "good-enough" account would be one that could somehow take into consideration

their conflicting experiences, or, should we say, their conflicting perceptions.

In a session with the older couple early in the therapy, I was
trying to understand why they had sought me out and what they
thought they were doing in therapy. The husband said, it's simple.
He then proceeded to describe South Africa's Truth and Reconciliation Commission. "They've got the right idea", he said with passion,
"Mandela is right—there can't be any reconciliation until there is a
confronting the truth of what has happened." What followed was an
interesting exchange. His wife talked about each of them having his
or her own views of what had happened between them. When they
came to a critical point where they had ardent, animated, but also
radically different, memories, she tried to retreat using the plea,
"You have your truth, your experience, and I have mine". He ex-
ploded:

> "Experience! Experience! I hate that word. The point is what hap-
> pened! We have to get at the truth, and if we don't, well there just
> can't be any reconciliation without finding out what happened."

The intensity of his outburst took me aback. There flashed through
my mind the occasions in the short time I had known this couple
when I had talked about the importance of being able to think about
their experience. I was conscious of how difficult it would be to find
a way of talking with this couple. With her, I shared a tendency to
think in terms of their, and my, *experience*. And yet I shared with him
a passion for *the truth*. It was difficult to find a way of acknowledging what one was saying without at the same time denying what
the other was insisting on. Although they were one of the most engaging and, for the most part, quietly thoughtful couples I have seen
in therapy, they were both trapped in a rigid world marked by a
persistent *either/or*—an either/or that announces the struggle for
survival, often on the edge of the most civilized violence. Each is
terrified that any accommodation can, in effect, lead to annihilation,
indeed that accommodation has led each of them to feel annihilated
as a person in this relationship.

The younger couple, although they did not share a long history
together, had nevertheless this same sense that they each could acknowledge what the other said about what had gone on between
them only at the cost of denying what they each *knew* in their heart to

be true. This dilemma of two conflicting accounts was echoed in their experience that, when he made it clear that he wanted to get married, she was flooded with doubts and drew back. And when later she was desperate to marry and for them to get on with their lives, make provision for children, and so on, he was the one flooded with doubts. This *either/or* dynamic not only marked their swings from feeling abandoned to feeling trapped in the larger scale of their relationship, one could also track it moment to moment in a session with them.

Some of that spirit can get into our professional life when advocates of different theoretical orientations act as if they were trapped in an *either/or* world, again almost as if accommodation could lead to annihilation. This can lead therapists to a kind of *relativism* based on an implicit assumption that *valuing* truth is tantamount to a claim to *possess* the truth. This seems to require that if one is to speak of truth it must be only speaking about *my* truth and *your* truth. This way of thinking claims that we all have our own truth, that there is no absolute truth. Already we hear echoes of an insidious either/or relativism or absolutism. But are we really forced into this dichotomy?

In a recent lecture at the Tavistock, a leading systemic family therapist was cautioning against any therapeutic approach that placed a premium on truth and on the search for truth. Illustrating how important it was in the systemic way of working that therapists should avoid falling into the trap of believing that their "truth" was the only truth, he reminded us of a familiar motto: *Never fall in love* . . . —he paused, and something clicked in my head at that point, although he had not finished his thought. *Never fall in love . . . with your own hypotheses* (Campbell, 1998)!

Good advice. And not just for those working systemically. Therapists working psychoanalytically can easily fall in love with their own formulations. But, I was still stuck on that *"Never fall in love. . . ."* We might say that *you* can have *your* view, and *I* can have *mine*—*she* can have *her* "truth", and *he* can have *his* "truth". We might say that one can sustain a kind of "live and let live" policy regarding differing perspectives, differing beliefs and convictions, as long as they do not intersect in any way that has real consequences. Falling in love with someone means that there are consequences that cannot always be avoided or evaded when the other person's perspective or belief differs from your own. It is when you care—and I mean care deeply—about *my* truth, and I care—care deeply—about *your* truth, that we cannot simply ignore the consequences of our conflicting realities. It is at this point that this notion of truth becomes problematic in a way that I think no easy relativism can constructively help us avoid.

Certainly, with couples in therapy, I think that if we avoid this issue of truth we deprive ourselves and the couples of the cutting edge of a psychoanalytic approach. In a sense, Bion's major contribution to contemporary psychoanalysis has been *both* his reminding us that since Freud the psychoanalytic aim has been the pursuit of truth *and* his making clear the qualities required for two people together to pursue the truth. Although we do not always use the language of truth in the context of the mother–infant relationship, one can say that Bion was describing the qualities that the mother must have in order that she and her infant can pursue the truth of the infant's experiences, experiences that otherwise are bewildering to the infant. Without that capacity of the mother, which Bion described as containing, the infant can only escape to an *either/or* world with everything split irrevocably into good and bad, accepted and rejected. Instead of a splitting that forms the basis of healthy discrimination, there is what feels like an unreconcilable world of exclusive disjunctions—one or the other, but not both.

While sometimes locked in an either/or world, my "Truth & Reconciliation" couple also seemed genuinely touched by the mood of the South African experiment and recognized some similar need in themselves to base their hoped-for reconciliation on a seeking and facing *together* the truth of their previous experience. It is unnecessary at this point to go into the details of their story, except to say that I was moved, and sometimes even shocked, both at the kind of traumas that they had shared and even more at the difference in the ways they individually had experienced those traumas. The reader with experience of therapy with couples will have had similar times when it was difficult to believe that the two otherwise apparently sensible people in the couple were attempting to describe the same event. For a long while in the therapy with my "Truth & Reconciliation" couple, my role seemed to consist in pointing out the junctures at which they were each torn between turning away from the truth of their own experience, and demanding that the other turn away from the truth of his or her own experience.

Surprisingly, the young couple who came to me for "pre-marital counselling" also were remarkably reasonable, listening carefully and thoughtfully to what I had to say. But they were always on the edge of handing over to me all responsibility for their fraught situation. Having set a deadline for their return to their home country, with commitments that they could not ignore, they felt that the decision they had to make would mean either that he would feel trapped and she abandoned, or she would feel trapped, and he abandoned. Although we knew at the beginning of the therapy that they would have only a short time, the deadline created a sense both of our being trapped, with a rapidly escalating feeling of panic, and an inevitable feeling that I was abandoning them at a critical juncture for both of them individually and for their future as a couple. What is it that leads to such a sense of crisis for these two couples?

We might say that there are two stages in the developmental process which lead to a capacity to pursue and face the truth. We might characterize the *first stage* of the developmental process as the development of a capacity to face the reality of our own experience. The *second stage* involves the capacity to face the truth of someone else's experience at the same time as not losing or denying the reality of one's own experience. The second is what Bion described as the "capacity to tolerate stresses associated with the introjection of another person's projective identifications"—that is, "a capacity for containing the discarded, split-off aspects of other personalities"—*while retaining a balanced outlook* (Bion, 1967, pp. 88–89). In the next section, I want to explore the possibility that the achievement of the first stage may be dependent on an intimate relationship with someone who has achieved the second stage.

## The capacity to face the truth of one's emotional experience

It is interesting and important to consider the relational dimension of the capacity to face the truth of one's own emotional experience. Turning away from emotional reality can lead to what Helene Deutsch (1942) described as the "as-if" personality, Donald Meltzer (1967) termed the "pseudo-mature" character structure, and Donald Winnicott (1960) described as the phenomenon of the *false self*. Although these different designations emphasize different aspects of this personality structure, they all point to a distinct and familiar phenomenon. For the moment, I want to concentrate on Winnicott's discussion because of its emphasis on the interpersonal dynamics related to this *as-if, pseudo-mature, false-self* state of mind.

Winnicott outlined his understanding of the false self in terms of the infant's relationship with what he terms the *not-good-enough mother*. In his well-known concept of the "good-enough mother", he included the mother's ability to recognize and to respond to the *spontaneous gestures* of her infant. What Winnicott described behaviourally as "spontaneous gestures" we can imagine as, in part at least, linked with what Melanie Klein described as the infant's intolerable emotions which are projected into the mother. Where Winnicott highlighted the mother's recognition and response to the infant's gestures, Bion emphasized the mother's capacity to take in and identify with the infant's projections, as the infant *both* seeks to get rid of disturbing feelings *and* to communicate in a primitive way what it can neither understand nor tolerate.

In an earlier paper, I described this relationship between mother and infant as a prototype of what I suggested was a "false-self couple" (Fisher, 1993). Winnicott makes clear in his paper "Ego Distortions in Terms of True and False Self" (1960) that the development of a false self was linked with the infant's early experience with the mother. He suggested that when the mother is unable adequately to recognize and respond to the infant's gestures, there is a temptation to substitute her own gestures for those of the infant. The use of the term "gestures" is interesting here. In a recent paper, Warren Colman has discussed Winnicott's analysis, suggesting an interactive field between mother and infant which he then goes on to use to describe the adult intimate relationship (Colman, 1995). Colman feels that this gives a richer conceptual range for understanding couple dynamics, which have traditionally been described in terms of projective identification.

The notion of *gesture* is indeed suggestive for thinking about the capacity to face the truth of one's own emotional experience. Gestures are not random movements. Of course, many of the infant's movements may be random, but under the rapt gaze and encouraging attention of the parents such movements are seen as meaningful gestures, and in the developmental dance of parent and child they do indeed become genuine gestures. This aspect of gesture—that it is a mode of communication—emphasizes the importance of the other, the one who is meant to, or it is hoped will, understand. That is, it is a moving of the body or some part of the body in a way that is *pregnant with meaning*, expressing or giving emphasis to an idea, a state of mind, or an emotion. That image of pregnancy derives, of course, from the literal meaning of the word, since "gesture" comes from the Latin meaning "to bear" and is related to "gestate", to carry in the uterus during pregnancy. A gesture gives birth to a meaning in that it is a gesture from someone, to someone.

Winnicott's point about the generation of a false self is that when the mother is unable to recognize and respond to the infant's gesture, not only is she tempted to substitute a gesture of her own, but the infant is in the helpless position of having to give sense to mother's gesture by its compliance. In my paper "The Impenetrable Other", I suggested that this relationship can be seen as a *false-self couple* (Fisher, 1993). This couple is constituted in the dynamic in which the one (the mother) substitutes her own gesture for that of the other (the infant), plus *the other's compliance* which in effect substitutes the gesture of the other (the mother) for its own (the infant). The infant loses contact with its own emotional experience and is unable to acknowledge what it is feeling because there is no other, no mother, able to acknowledge its gesture, to acknowledge what it is feeling.

One of the most distressing scenes I have seen in the attachment research videotape studies of mother–baby relating was one in which the baby was crying hesitatingly and, in the opinion of the researcher in the room and those watching the tape, was in some distress. The mother looked nervously at the researcher and then at the baby and said: "Oh look, he's laughing." It is an uncomfortable but not an unfamiliar scene. More than once in the consulting-room with couples, one or other partner has begun laughing for no apparent reason, and in fact quite contrary to the mood of what was being talked about. And more than once I have commented on it as strange, only to have them acknowledge that if they were not laughing they would be crying, crying unbearably and uncontrollably. They had learned to laugh, not cry, to substitute some other person's idea of the appropriate gesture for what they were actually feeling. At least in this case it seemed possible to recover the genuine feeling, the spontaneous gesture, behind the learned compliant behaviour. That is not always easy, and sometimes can almost feel impossible.

In Bion's terms, this describes the mother who is unable to take in the infant's projections, who becomes, to use Michael Feldman's language, impenetrable (Feldman, 1989). In a very important paper for understanding this dynamic, Feldman describes how the infant confronted with an impenetrable mother or parental couple becomes increasingly desperate and this gives rise to two alternative patterns. Either the infant makes increasingly violent attempts to get through to this impenetrable object, or it withdraws to the blankness of a hopeless situation that it cannot face. Probably with most infants in such a situation, the former gradually gives way to the latter. Certainly in adult couples we often see an oscillating and escalating pattern in which one becomes increasingly violent in an attempt to get through to the other, while the other increasingly withdraws into impenetrable blankness.

We might say that somewhere in this dynamic there emerges Winnicott's compliant infant "making the best of a bad job", another of those phrases we shall come to when we consider Eliot's *The Cocktail Party*. This capacity to make the best of a bad job, so useful in some ways, can disguise a development that over the years leads to a firmly fixed pattern of false-self relating. In "The Impenetrable Other", I also pointed out that the false-self couple needs a term for the other, for the one who is in the position of the not-good-enough mother who can neither recognize nor respond to the gestures of the infant (Fisher, 1993). I suggested that the substitution of her own gestures for those of the infant's is a tyrannical move.

Every couple whose relating is structured on this pattern—every *false-self couple*—is made up of either a *compliant self* and a *tyrannical other*, or a *tyrannical self* and a *compliant other*. Every false-self personality structure hides in it the tyrant, and one has only to observe such compliant persons when the tables can be turned. What we see is that the false self both complains about the tyrannical other *and, given the opportunity*, becomes that tyrannical other demanding compliance in return. Those are the only two options! It is an either/or world, either tyranny or compliance, either being a bully or being bullied. We see this dynamic of tyranny and compliance at any age, even dramatically at the end of life, as Hess shows in his study of *King Lear* and old age (Hess, 1987).

## Distinguishing between self and other

Let me introduce you to a young patient of mine who is struggling with her panic at the prospect of a *de facto* marriage as her boyfriend of some years proposes to move back in with her on an "experimental" basis. It was, she said, like "reality kicking in", giving up, settling in, "the end". But why? A year previously he had said that he needed space to sort himself out and had moved out into the country four or five hours' drive away. This was traumatic for her, but over the year she got used to a commuting relationship and bought a large flat with rooms she could let to flatmates of her choosing. When she came to her session after her boyfriend's announcement that he was moving back in, she had been awake most of the night. She felt as if she had been burgled, except instead of someone breaking in and taking valuables, she felt oppressed at the "invasion" of all her boyfriend's things.

Her picture was that it would no longer be *her* bedroom, but *theirs*, his possessions, his depression, everywhere permeating all the spaces. It was, I suggested, as if there were no doors in this flat, at least none that could be closed. She responded that it was crazy, but she lay awake in the middle of the night thinking of her plates and his plates side by side in the cupboard. How would they tell them apart! Immediately she began talking about the horror of her parents' divorce, the painful, hateful, and impossible task of separating what belonged to whom, ripping apart things that belonged together.

I suggested to her that she was in fact describing a nightmare, a dream of a little girl, listening anxiously to what mummy and daddy were doing in their bedroom—doing something that got everything all mixed up together, her picture of intercourse. My patient responded testily that there was no relationship on earth where people don't want to destroy each other. It was possible then to talk about her fear in her relationship with her boyfriend, and in the relationship with me, that intercourse means things getting all mixed up so there is no "yours" and "mine". Of course, as she pointed out, the plates were very distinct, with different patterns. Factually, it is easy to tell them apart. Like her thoughts, and my thoughts. But emotionally coming together intimately means *con-fusion*, literally "fusing with", the end. But separation, too, was the end, since it meant, inevitably, as another patient insisted, divorce—and divorce, he growled, *is the end*.

How does one safely distinguish between self and other, between *me* and *not-me*? I want to take us right back to the beginning, to thinking about the primitive experience of recognizing what belongs to me and what does not. My experience of the psychoanalytic process with couples is that we are almost continuously taken right back to the most primitive dynamics of the confusion of self and other. Clarity about these primitive dynamics, I think, helps us as therapists in the heat of the consulting-room to retain what Bion called "a balanced outlook".

I do not think that it is necessary for our purposes here to turn aside to questions about the distinction between *self* and *other* which belong in the domain of developmental psychology and are the subject of empirical research. While this is not a discussion I will explore here, readers of this book who are interested in this subject will probably find most intriguing the work of Peter Hobson, who brings a unique combination of psychoanalysis and post-Wittgensteinian philosophical understanding of subjectivity to his developmental studies (Hobson, 1993a, 1993b). Although I am very interested in this area and have begun my own exploration in my paper "The Domain of the Self " (Fisher, 1996), here I want to focus on how we think about the distinction between self and other in intimate relationships, whether in marriage or in the consulting-room.

Intuitively, when we look at adult relationships we might wonder how my patient, or any of the otherwise sensible couples we see, could become confused about what is self and what is other. However, if we look at the infant's experience we might wonder just the opposite. How does the infant come to distinguish what is and what is not self? We know that there is a long and intricate process of reality-testing which leads to a capacity to recognize and acknowledge what is real, true, genuine. The development of what Freud called a *reality-ego* includes a capacity for relationships in which there is both emotional intimacy and a recognition of the emotional reality of what belongs to the self and what belongs to the other.

Consider with me for a moment what we might describe as Freud's "fable" of the developmental process leading to an acknowledgement of reality—what he calls the "reality principle". I believe this fable is not as far from Wilfred Bion's ideas as at first it might seem. The basic struggle in Freud's imaginative story is the move from what he called a *pleasure-ego* to a *reality-ego*. That is, we should say a "mature" reality-ego, since Freud imagines an original "reality-ego" that was able in a primitive, but effective, way to distinguish between internal (subject, self) and external. He invites his readers to picture a helpless living organism as yet unorientated in the world and receiving stimuli, and he offers this account of how this original reality ego might function:

> This organism will very soon be in a position to make a first distinction and a first orientation. On the one hand, it will be aware of stimuli which can be avoided by muscular action (flight); these it ascribes to the external world. On the other hand, it will also be aware of stimuli against which such action is of no avail and whose character of constant pressure persists in spite of it; these stimuli are the signs of an internal world, the evidence of instinctual needs. The perceptual substance of the living organism will thus have found in the efficacy of its muscular activity a basis for distinguishing between an "outside" and an "inside". [Freud, 1915c, p. 119]

We are being invited to imagine how a primitive distinction between inside and outside arises in the infant's awareness. How does the organism come to distinguish between what belongs to its "self" and what belongs to some "other", or, in the language of personal pronouns, what is "me" and what is "not-me". It is simple, at least in this appealing fable. The external is that from which I can escape, for example, by moving some muscles. Something hurts my hand— something sharp, say. I move my hand, and then it no longer hurts. But, if I move my hand *and it still hurts*, no matter what or how I move, it must be me.

It is simple, perhaps too simple, although fables generally are. But stay with me, or rather with Freud, for a minute. Why? Because this simple capacity to distinguish internal and external reality, self and not-self, is almost immediately affected by what Freud called the "pleasure principle". According to this basic assumption, organisms move towards what feels good and away from what feels bad. And this undermines the original reality-testing capacity. Thus, in Freud's fable, the original "reality-ego" gives way to the "pleasure-ego", with the result that the boundaries between self and other, between internal and external, are re-drawn.

I think Freud is suggesting that this intrusion of the pleasure principle is the beginning of a basic confusion—or at least I am reading him that way. Much of subsequent development can be seen as a struggle with this self-interested attempt to redraw the boundaries between self and other, this "gerrymandering" of reality if you please. Success in challenging this gerrymandering can be described in other language as the resolution of the depressive position.

Consider what the pleasure principle does to the original distinction between self and other. Insofar as the self encounters objects that appear to be sources of pleasure, it takes them into itself, or, Freud says, to use a term of Ferenczi's, it *introjects* them. On the other hand, quite conveniently, Freud suggests, the self, the ego, expels whatever within itself becomes a cause of unpleasure (i.e. what the original reality-ego recognized as stimuli that it could not get away from). Thus we find that the pleasure-ego has redrawn the boundaries of internal and external, or, should we say, *gerrymandered* the boundaries, to its own advantage:

> For the pleasure-ego the external world is divided into a part that is pleasurable, which it has incorporated into itself, and a remainder that is extraneous to it. It has separated off a part of its own self, which it projects into the external world and feels as hostile. After this new arrangement, the two polarities coincide once more: the ego-subject coincides with pleasure, and the external world with unpleasure (with what was earlier indifference). [Freud, 1915c, p. 136]

This is, I am suggesting, a lively and early version, a fable, of the dynamic familiar to us now under the term *projective identification*. Melanie Klein introduced the term projective identification to make clear that what is split off and projected is a part of the self (Klein, 1946). How often we in our personal lives, as well as the patients in our consulting-rooms, recapitulate Freud's fable of the developmental process. It usually sounds something like this: what is good belongs to, or comes from, me, and what is bad belongs to, or comes from, you—or one of the many variations of this gerrymandering of reality. Most, if not all, of the couples I have seen in therapy have had versions of this exchange in which they seem to want to con-

vince me, or themselves, of this way of drawing the distinction between what is internal and what is external, what is his responsibility and what is hers.

Of course I am oversimplifying here, but I only want to emphasize
the familiarity of Freud's intuition. In his paper "Negation" in 1925,
Freud comes back to the characterization of this stage of development as the pleasure-ego, which "wants to introject into itself everything that is good and to eject from itself everything that is bad". The
consequence of this perversion of reality, for that is what this gerrymandering is, is that the capacity to face reality becomes the basic
achievement of the developmental process. Melanie Klein, Roger
Money-Kyrle, and Wilfred Bion among many others have brought
psychoanalysis back to a focus on this aim, the importance of the
capacity to face the truth of one's experience of both self and the
external world.

My aim here is to emphasize the momentous task of coming to
terms with what is self and what is the external world when the
"external" means another person who is also a subject, a self. This is
an essential stage of the developmental process, the encounter where
the other in my external world also has a subjective struggle with his
or her experience of me as an external other, and we both are trying
to come to terms with a shared external world. Structurally, this can
be described in terms of the Oedipal drama, especially in the way
Ronald Britton has drawn attention to what he calls the "triangular
space" which marks the achievement of an emotional capacity to
face the turmoil of being excluded from the parental couple, as well
as being part of a couple that excludes an other.

Perhaps participating in the psychoanalytic process with a couple
gives us a particular viewpoint from which to observe the dimension
of this developmental achievement I want to highlight now. There is
a sense, I think, in which the classical Oedipal picture can distort our
picture of this process of facing reality, the development of what is
called the "reality-ego". I began with *The Winter's Tale* because I
think that what I have been calling the Leontean drama gives us a
different perspective on the facing of reality, one that emphasizes
how intercourse can lead to a third, where a genuine intercourse
with the reality of the other leads to a third reality that participates
in the reality of each but is identical with neither.

Ironically, the classical picture of the Oedipal drama can lead to a distortion of the pursuit of truth. It need not, but I want to explore how it can, mistakenly, be linked with the child's appeal to the parental truth, an appropriation of the parental prerogatives. On the other hand, the Leontean drama emphasizes the pursuit of truth as an intercourse with the other and the taking of responsibility for the outcome. These are two different models for the encounter with the truth of the other.

## Models for the encounter with the truth of the other

The two models that I want to describe for this second stage of the facing of truth, this encounter with the truth of the other, are based both in unconscious phantasy and in conscious fantasies about the nature of knowing. They are also rooted in the experience of knowing in the context of early family dynamics.

The first has to do with an external, "objective" authority, and we might call it the "mother knows best" or the "father knows best" version. It contains the wish, and eventually the expectation, that we can find a way to assume this parental (or divine, or at least supra-human) prerogative. This model has its origin in sibling rivalry as children squabble over who is right, each seeking to establish his or her own experience as *the truth*. The assumption, at least for the earliest years of life, when it has its greatest plausibility, is that there is someone—the adults, in particular the parents—who has access to, or in some cases, determines what is true. In its earliest form, and in the form that gives it its power, it is true that for the helpless infant, reality and thus survival is in the hands of the parents. Later on, this authority shifts gradually to other adults, and ultimately to the fantasy of the truly objective outsider.

For some, this fantasy is never challenged. As our understanding has increased and science has taught us that standing outside is conceptually impossible, this fantasy survives perhaps most dramatically in religious belief—not in the gods say of ancient Greece who were hardly "outside", but in the Wholly Other, a fully transcendent God. Without pursuing the point here, I just note that in Christian theology the attempt to imagine a Wholly Divine Other who becomes part of human experience—and if God could not know what it is like to be human, he could not be omniscient (that is, all-knowing)—resulted in just the kind of conflict I am trying to describe. That is, the God-the-Son exclaims (and believes), my God, my God, why hast thou forsaken me. But God-the-Father knows he has not forsaken his son. To pursue this further might take us into struggles in the ancient Christian church—for example, over the Homoousian (Father and Son were the same, consubstantial), Heteroousian (Father and Son were other), and Homoiousian (Father and Son were like but not identical) doctrines.

These are powerful mythical images of fundamental unconscious assumptions about the nature of intimate relating, whatever we think about the great theological and philosophical debates in which they enter into the language of our culture. Similar conflicts take different forms in different religions and cultures, but the themes are universal, as universal as the intercourse-of-two-giving-birth-to-the-third. It is the struggle between reproduction through intercourse versus reproduction through identification or identity.

There are powerful and complex reasons why we persist in this wish to be in a relationship, and therefore have the point of view we have, and at the same time stand outside it and know something— the truth—as only a genuinely objective outsider could know it. It is not possible—but we are reluctant to give it up. We all still want a parent who knows, *and* we want access to this *objective truth*, and sometimes claim to have it, even though it is impossible!

It is important to keep in mind that, when we talk about the capacity to acknowledge the truth of our experience, we are talking about the truth of our emotional experience, the meaning, the emotional meaning, of our experience. I can *learn about* the meaning of my parents' intercourse. At one level, the answer to the child's questions "how did I get here?" and "where did I come from?" is the same: daddy and mummy had intercourse. Just as the child continues to be dependent on the intercourse of the parents with the world. But the emotional meaning of that intercourse lies hidden behind the bedroom door. My exclusion from that couple and their intercourse is the truth of my dependence on them and the truth of the difference between the generations. Of course, I can imitate my parents and seem to know what they know by trying to identify with them. But that illusion of meaning, the illusion of my experience having a meaning because I imitate them, leads to a pseudo-adult state of mind, what we described in Winnicott's terms as a "false self", or what Meltzer calls the pseudo-mature person, or what Deutsch called the "as-if" personality (Deutsch, 1942; Meltzer, 1966).

On the other hand, I may aspire to something meaningful because the emotion of their intercourse gave birth to certain feelings in me, but that is something very different from identification or imitation, and something much more like aspiration or inspiration. It is something much more like intercourse. This leads to an alternative to this model of the "objective" parental other, access to whose truth we seek. The dynamics of this knowing is grounded in both unconscious and conscious phantasies about procreative intercourse. In emphasizing the other side of the Oedipal drama, the Leontean drama, I want to call attention to the anxieties involved in two people, each with different realities, coming together in a creative intercourse, a *knowing* of the other in the biblical sense. The anxieties have to do with the potential of the creation of a third, related to each of these two different people *but identical with neither*.

Were either of the procreative couple to try to become identical with the other, intercourse would become impossible. I want to emphasize the obvious: intercourse is the coming together of two *different* people, two different realities, two different truths. Of course, there must be the possibility of a coming together, there must be a complementarity, complementary differences. Otherwise, there can be no coming together at all. But reproduction that is not based on the intercourse of two who are different must be some version of cloning. In a recent dream, one of my patients, a computer specialist, described it as the making of a "back-up file"—that is, "perfect" reproduction.

But genuine intercourse means engaging one's truth with the truth of another, being willing to *risk creating together the child, the truth of that intercourse*. And one persistent anxiety is the anxiety that it will be a bastard child, a child who does not bear the stamp, the imprint, of the parent. Procreation is risky because the coming together does not *re-produce* the two, not exactly. Like Leontes' anxiety about his son Mamillius—does the son resemble him, how can he know he is really his, that there is not too much of his mother Hermione in him—the hatred of difference extends to the offspring.

We have been considering this dynamic in interpersonal terms, but it is interesting to return to Bion and his analysis in terms of

mental processes. Once we begin to take seriously the relational nature of the developmental process, it perhaps comes as less of a surprise to find that there is an intimate interplay between the processes
that shape interpersonal dynamics and those that shape mental functioning. In his paper "Differentiation of the Psychotic", Bion notes
that destructive splitting in a psychotic state of mind attacks the very
thought processes themselves (Bion, 1967). I quote him at length because his comments are germane to what might be termed psychotic
processes in the couple relationship.

> All these [links] are now attacked till finally two objects cannot be
> brought together in a way which leaves each object with its intrin-
> sic qualities intact and yet able, by their conjunction, to produce a
> new mental object. Consequently the formation of symbols, *which
> depends for its therapeutic effect on the ability to bring together two
> objects so that their resemblance is made manifest, yet their difference left
> unimpaired*, now become difficult. [Bion, 1967, p. 50, italics added]

Bion goes on with an even more pertinent observation that this does
not mean that a coming-together is impossible, only that the coming-
together is "impregnated with cruelty":

> This last does not mean that objects cannot be brought together; as
> I shall show later when speaking of agglomeration, that is by no
> means true. Further, since that-which-links has been not only
> minutely fragmented but also projected out into objects to join
> other bizarre objects, the patient feels surrounded by minute links
> which, being impregnated now with cruelty, link objects together
> cruelly. [Bion, 1967, p. 50]

One could hardly imagine a more apt, concise description of the
dilemma of the couple caught in a process of psychotic relating. In
the stories we shall explore in this book, we will see time and again
versions of this resorting to a fragmentation of emotional experience
in an attempt neither to acknowledge nor to think about emotional
reality. The mark of this kind of fragmentation, as we shall see all too
often, are links "impregnated with cruelty". It is the dynamic described in chapter eleven as the sado-masochistic *folie-à-deux* relationships.

Therapists new to working psychoanalytically with couples are
often puzzled about what holds two people together when almost

every moment of their relationship is permeated with cruelty. Until one has experienced the power of this psychotic process to lock two people together in what feels like hell to both, it is, I acknowledge, difficult to credit. And because it is a deeply psychotic process, the temptation to reason with the couple not only leads to frustration for both therapist and couple, but it also profoundly misunderstands the nature of the dilemma.

The Othello story, like *The Winter's Tale* and many other of Shakespeare's dramas, as well as the story brought to us by so many of the couples who seek out therapy, is the story of the hatred of just those differences that make procreative intercourse possible. In the final chapter, I want to turn to *Othello* in some detail, in the way we considered *The Winter's Tale*, since it is one of the most shocking versions of a story that we will explore in some of its many guises.

To recapitulate: I am suggesting that the capacity to pursue the truth of one's own experience and also to tolerate the truth of another's experience, acknowledging and taking in the meaning of the other's experience without losing the meaning of one's own, especially when these experiences not only differ but conflict, is a major developmental achievement. It will be clear to those familiar with the contributions of Melanie Klein that this is one way of describing what she called the *depressive position*. The achievement of this capacity is not a fixed state, and in intimate relationships we are always under the pressure of our infantile wishes, fears, and anxieties to redraw the boundaries between self and other. The bad, the undesirable, the persecuting, and so on we are always tempted to project into the other, appropriating to ourselves the good, the desirable, and so on.

With these theoretical considerations in mind, I want now to take us into the consulting-room for an extended look at the therapy with one couple which illustrates some of the themes that I have outlined in this chapter.

# CHAPTER THREE

# The gathering of the transference

You might say that the development of a psychoanalytic understanding of the couple relationship began with the beginning of psychoanalysis itself, and thus with the pioneering work of Sigmund Freud. It is true that the couple in which Freud took the greatest interest was the analyst–analysand couple; at least, it was the couple relationship that he explored in some detail. However, the development of a psychoanalytic approach to psychotherapy with couples begins much later. I am tempted to claim that the first couple psychotherapy session was described in 1949 by T. S. Eliot in his play *The Cocktail Party*—a somewhat tongue-in-cheek claim that I will present in subsequent chapters. How psychoanalytic the "therapy" described by Eliot in that play is, the reader will have to decide after reading my commentary on it.

In a more sober mood, I want to acknowledge the work of two of the pioneering institutions in the application of a psychoanalytic approach to therapeutic work with couples: the Family Discussion Bureau (FDB), as the Tavistock Marital Studies Institute (TMSI) was originally known, and the Marital Unit of the Tavistock Clinic. Both of these units still exist, although only the TMSI has instituted a formal training and qualification specifically in psychoanalytic marital psychotherapy, and in consequence there is now a Society of Psychoanalytical Marital Psychotherapists (SPMP) which carries forward this tradition. The Marital Unit in the Adult Department of the Tavistock Clinic includes some experience with couples as part of its adult psychotherapy qualification. Since I do not intend to take a descriptive historical approach here, the reader who wishes to look back may want to consult *Psychotherapy with Couples* edited by Stanley Ruszczynski (1993) as well as *Marital Tensions* by Henry Dicks (1967) for an appreciation of the work and thinking of these two sister organizations, although there is no history as yet which includes the story of the SPMP.

However, there is one sense in which I do want to look back. Having begun with the story of Leontes and Hermione in *The Winter's Tale*, I now want to invite you, the reader, to consider with me what is genuinely one of the earliest accounts of a psychoanalytic approach to couple therapy. It was published originally in a book that recorded some of the cases that epitomized the pioneering work of the Family Discussion Bureau. For decades it was a standard text for couple therapists and counsellors. Edited by Lily Pincus and based on clinical work done in the 1950s, it was often referred to over the subsequent three decades after its publication as simply "the Marriage Book". I propose to use it as something of a springboard for my account of some current thinking about the application of psychoanalysis to a clinical setting where the patient is a couple.

## "The Marriage Book"

In his introduction to the Marriage Book, formally titled *Marriage: Studies in Emotional Conflict and Growth* (Pincus, 1960), psychoanalyst Geoffrey Thompson characterizes the five case studies that make up the bulk of the book as representative both of the types of marital problems brought to the FDB and of the therapeutic work done with the couples. The detailed descriptions of the interaction between the "caseworkers", as the therapists were then known, and each partner in the couples, give a lively sense of the kind of thinking that informed the work at this early stage in the history of couple therapy.

What strikes me now re-reading the Marriage Book is both how familiar and yet at times how distant it can sound. For example, the fact that the therapists were known as caseworkers shows the strong link with the Social Work profession. I will, for convenience, refer to them by the terms currently in use in this emerging speciality of psychoanalytic psychotherapy: marital psychotherapist, psychotherapist, or simply therapist. There is also the matter of how to refer to the couples who come for therapy. In the FDB days, they were known as "clients", and many therapists today still prefer that term. I tend to prefer the term "patients", in the etymological sense of "those-who-suffer", accepting the risk that for many people the term inevitably suggests a medical model for the work of therapy.

Looking back at the Marriage Book, we very quickly see that the key psychoanalytic idea that shaped the work in the FDB was the concept of the splitting off of parts of the self and projecting them into someone else, primarily the partner, although occasionally the therapists are described as the recipients of the projections. Thus we read of the couple whose pseudonym was Mr and Mrs "Clarke":

> We have seen in this case that these two people had chosen each other partly because each fitted so well the other's needs to project on to the partner those parts of his personality which he had hitherto disowned in himself. Each, then, in using the partner to carry his or her own repressed parts, contributed to the exaggerated expression of these by the partner—which then invited condemnation, and evoked guilt and anxiety. They had chosen partners who were only too able and willing to accept and react to these unconscious projections, thus giving to one another an initial feeling of acceptance but at the same time perpetuating the denial and restricting the growth and adaptability of both personalities. [Pincus, 1960, pp. 56–57]

This splitting and projection is closely related to the notion of "fit", or "marital fit" as it came later to be expressed, and is more familiar to us today in terms of the primitive narcissistic defence termed "projective identification" by Melanie Klein (Klein, 1946). Throughout the Marriage Book, reference is made to "projection", but only once, in her introductory theoretical chapter, "Relationships and the

Growth of Personality", did Lily Pincus actually use the term "projective identification" (Pincus, 1960, p. 23). It should be remembered that the work reported in this book was done in the late 1950s, when the understanding of projective identification was just beginning to be influential in the psychoanalytic world, particularly at the Tavistock.

Whatever the extent of the acknowledgement in the FDB of the Kleinian origins of their thinking, their description of the splitting of the self, or "personality" as these therapists seem to prefer, makes their use of the notion of projection very close to the Kleinian notion of projective identification. A paper written in 1966 by Guillermo Teruel makes clear just how central the Kleinian concepts of internal objects, projective identification, part objects, whole objects, the paranoid–schizoid position, and the depressive position were in the Tavistock Clinic's Marital Unit, the sister unit to the FDB (Teruel, 1966). Given the close proximity of the work of these two pioneering units specializing in psychotherapy with couples (both in the Tavistock Centre), it is not surprising that these concepts came to be central to both, although it is true that the FDB publications laid much less stress on theoretical concepts (Dicks, 1967, pp. 233–234).

We will see in the case study I have selected for examination—the therapy with a couple who were given the pseudonym "Mr and Mrs Webb"—that there is little discussion of theory or technique. However, the description of the progress of the work with this couple and their two therapists allows us to see something of how the therapists in the FDB thought and what they said to the couple. Because the Marriage Book is now out of print, I have decided to reprint the whole of the story of the "Webbs" so that readers can follow it as I comment from a contemporary perspective on this work. The text of this case study, including observations and discussions of the material presumably written by the therapists and the editor are set in a different typeface so that the reader can clearly distinguish the case study from my commentary on the text. Also, the reports of the therapy are printed in regular type whereas the editorial comments by Lily Pincus are in italics. Page references in brackets following each excerpt are to the original Marriage Book (Pincus, 1960).

## The first sessions with Mr Webb

This couple was of a type well known to social workers. Their marriage had been unhappy almost from the start, and they had sought help, over the years, from almost every agency and clinic in their district. At the time of their referral to the Bureau they had been married for nine and a half years and had two children, the first conceived before marriage. The husband complained of his wife's behaviour with other men and of his own headaches and insomnia. The wife complained of her husband's jealousy and sus- picion and of his violence towards her. She had been refusing intercourse for some months before this time and was daily threat- ening to leave the family.

Mr Webb was a qualified electrician working for a local Board. He had studied for his National Certificate during the marriage, having been previously only a labourer. He was thirty-five, his wife twenty-eight, and they had a son aged nine and a daughter aged four. [p. 58]

To my knowledge, no notes on the production of this book still exist, so it is impossible to know to what extent these details have been altered or whether this particular couple was consulted about the publication of this case study. In her Acknowledgements, the editor expresses gratitude "especially to those who have given us permis- sion to use some of the material of their interviews at the Bureau". She also says that "all factual details have been altered to conceal identity", although that must surely be taken to refer only to poten- tially identifying factual details (Pincus, 1960, p. ix). The question remains for anyone who publishes reports of clinical work how and which details to change or omit. For example, how important are the details about the "Webbs" which are given to the reader at the outset of the description of the work with them? They create a picture in our minds, a picture whose texture and colour emerge out of the details of the account. After nearly four decades, we might think that the issues of confidentiality have receded sufficiently for us not to be concerned, although, of course, they never disappear entirely no matter how long after the therapy ended that we publish the ac- count.

As we meet the Webbs, out of all the details that these therapists might have shared with us, what do we make of what we are told?

As readers find their own thought taking form, I will offer comments, not as a reinterpretation of this work, but as a kind of dialogue between me, the Webbs, and their therapists, with an invitation to you, the reader, to join in. It is an invitation to intercourse. And the truth of the story is the offspring of that intercourse. One joy of reading a case study like this is that the style of writing means that it is possible to engage in thinking with these therapists, to join in the struggle to think in the face of confused emotions and sometimes-intense anxieties. At least, I suggest that this is the way to read such material, as if one were participating in a clinical seminar.

My first thought, which I imagine will not surprise you, is that immediately I feel we are emotionally in the world of Leontes and Hermione and *The Winter's Tale*, even though in this tale of the Webbs set in working class Britain of the 1950s we are a long way away from Leontes' court and international royal society. That husband, too, "complained of his wife's behaviour with other men" which gave him a headache and sleepless nights. And Hermione would certainly join Mrs Webb, who "complained of her husband's jealousy and suspicion and of his violence towards her". There are about as many plots, and as few, in marital therapy as there are in Shakespeare's dramas.

Already at the outset of the encounter with this couple, some ideas begin to take shape, ideas that we will want to test out with further observations as we proceed. Mrs Webb's withdrawal, her refusing intercourse and threatening to leave, her "turning to stone" to use an image from *The Winter's Tale*, linked with Mr Webb's jealous suspicion suggest a pattern that I would think of as the couple's narcissistic dilemma. He feels that she escapes the orbit of his control, that she has a mind of her own, which he experiences as betrayal. Of course, we need to know just what it is that he sees as betrayal, assuming that he is describing something very real to him in his experience.

She cannot find a way to confront this with him, trapped in an *either/or* world where her only options feel to her to be capitulation or escape. There is no intercourse in this marriage, not just in that she is refusing a sexual relationship with him, but in that neither can be sufficiently separate to be properly linked. Of course we need to listen to find out just why it feels impossible to confront his suspicion and hostility in a way that can lead to a resolution. Why does she think fleeing is the only viable alternative for her?

The therapy is under way. The fact that they have sought help "at almost every agency and clinic in their district" can be seen as threatening despair for the therapist—or it can be seen as offering hope. At least we can say: this is serious. We are at the end of the line, and now it is time to get down to business with genuine urgency. That is no bad thing. The fact that couples often come to therapy in crisis is one thing that gives the psychoanalytic process the urgency that in other forms of psychoanalytic therapy can take months and even years to achieve.

> Mr Webb was seen first. He was a tall thin man, shabby and untidy, with a strong cockney accent. He seemed nervous and confused and spoke in an extremely subservient manner. He gave no impression of having the necessary intelligence to qualify for the job he in fact held.
>
> He began by expressing gratitude to the caseworker for seeing him, and called her "Madam". Then he poured out his complaints against his wife. He told stories of her flirtations with other men, and particularly of her interest in "inferior" men, for instance, dustmen and coalmen. He said she delighted in humiliating him before such people, and added that she had had a bad mother who had had children by several men. He went on and on pouring out these confused stories, endlessly detailed but often mutually contradictory, but when his caseworker, Mrs A, made any comment, however trivial, he immediately returned to his subservient and placatory manner, turning the comment into words of wisdom: "Oh, thank you, Madam. You would advise me to do that, would you, Madam?" [p. 58]

When I read detailed physical descriptions such as this of Mr Webb, I am reminded of Bion's subsequent reflections on some of his own previously published clinical papers when he republished them in the book he entitled *Second Thoughts*. In the Introduction he urges caution with regard to "facts" and suggests that we think instead about how these accounts contain a *pictorialized communication of an emotional experience*:

> I do not regard any narrative purporting to be a report of fact, either of what the patient said or of what I said, as worth consid-

eration as a "factual account" of what happened. . . . Therefore in
any account of a session, no matter how soon it may be made after
the event or by what master, memory should not be treated as
more than a pictorialized communication of an emotional experience. [Bion, 1967, pp. 1–2]

Bion is here inviting us to see such descriptions as attempts to communicate something of our emotional experience of these couples. It
is not so much that memory, and hence the account the couple bring,
is full of what Bion called "involuntary distortions", although that is
obviously important. What is more interesting to consider is how our
perspective changes when we think of these "stories", these "factual
accounts", as attempts to communicate emotional experiences.
Thinking of the description of Mr Webb this way gives us an interesting insight into the countertransference experience of his therapist, and it might give us pause for thought when we look back over
ways we have described couples to ourselves or to our colleagues.

Already we have a vivid picture of the therapist's encounter with
Mr Webb as well as what we can imagine about his encounter with
her. I should point out that it was the convention in the Marriage
Book that the therapist for the husband was called Mr or Mrs A,
while the therapist for the wife was called Mr or Mrs B. At that time,
and for a couple of decades, it was the practice in the FDB for each
partner in a couple in therapy to have a therapist. For the most part,
each was seen individually in parallel sessions, only occasionally
being seen together with both therapists in a "joint" session. The
couples were made aware that their two therapists would meet and
confer regularly throughout the therapy, with a clear emphasis on
the "marital" therapy and the active partnership of the two therapists. This practice changed over the past three decades, and it has
now become the exception for each partner to be seen separately,
couples generally being seen in (con)joint sessions with either one
therapist ("threesomes") or two therapists ("foursomes").

I am curious that in the first meeting we hear about Mr Webb's
"subservience" and the apparent lack of evidence of the intelligence
his therapist expected from him. Is there a link with his complaint
about how his wife "humiliated" him, especially with "inferior
men", and how he experiences the FDB in the person of his therapist
Mrs A? Donald Meltzer talks about the notion of what he calls a

"pre-formed transference" which has to be "dismantled" before there is room enough for a genuine transference response: "when the patient comes originally, he has a professional pre-formed transference, usually full of ideas and full of expectations and full of limitations and doubts and misgivings" (Meltzer, 1995, p. 119). In the case of Mr Webb we are struck by the pervading sense of an emotional world in which he appears to live and which is divided into those who are superior and those who are inferior.

With such a powerful pre-formed transference, it would be a question for any of us how soon we would feel prepared to take it up. Mr Webb's outpouring of confused stories no doubt contained much that could have been taken up that would have been of interest and might have helped Mrs A to understand this desperate man. And he also has his own "theory" for why things are as they are—namely, because his wife had a "bad" mother who had had children by several men. Does this "bad" mother denigrate, use, and humiliate men, and how is she related to his own mother? Can he hope for anything else? In this, Mr Webb begins to sound as if he shares something rather fundamental with both Leontes and Othello, who are all too ready to believe the worst about the one woman in their lives whom we might expect them to treasure. It is interesting, therefore, to see how the therapist in the late 1950s at the FDB responded to this presentation.

> After some time Mrs A commented on this [Mr Webb's subservient and placatory manner], and said that her client seemed to be trying to pretend to himself that he was already getting a lot of help and advice from her. She said she wondered if he was expecting nothing, and was trying to ward off his disappointment and the anger and despair he would feel about it. [pp. 58–59]

Mrs A immediately and courageously takes up the transference which seems to contain such a direct and powerful reflection of Mr Webb's perception of his relationship with his wife. She does not tell him what he is feeling, but rather she invites him to think about the possibility that there is a familiar story lying behind the way he relates to her: a woman in a position of dominance over him who will humiliate him, pointing out how "inferior" he is just by the fact that he needs her. His only option, it seems, is to hide any feelings of disappointment, anger, and despair. Already we see, highlighted in sharp relief, something of a potential map of the links between the transference in the marital relationship and the transference relationship to the therapist.

In psychoanalytic psychotherapy with couples, it is not a matter of either/or with regard to transference to the therapists and the dynamics within the marital relationship. Mrs A is not avoiding or neglecting the marital relationship, and she certainly could have begun by exploring Mr Webb's perception that his wife "delighted" in humiliating him. She could not have been oblivious to the link between this "humiliation" and his subservient and placatory manner towards her. Instead, she chose to take up what was so emotionally alive at the moment, the emotional *edge* as one might call it.

The response was dramatic, and it makes clear just how important it was to take up the emotional point of contact. In fact, Mrs A reports quite candidly how Mr Webb's response to her comments surprised her.

> Mrs A had thought hitherto that he was too nearly deluded to make any actual contact with her, and was surprised when he reacted to this. He did not answer directly, but left the stories about his wife and began to talk more rationally. He told Mrs A that he had been discharged from the Army with psycho-neurosis and that between that time and his marriage he had lived with his parents, quarrelling with them most of the time. "I was awful to my mother. I don't know how she stood me", he said. [p. 59]

In Mrs A's report of Mr Webb's "stories" as confused and often mutually contradictory, we can now see her emotional experience of him as almost "deluded". He confirms her alarmed feelings by reporting a mental illness serious enough for him to be discharged from military service and followed by his returning to live with his parents until he married. He himself makes a connection between his internal experience of a "humiliating/humiliated" world, mental illness, and his close relationships with his mother and his wife, all of which is now focused in his experience of Mrs A, a woman to whom he felt he had to be subservient and placatory. The stories now seem to have been the anxious out-pouring of the nightmares of his internal world, something that he could now for a moment leave to speak *more rationally*.

At this point we might note some similarities between Mr Webb and the patient Wilfred Bion discusses in his paper "On Arrogance" which we considered in the previous chapter. Of that patient, Bion wrote in 1957 (which interestingly was about the time that the therapy with the Webbs was taking place):

> The patient in question did not at any time behave in a way which in my view would warrant a diagnosis of psychosis; he had, however, displayed the features I have mentioned, namely, scattered references to curiosity, arrogance, and stupidity. . . . He described his behaviour in the sessions as mad or insane, and he showed anxiety at his ability to behave in a way which his experience of analysis had shown him to be helpful in furthering analytic progress. For my part I was impressed by the fact that for several sessions at a time he seemed to be devoid of the insight and judgement which I knew from previous experience he possessed. [Bion, 1967, p. 89]

Although we need to be cautious about making too much of the similarities between Bion's patient in analysis and Mrs A's patient in once-weekly couple therapy, it is interesting to think about the link between stupidity and the fear of madness. Bion goes on to say that the material in the sessions with his patient resembled that which he experienced in his work with psychotic patients, especially in that "projective identification was extremely active". We might say that Mrs A took up Mr Webb's splitting off of his capacity to think and projectively identifying it with his therapist, this helpful, wise woman. By interpreting his projection, pointing out his need to "pretend" that he was getting a lot of help from her, he could begin to re-find his own "rationality".

The transference that Mrs A addressed right at the beginning was a *negative* transference, although hidden under the cloak of a subservient and placatory manner. That is, it was hidden only from Mr Webb, who would have doubtless denied any hostility, while Mrs A can hardly have failed to experience in her countertransference this subservience as hostility. His subservience reflected the arrogance that he was projecting into her, an experience that we can imagine would have made it difficult for Mrs A to think clearly. Her temptation would likely have been to become very defensive at this implied arrogance on her part. And had she failed to take up this negative transference we can well imagine that Mr Webb would have continued to bombard her with his desperate and confused stories about his wife, since they were to some extent an expression of his internal world, in which we can imagine he was bombarded by one humiliation after another.

Melanie Klein described as early as 1926 her experience of the consequences that commonly follow the interpretation of the negative transference with children—for example, it can lead to the dissolving of inhibitions of play, the reduction of immediate anxiety, and a change to a more positive relationship with the analyst (Klein, 1926, p. 137). She also notes that it was her impression that the interpretation was initially only *unconsciously* assimilated. The first observable result that the interpretation had been taken in was that the emotional relationship of the child to the parents improved. Conscious understanding, she suggests, comes only later.

This description of the result of the interpretation of the negative transference with children in analysis would seem to have a parallel in the way that Mr Webb responds to Mrs A's taking up his unconscious hostility. Rather than continuing to bombard her with his confused stories, he begins to engage more directly with her and offers helpful information about his previous experience. Mrs A describes this as his beginning "to talk more rationally". We shall see this process repeated several times in the work with Mr Webb, as the interpretation of the negative transference is followed by more positive engagement, only to be followed by the re-emergence of the negative. We could almost say that the case study of the Webbs is one *locus classicus* of the effect of interpreting the negative transference in analytic work with couples, in the spirit of Melanie Klein in the "Symposium on Child-Analysis" in 1927 where she observed:

> My experience has confirmed my belief that if I construe this dislike at once as anxiety and negative transference feeling, and interpret it as such in connection with material which the child at the same time produces and then trace it back to its original object, the mother, I can at once observe that the anxiety diminishes. This manifests itself in the beginning of a more positive transference and, with it, of more vigorous play. . . . By resolving some part of the negative transference we shall then obtain, just as with adults, an increase in the positive transference and this, in accordance with the ambivalence of childhood, will soon in its turn be suc-

ceeded by a re-emerging of the negative. *Now this is true analytic work and an analytic situation has been established.* [Klein, 1927, pp. 145–146, italics added]

> Then he quickly asked if his interviews could be arranged at such times that his employers need not know about them. He was frightened that they would think him neurotic or mad. Mrs A said that he seemed very uneasy about what people would find out about him and was perhaps trying to warn her that she might not be able to stand him either. Again he looked at her as if he had heard what she said and seemed relieved by it. He could not leave without shaking her hand at the door and thanking her warmly. [p. 59]

Here again we see this oscillating dynamic, just as Melanie Klein described it, in the moment-to-moment shifts in the first session with Mr Webb. Having experienced some relief following the first transference interpretation, his anxiety resurfaces, ostensibly in reference to his employers who might think him neurotic or mad. We know from the bit of history he has just shared that he has had some difficult experience resulting in his being judged mentally ill, and it seems here that this anxiety may be connected with his needing to ask for help regarding his marriage. "Is he mad to need therapy" seems to be his implicit question to Mrs A. And, if so, might Mrs A, like his employers, write him off or kick him out?

In my experience, this kind of anxiety hovers in the background for many couples presenting for therapy, sometimes forcing its way into the foreground as the anxiety becomes acute. And often the couple's anxiety will be split, one partner desperate for therapy and the other voicing concern about, for example, getting trapped in a therapy from which escape will be impossible.

In one couple I have in mind, the husband will predictably express a wish to start thinking about ending therapy whenever a holiday break is on the horizon. Just before a recent longer-than-usual holiday break, he quoted an experienced psychologist he had met at a party who said the problem with psychotherapy was that it can go on for years. Seven years, he recalled her saying, fostering a dependency that was hard to break. Were they going to have to come to therapy for the rest of their married life! Since we had been through this kind of expression of anxiety many times in the several years they had been in therapy, I could joke gently that he seemed to have heard this psychologist say "seventy times seven" and wondered with him if he was concerned whether his therapist would "stay the course".

In fact, his wife was pregnant, and she gave voice to their desperate hope that this time the pregnancy and birth could be a positive experience in which they could support each other. He could consciously share this hope, but unconsciously he shared with Leontes a fear that he might be trapped, betrayed either by never being able to escape—a child was a reality he could not walk away from—or by being abandoned, as his wife increasingly turned to the baby inside her and his therapist turned away to his holiday. The longed-for birth of the baby contained the longed-for birth of the couple for which they despaired. Would I see it to term with them, and could they bear the feelings of vulnerability in their dependence on me?

Mrs A takes up Mr Webb's negative transference directly in relation to herself, his "warning" to her about her not being able to stand him and his "madness". And once again this comment seems to have an *unconscious effect* rather than leading to his *conscious assent*. Melanie Klein's analytic work with children helps us to attend to the behavioural expression of unconscious communication. Unconscious assimilation of the therapist's communication precedes conscious understanding, and often our preoccupation with the latter can distract us from our observation of the evidences of the former.

The observation about how Mr Webb left the session leaves us in some doubt as to how to understand it—indeed, it perhaps suggests that the manner of leave-taking was itself ambiguous. We can well imagine that he experienced some genuine gratitude to this stranger who attended so thoughtfully to anxieties that he could hardly begin to formulate for himself. And yet it seems to have something of the subservient and placatory manner that marked the beginning of the session. No doubt this manner has become an externalization of his "humiliating/humiliated" internal world, and we would expect it to be repeated throughout analytic therapy until it can be worked through. Mr Webb will need time and patience as he works through the dynamics of responding to an emotional world of humiliation in a placatory manner (what Klein called the paranoid–schizoid position) towards the genuine gratitude of an emotional world where one can care and be cared for (what Klein called the depressive position).

Mr Webb's comments at the beginning of the next session reveal just how contaminated his gratitude was at the end of that first session. That is not to say that it was not genuine gratitude, but that omnipotent infantile dynamics had infiltrated the gratitude and dependency by means of an omnipotent identification with Mrs A—as if a latency little boy in omnipotent projective identification with a grown-up, wise mummy was now trying to control his little sister–wife. It suggests that in addition to his gratitude to Mrs A, he also felt controlled and "psychologized" by her—the humiliation with which he was so familiar and which seemed to dominate any emotional world he inhabited.

> He opened the next interview by saying that he had read books on psychology and had tried to explain to his wife why she behaved as she did, but it was of no use, she just wouldn't understand, and that made him furious. Mrs A said that he was perhaps wondering whether it would make her furious if he "just wouldn't understand", or whether he was afraid he would get furious and frustrated when she failed to understand him, as she often would. [p. 59]

Once again, Mrs A focuses on the present relationship in the room and Mr Webb's immediate anxieties. It is as if she links the image of Mr Webb reading his psychology books and lecturing his wife with explanations of her behaviour with another image, the image of what is happening in the interaction between the two characters present in the room. The drama comes alive. As Henri Rey liked to ask in clinical seminars: "Who? . . . is doing What? . . . to Whom?"

By standing back, and inviting our patients to also stand back, we can see a more thematic image, a drama of the internal world which, when externalized, can be peopled by different people at different times as they make themselves available for these roles. We could say that psychoanalytic therapy is a setting in which we as therapists make ourselves available for those roles as a way of allowing the patient to communicate something more primitive and profound than can at that moment be captured in our often too limited and wooden adult emotional vocabulary. Similarly, with clinical reports, we must respect the therapist's experience, since important aspects of the communication between therapist and patient cannot be conveyed simply by a record of the words spoken. We must assume that Mrs A sensed an anxiety in Mr Webb—anxiety that neither would she understand him nor would he understand her, and that this could lead to conflict, with one of them getting angry.

Again, Mrs A chooses to comment on the immediate transference dynamics, although she would no doubt have noted to herself Mr Webb's omnipotent identification with her in the story that he told—she must have been the archetypal "reader-of-psychology-books" for him. Again, the marital dynamics and the transference dynamics are closely linked, although not yet explicitly explored by the therapist. We might say that his anxiety about not understanding or not being understood is linked with his use of projective identification. That is, his omnipotent *being* Mrs A—which he does by reading books perhaps more out of imitation than out of a desire to learn—is met by frustrating failure, his wife standing in the story for the part of himself on the receiving end of a "lecturing-Mrs A-part-of-himself" (in other words, the internal object that is always humiliating him).

Whatever way one reconstructs the details of the unconscious links between Mr Webb and Mrs A (and Mrs Webb), the choice that the therapist made to comment on (potential) negative feelings about (potential) conflict seems to have touched something important unconsciously for him. The difficulty of trying to analyse a clinical report published by someone who is not here to elaborate on it is that we must rely on our imagination and our own clinical experience.

The next exchange shows how the process is both repetitive and yet moves forward ever so slowly in the moment-to-moment of the session.

Again he seemed relieved and then asked if he might take notes or be given definite problems to think about between meetings. Mrs A said that she felt it was hard for him to bear the slowness and vagueness of this work and that he seemed to be trying to find a way of keeping at bay his frustration and anger about it. This time he replied directly, admitting his impatience and saying desperately that there wasn't much time to spare. He didn't think he could bear the situation much longer. [p. 59]

There cannot be many readers of this book who have not experienced a request like this from someone very much like Mr Webb. It is difficult, sometimes virtually impossible, to believe that someone else, your therapist or analyst, is actually interested in you. Surely one has to produce something interesting, make some progress to satisfy the therapist. He wants to take charge of this process of growth, afraid that his infantile self will not be able to sustain what is happening and feeling increasingly vulnerable in his dependency on his therapist. Mr Webb shows her his "latency self", the one that is so good at lecturing the infantile self, ostensibly out of a desire to learn, but born more out of the anxiety and impatience with the dependency of the analytic relationship.

But Mrs A's persistence pays off as she attends to these apparent negative feelings just under the surface which seem to have kept Mr Webb at a distance emotionally from her in these first two sessions. Despite the fact that there is a lot of open hostility between him and his wife, we might imagine how his inability to face *and think about* these negative feelings keeps him at a distance emotionally in a similar way from his wife. However, his response to his therapist is now more direct and open as he acknowledges his impatience and sense of urgency. Mr Webb, like all patients new to this strange analytic encounter, discovers in the relationship with the therapist the wonder of this "conversation" in which someone attends with care to the most intimate and threatening anxieties.

There are differences of views about the initial sessions with a new patient—how much one prompts an exploration of the patient's early family history, for example. This session with Mr Webb is interesting in the way that the therapist attends to the current anxieties with the result that there is an apparent diminution in those anxieties. And, as with Melanie Klein's description of how a child in analysis will return to its playing following the interpretation of anxieties, Mr Webb now unprompted turns to his own personal history. One has a sense that such spontaneous reports of history are alive with meaning in a way that the recounting of history in response to prompting by the therapist is often lacking. What follows in his talking about some of his early experience is as dramatic as it is spontaneous:

Then he began to talk, unasked, about his own history. He had been the youngest of six children in a very poor family; his father had had long spells of unemployment. He felt he had always been "picked on", blamed for everything, and made into the family drudge. He said finally that his mother had had a breakdown when he was born, and had been in hospital for six months. He did not know how he had been looked after, "I don't think I was properly fed as I was always going into convalescent homes later on".

Then he suddenly returned to his stories about his wife's behaviour and went on pouring these out until the end of the interview. They were of an even more confused nature than those he had told before, stories about the sexual depravity of other people not connected with his wife, stories about his colleagues, and about people whom he met in the course of his work.

Again he shook hands warmly before leaving. [pp. 59–60]

This material is particularly interesting because it points us in two directions. Coming spontaneously after Mrs A had persistently focused on his apparent anxieties in meeting this woman on whom he immediately seemed to feel so dependent, this story of his place in the family seems dramatically to reflect an internal world of anxiety about anyone on whom he is dependent. What he remembers is being picked on and blamed for everything, poorly fed and cared for by an ill mother. It seems particularly significant that he mentions not being properly fed in a context in which he so clearly seeks to get something nourishing from Mrs A.

This spontaneous recovery of a memory functions like the recounting of a dream in the session. It is *both* an important bit of his personal history *and* something like a version of an unconscious phantasy that shapes all his intimate relationships. In effect, he says to this strange woman who now attends to him so carefully: *this is why I am filled with anxieties and why I keep myself at a distance emotionally by my deferential, placatory behaviour.*

As well as pointing back in time and inwardly to his chaotic internal world, it points towards his unhappy relationship with his wife. It is as if when his therapist makes contact with those anxieties and he feels safe enough to allow himself to think about them, he becomes overwhelmed. These stories, the details of which we are not told—perhaps because they were so chaotic and confusing that the therapist could not hold them in her mind—are the outpouring of his near-psychotic anxieties projected into the world around him, and, in particular, into the person closest to him, his wife. Clearly something very important has begun to happen in these first two sessions for Mr Webb. We could surmise that what has happened is that his analysis has begun; in the words of Melanie Klein: *"Now this is true analytic work and an analytic situation has been established"* (Klein, 1927, p. 146). That there is sufficient containment for this beginning seems to be evident in the manner of his leaving, despite his out-pouring, and despite the fact that his gratitude is doubtless contaminated by his defensive placatory manner which protects him from those very anxieties.

## Early reflections on technique

One might be tempted to think from the title of this chapter that the "gathering of the transference" is an active process, related primarily to the capacity of the therapist to take up evidence of negative, hostile, or persecuted feelings in order to facilitate the evolving transference relationship. In a sense this is true, and we have seen how Mr Webb is freed up by Mrs A's interpretations of his negative feelings. It is worth stopping for a moment to think about some questions of technique, particularly in terms of awareness of transference dynamics.

I find Donald Meltzer's later reflections on this process to be particularly intriguing:

> As this infantile transference is freed, bit by bit, it "comes home" on its own, so to speak, like Little Bo Peep's sheep, attracted by the atmosphere of the consulting room, and visibly affected by the suffering resulting from the interruption of the usual rhythm of sessions during weekends and holidays. It is this return "home" that I call "the gathering of the transference", in an intransitive sense, as one might speak of "the gathering of the clans of Scotland". As this infantile transference gradually begins to appear in the material in the form of bits of "acting in" or "acting out", of memories or dreams, their recognition and investigation sets in motion the analytic process. [Meltzer, 1986, p. 556]

My experience with couples suggests that it is often much less gentle than this might imply, as the intense acting out and acting in sweep the therapists up as if they had awakened to find themselves in someone else's nightmare. With the Webbs, there does seem to have been something more like Bo Peep's sheep shyly emerging through the rigid pre-formed transference with which they arrived.

Perhaps that is because the husband and wife were seen individually, whereas our practice today almost exclusively means meeting the two together.

It is interesting, therefore, to consider the reflections on the technique of analytic therapy with couples in the editorial commentary in the Marriage Book, written presumably by Lily Pincus herself. In contrast to the clinical material, it is rather sparse and seems tentative and strangely reticent.

> Many readers may wonder why Mrs A said the things she did, and will think of other possible comments. Clearly many different things could have been said which would have been equally relevant and helpful. The important thing seemed to be to cut through the outpourings of this distressed and almost deluded man, and to make contact with him at some level at which he could feel the caseworker's recognition that he was trying, despite all his difficulties, to make a relationship with her. His material was too confused to be used helpfully, but he seemed to respond to the awareness of his needs and fears and, although he rarely replied directly, he gave the impression of "hearing". Even in the first interview he was then able to stop abusing his wife and to comment on his own "awfulness" and, in the second interview, to mention his own anger with a "bad" mother who had deprived him of food and severely damaged him. [p. 60]

In one sense, one can feel amused by the hesitant way that the editor refers to the interpretations made by Mrs A, even if at the same time we feel disappointed that she did not take this opportunity to explore with the reader the nature of the analytic work that had such an effect on Mr Webb. This is typical of the reports of clinical work in the FDB in this early period. We know from accounts of participants that in the clinical case-discussion groups they did not fail to explore relevant theory. Perhaps there was a feeling that the readers of the Marriage Book would not be interested in theoretical discussions.

One key aspect of the theory that appears to be operative in these editorial remarks is the idea that it is important for Mr Webb to have his therapist recognize that he is trying to make a relationship with her. As therapists, we would be interested in the anxieties that interfere with his capacity to make intimate relationships, as well as in the defences that protect him from an awareness of those internal conflicts. Mr Webb's ability to recognize negative feelings in himself, as well as perhaps taking some responsibility for his part in a relationship instead of "abusing his wife", suggest that there is reason to be hopeful about the therapy.

When Lily Pincus says that in large part the material in these two sessions was "too confused to be used helpfully", we must assume that she has in mind using this material for a conscious, rational discussion of his difficulties. If, instead, we viewed these "stories" as something more akin to dreams, shaped by the dramas of the internal world and peopled by characters who represent in some way the internal objects whose "stories" are the stuff of our nightmares, we might listen and respond to them with a different kind of attention. We will want to return to this topic to look in greater detail at these "stories" that couples bring to therapy, as well as at different ways we can see and hear these "stories".

I think these editorial remarks suggest that some therapists in the FDB, influenced and supervised by experienced psychoanalysts, were attempting to interpret unconscious anxieties and phantasies with couples (or with one partner in a couple). Others, perhaps, were using a psychoanalytically informed understanding to work at a more conscious level with couples. Both approaches have their adherents who can argue for their strengths and advantages, and, no doubt, the actual practice of psychotherapists working with couples (as well as with individuals) includes variations on both.

Because so little of the analytic work was systematically written about, and the technical and theoretical issues were examined in such a sketchy way, much of the development of a psychoanalytic approach to therapy with couples has been lost as those early generations of pioneers died out. Anecdotal accounts of their case discussions suggest a high level of theoretical and technical sophistication, but, as these editorial remarks on the work with the Webbs illustrates, not much of it found its way into the FDB publications. One might say that, to a much greater extent than is true with psychoanalytic therapy with individuals, the psychoanalytic tradition of therapy with couples has remained an *oral tradition*, passed on in supervision and in clinical seminars. One of the aims of this book is to encourage more publication of thinking about clinical experience of working psychoanalytically with couples.

# CHAPTER FOUR

# Duet for one?
# Two people or a couple?

Having had this report of the first two sessions with Mr Webb, the reader may be a little uneasy about the marital dimension of the work. What distinguishes these sessions from initial sessions with an individual patient? One essential *boundary* of psychoanalytic psychotherapy with couples has to do with the psychic reality that the analytic work is with two people linked in a particular intimate and powerful way. It is important to keep that in mind even in this early way of working in which each marital partner was seen individually. Before we explore this issue of boundaries in couple psychotherapy, perhaps we ought to meet Mrs Webb.

One might note here the importance of the fact that Mrs Webb was seen, in parallel individual sessions, by a therapist who would meet regularly with her husband's therapist throughout the therapy. This reality shapes and informs the analytic work in a powerful way. *He*, Mr Webb, is always there in a unique way in all her sessions, "listening and watching" in a way that is not always literal (confidentiality being maintained for each partner) but is more than metaphorical—just as *she*, Mrs Webb, is there in his sessions.

## The first sessions with Mrs Webb

At last we begin to hear directly about Mrs Webb's experience.

> Mrs Webb came to her first interview looking drab and untidy though she was a tall and quite nice-looking woman. She seemed to be at the end of her tether and said that she had no love left for her husband and could not stay with him much longer. His irrational jealousy and tempers were quite impossible. Every day he made scenes about nothing, and had recently begun to smash crockery and damage her possessions in his outbursts. He treated her as an inferior and continually accused her of being a "bad woman". She said that there was really no point in talking about the marriage. The only problem for her was how to get away, since there were two young children whom she did not want to leave. [p. 60]

Again, we are reminded of Bion's remarks about memories in the form of descriptions about, for example, the therapist's accounts of the physical appearance of the patient. What "pictorial communication of an emotional experience" do we imagine to be captured in this description of a "tall, nice-looking" woman who appeared "drab and untidy". Her capacity to be attractive (and perhaps sexually appealing) is disguised and perhaps even attacked by her neglect and despair. Having heard about the first two sessions with Mr Webb and his therapist, we inevitably begin to think about the encounter with Mrs Webb and her therapist in terms of that relationship and how the account of each must somehow in the mind of each therapist be brought together to shape one interactional account.

This is what we mean when we say that for couple psychotherapy one essential "boundary" is the focus on the relationship (Stokoe, 1995). In the history of the TMSI, this has been expressed in various ways, perhaps most clearly in the idea that "the relationship is the patient" (Ruszczynski, 1993). The point that I think is central, however it is expressed, is that the psychic reality of the relationship between the therapist and the couple, or between the therapist and each partner, is that the other is *always present* emotionally if not physically, and therefore every aspect of the relating is psychically *in the presence of* the other. Because we had not yet met Mrs Webb, so to speak, we could only take account of her via our imagination, reconstructed out of his comments and behaviour and our intuition. That now changes profoundly for us, just as the relationship between Mrs

A and Mr Webb must have changed from the moment Mrs B met Mrs Webb and then spoke to her co-therapist about that encounter. We minimize or neglect the importance of that moment at our peril in analytic work with couples.

Some psychoanalysts believe that couple therapy can be an integral part of the analytic process, but in the limited sense of preparation for full participation of one or other partner, or both, in the analytic relationship. For example, a North American psychoanalyst, Arnold Rothstein, interestingly argues that the couple therapy may help the spouse of an analysand accept the recommendation to begin analysis himself or herself (Rothstein, 1992)—with another analyst, I should make clear. He also sees it as an advisable course in stalemated analyses where resistance to analysis is "externalized" in the marital partner. I doubt that this is a widely shared view, since this practice is as likely to stimulate fantasies as to dispel them, and in a way that could be quite intrusive. One way to deal with the potential intrusiveness is for couple therapists to open themselves to the full participation of the partner in the analytic process, although I want to emphasize how important it is to have good reasons for opening the analytic process to a couple rather than limiting it to the analyst–patient dyad.

This is an issue that we must continue to struggle with since it is fundamental to an understanding of the analytic process with couples. One is very conscious of this dimension when occasionally a therapist continues to see one partner alone after the departure of the other from the marriage and from the therapy (or, in thankfully rare cases, after the death of the partner). The physical reality that the partner is no longer there has an emotional counterweight—that is, the psychic reality is that the therapy that continues is always *in the presence of the other*.

In this encounter with Mrs Webb, we hear a theme of Mr Webb's sessions, but played in a different, a complementary key, as it were. Where he felt "humiliated by her", she feels that he treats her "as an inferior". His violent behaviour and accusations have destroyed her love, and she seems intent on trying to get away from him. Where he brought her to therapy, so to speak, as a problem that needed fixing, she brings him as a problem she needs to be rid of. In a sense, neither wants to talk about the relationship, what each contributes to it, or what each could do to improve it. The problem is located in the other, and hence there would be no reason for either of them to seek therapy or analysis for themselves.

This is very important in understanding the analytic process with a couple—why some people engage in a psychoanalytic process *as a couple*, whereas it is much more common for people to come to psychoanalysis as individuals. It is interesting to note that Mr and Mrs Webb were described as "of a type well known to social workers", what today are often called "multi-agency families". It is also the case that sometimes couples present for therapy when the therapist describes them as "not being sure whether they have a marriage or not" (Colman, 1993, p. 72). Lily Pincus and her colleagues obviously felt the Webbs were not a couple who were able to use what the FDB had to offer, at least not in a straightforward way. At the conclusion of the case study, they comment on this and suggest, as a matter of some surprise, that the FDB often makes a "greater impact upon these clients than upon more sophisticated and more stable ones" (Pincus, 1960, p. 73).

The reason for this effectiveness, I think, is that to a significant extent the FDB was working analytically with the transference with these couples rather than in a psychodynamically informed counselling approach that one can use with couples who are prepared to reflect together about how each contributes to the marital difficulties and how each might contribute to an improvement in their relationship. Not that all couples who say that actually behave in that way. All therapists will have been frustrated by the "rational, psychologically informed" patients whose very "cooperation" is the most successful defence against any real emotional engagement in the analytic process.

The Webbs, I suggest, are just the kind of couple who need a psychoanalytic approach because the turmoil of the internal world with the damaged internal objects is so successfully and unshakeably located in the partner and the relationship with the partner. Mr Webb comes primarily because his wife is for him a problem, representing for him his damaged and damaging internal object. Mrs Webb comes primarily because she wants to get away from him, representing her damaged and damaging internal object. We will continue to examine this dynamic—so critical to understanding the analytic process with couples—in chapter seven, where these ideas are traced from the work of Joan Riviere to that of Henri Rey and others.

> Mrs Webb then expressed considerable uneasiness about the purpose and methods of the Bureau, and said that her husband had told people that she was mad and that he was bringing her here for treatment. The caseworker, Mrs B, discussed this with her and then, listlessly, and apparently only because she thought this was wanted, Mrs Webb outlined her own story. She said she had been the younger of two daughters and had been extremely fond of her mother. When she was seven she had gone into hospital with diphtheria and had returned home to be told that her mother had died while she was away. Her father had remarried two years later, but she had hated her step-mother and had left home at seventeen. Soon after this, she had had a love affair, but the man had left her after a few months, and she became promiscuous for a time. Then she had met her husband and become pregnant by him and married him as a result. She said that the only time she had had any satisfaction from sexual intercourse was before marriage. Mrs B said that Mrs Webb seemed to have experienced a number of desertions in her life and the client replied that she had felt "utterly abandoned" when her mother had died. She said that her husband accused her of not being fond enough of the children, but she felt it was wrong to give "too much love". She added that he was himself very good with them, and very concerned about the effect the situation in the marriage would have upon them. [pp. 60–61]

We now get a glimpse of Mrs Webb's pre-formed transference, affected no doubt by the attitude of Mr Webb, an attitude that she perceived quite accurately, as we know from the two sessions with him. We understood that he was bringing a damaged and damaging internal object firmly located in her. That is, he was bringing "her" for treatment, with emphasis on the ambiguity of the reference for that pronoun. We should not be surprised that she suspected the FDB of collaborating with that intention, especially since he had been seen before she had been. She might, therefore, quite reasonably imagine that he had already "recruited" both his therapist and, by inference, her therapist as well to his point of view.

What is striking here is the difference in the approach we might infer that her therapist, Mrs B, took. Again, we do not have access to the original notes for the book, so we do well to be cautious about any conclusions that we draw from the minimal evidence of the text as published. Nevertheless, our interest here is not to offer an *exegesis* of this text, but rather to take a contemporary look at it, drawing attention to how we might think about this material today. Reading the Marriage Book, one is aware that the eight therapists worked in slightly different ways. In this excerpt there does seem to be a striking difference at times between the way Mrs A took up the material from the way Mrs B did.

We note that "Mrs B discussed this with" Mrs Webb. What she might have done is to interpret the anxieties lying behind Mrs Webb's concern. We suspect that what she did was to reassure Mrs Webb that she was not mad and that, for example, the "marriage was the patient", not her. If that is what happened, we should not be surprised that her response was so different in tone from that of Mr Webb when his therapist courageously took up directly the negative transference. What we know from the text is that "listlessly" she outlined her own story "only because she thought this was wanted". Reassurance in a situation like this can often be experienced by the patient as if the therapist were anxious, and perhaps even defending against her own thought that perhaps this woman was mad. What may have been missed was an opportunity to let the patient know that her therapist recognized her deep anxieties and was able to talk with her about them.

The story that she tells is a remarkable one about abandonment and a profound confusion about her sexuality, leading to promiscuity for a time and ultimately to her lack of sexual satisfaction in the marriage. The link between these two is not obvious. Rather than take up this missing link, Mrs B chose simply to call attention to the number of desertions Mrs Webb had experienced. Mrs Webb responds to this by emphasizing the "utterly abandoned" feeling when her mother died and revealing what must be an important defensive belief for her: "it was wrong to give 'too much love'." We might also imagine that the way she remarks on her husband's love and concern for the children suggests that she projects much of her capacity for love into her husband. If so, it would mean a profound dilemma for her when she sees her only alternative is to leave him. How can she re-capture this capacity to love her children and escape from this cold restriction against giving "too much" love?

At her second interview Mrs Webb still looked dreary and showed little animation. She reported further scenes at home during the week. Her husband complained that she was interested in everyone except him, and she couldn't give anything to him. She admitted that she could hardly bear him to touch her and felt quite dead sexually. She repeated her statement that she was remaining with him only for the sake of the children, as she did love them, although she could not show it. [p. 61]

We pause here to note again the deadness that seems to link her own experience sexually with her inability to show her love for her children. Her therapist must have been wondering about that link, and in re-reading what follows in this case study we cannot help but think that this woman was desperate to tell her story. When her therapist simply comments on her difficulty in showing love, the story pours out. Often it is not our clever interpretations but simply the fact that we are there, ready to hear a story, that is important to our patients.

Mrs B commented on this difficulty in showing love, and then Mrs Webb said that the only person she had ever wholly loved was her mother. She added, with a rush, that she had learned later (when she was about fourteen) that her mother had not died at the time she had been told this, but had gone off with another man—but this had not made any difference at all to her feelings for her mother. Mrs B said gently that Mrs Webb must have been very upset about this, and that some bit of her must have been very angry with her mother and might perhaps feel very guilty and very muddled about this and about sexuality in general. Mrs Webb entirely denied the anger, but said with some relief that she always felt herself to be bad sexually. Then, looking a little brighter, she asked if she might bring her little girl to the Bureau next time as she was "such a lovely, happy child". [pp. 61–62]

Both Mrs B and now the reader are given an experience that replicates the shock that Mrs Webb must have had at fourteen after having lived for seven years believing that her mother was dead. Even though Mrs B and the reader have to experience the death of the mother for a relatively brief moment, it is nonetheless a considerable shock both to hear that mother had not died and then to hear of her desertion and the father's deception. We can well imagine that Mrs

Webb was not consciously deceiving her therapist, but rather that she was communicating unconsciously something of what this experience was like. This is particularly important, if it is true, because it might suggest that Mrs Webb also attempts to communicate with her husband in a similar way—that is, by giving him a taste of her experience. It is certainly something one would want to take up with her, if only to find out how she understands the way she communicated this vital information.

It is also significant that Mrs Webb was told of her mother's desertion when she was fourteen, since now we can see a link between abandonment and confusion about her sexuality—although we are told nothing of the circumstances, we can imagine some adolescent confrontation about independence and sexuality when someone angrily throws at her the mother's "bad behaviour", perhaps even linking Mrs Webb's adolescent rebellion or "bad behaviour" with that of her mother. We know that her response to her therapist's comments about her possible anger with mother and resulting confusing feelings about sexuality was relief and an acknowledgement of always having herself to be "bad sexually".

Also important is the renewed evidence of a profound splitting in which Mrs Webb seems to need to protect the loving, good part of herself by splitting it off and projecting it into someone close to her. We saw how her husband can enact some of her loving feelings towards the children which she had to restrict in herself. Here we see the "lovely, happy" little girl part of her self quite dramatically and concretely projected into her daughter. It is a touching request. Can this part of my self be brought to therapy—or is it only the "sexually bad" girl/woman who is wanted here? It is also suggestive of a split transference, Mrs B being experienced primarily as the "bad" step-mother who is there only to criticize her; but at moments when Mrs Webb allows herself to hear the concern, Mrs B is perhaps experienced as the loving mother—the "only person" Mrs Webb had ever wholly loved. It is an important moment in the therapy and, therefore, one to which she must come back again as she seeks to discover how to recover for herself that loving part of herself, that "lovely, happy child".

## Early reflections on the marital dynamics

Now, in the text of this case study, we read the first extended editorial analysis of the marital dynamics in the Webb's relationship. Interestingly from our contemporary point of view, there are no comments on the transference or countertransference dynamics in relation to the two therapists, although the case material itself had given us a picture of some of those dynamics along with evidence of how the therapists had commented on the material.

> A good deal of what was going on in this marriage seemed very clear, though it was less easy to see what could be done to help. Mrs Webb seemed to have had a severe shock in her childhood which had left her both despairing about the value of giving or asking for love, and very unsure about her sexuality. In her late teens she had indulged in rather promiscuous affairs, probably in some muddled way both punishing her mother and yet seeking to justify her behaviour by copying it. By conceiving a child before marriage, she had ensured that she should not have a husband entirely for herself for very long. The man she married she knew to have been discharged from the Army with a nervous breakdown and she consciously saw him as someone for whom she could be sorry. She seemed thus to have tried to solve her confusion about her own goodness or badness as a woman by hoping to mother him and help him, but also by having a "bad" sexual relationship with him. She must have been partly aware that his instability would result in considerable suffering for herself and to have unconsciously sought this kind of punishment for her feelings about her mother, and perhaps, too, about her love for her father. But she had also played the part of the unloving abandoning mother to her husband, whom she knew to be very dependent upon her. In her relationship with her children, too, this anger about her own abandonment proved an inhibiting factor. Though she very much wanted to be a good mother, she found it hard to show them any love, and in her interviews usually talked of "the children", not distinguishing them by name or sex.
>
> She was clearly not able to show love to her husband at all; she soon began to dislike sexual intercourse and hated being pregnant. It seemed fairly certain that she did to some degree provoke and increase her husband's jealous phantasies by her own need to identify with the underdog, and to associate with, or seem to flirt with, men of that kind. [p. 62]

In my view, this editorial commentary by Lily Pincus is a good example of the lively and imaginative style in which the FDB used analytic understanding to paint a picture of the marital dynamics. At some points, it strikes me as going beyond the session material that had been presented, but we assume that it may have been derived from case conference discussions in which the therapists may have offered material that did not find its way into the published reports of those first sessions—for example, the idea that Mrs Webb hated being pregnant. One also wonders how much it represents an understanding developed with Mrs Webb, as opposed to reflections by the therapists and the editor *after the fact*. Obviously, it will not have benefited Mrs Webb until it became possible to explore, for example, her confusion about her sexuality and how it might be linked to her mixed feelings about her mother and her possible identification with her. In this sense, the commentary represents some of the future work of the therapy with Mrs Webb—and indeed this is what happened, as we shall see subsequently.

Most puzzling, perhaps, is the remark at the beginning about it being "less easy to see what could be done to help". This suggests a more active orientation in contrast to a more psychoanalytic one, although we are possibly laying too much stress on that one remark. Looking back after just two sessions, we are struck by the contact made, especially with Mr Webb, and we shall see that this couple made good use of their therapists' attempts to help clarify and put into words their internal conflicts which were being projected into the other. Those projections were the result of splitting processes that, for example, made it difficult for Mrs Webb to recognize and think about her own damaged and damaging internal objects and her projective identification with them. The internal mother seems split into an idealized mother—the only person she had "wholly loved"— and the sexually promiscuous mother with whom she identified (and not only in her late adolescence, but perhaps in her present flirtatious behaviour with other men). Surely "what is to be done" is to help her understand those internal infantile conflicts and how they affect her intimate relationships with her husband and her children—as there is every evidence that her therapist was trying to do.

*Mr Webb seems to have found in his wife an ideal object on which to put his divided feelings about his mother, the good woman whom he needed to love him and wanted always to placate, and the depriving, rejecting woman who starved him and deprived him of strength and manhood. This latter picture of the bad woman seemed also to include the sexual woman though, in fact, this client was obsessed less by suspicions about his wife's actual behaviour (he did not really believe that she had intercourse with other men) than with much more infantile images. He seemed to see her as the mother who gave her milk to others and not to him.*

*His despair at being deprived and rejected by her drove him into childish furies in which he abused her and occasionally attacked her physically—this behaviour driving her still further away from him. Her lack of response to the sexual relationship and her hatred of pregnancy increased his doubts and guilts about his own sexuality and his potency. Her misery and failure to defend herself against him were a continual reproach to him, and both increased his fear of his own destructiveness and made it harder for him to control it.*

*Despite the chronic difficulties in this marriage and the degree of disturbance in the husband, there seemed a ray of hope in the attachment of both partners to the children. There seemed, too, to be some real search for help.* [pp. 62–63]

When we are told that Mr Webb "found his wife an ideal object on which to put his divided feelings about his mother", we need to distinguish between his relating to his wife as he relates to his internal mother (both "good" and "bad") and his projecting his own ambiguous feelings into his wife/mother. His confused stories of sexual depravity in others might suggest confusion about his own sexuality, which then gets projected into his wife resulting in his humiliation by her "flirtations" with inferior men. On the other hand, like his wife, Mr Webb has an internal abandoning mother (the story he tells is about a mother who had a breakdown and was in hospital for six months after he was born), but whereas Mrs Webb seems unconsciously to have identified with the abandoning mother, he experiences his wife as that abandoning mother.

The editorial comment concerning Mr Webb's infantile images about the rejecting mother who gives her milk to others is particularly astute. Although she does not tell us on what she bases this observation, it suggests that he had no secure maternal presence when he was overwhelmed by genital urges, which he then projected into this rejecting mother. She consequently becomes "sexually depraved" in his mind. This link between rejection and abandonment on the one hand, and sexual promiscuity and depravity on the other, seems to represent a *shared unconscious phantasy* for Mr and Mrs Webb, a shared unconscious drama that they can only re-enact because they cannot bear to think about it, indeed perhaps do not have the emotional language with which to think about it.

Furthermore, since the abandonment and rejection are linked with destructive anger that also cannot be acknowledged or thought about, primarily no doubt since it is directed towards the good internal mother, the pent-up anger erupts into physical violence. For the most part, it is Mr Webb who enacts the violent feelings, while Mrs Webb consciously denies her anger, depriving her of the strength to challenge his violent behaviour except by the threat of withdrawal. It is interesting that the editor repeatedly comments on the "degree of disturbance in the husband". What comes across in these accounts is the degree of disturbance in the relationship, largely to do with splitting and projection.

The case study now telescopes the next period of sessions to focus on a joint session in response to the couple's insistence. This is one reason I chose this particular case for discussion, since it illustrates the view of joint couple sessions in the late 1950s. By the mid-1960s, joint sessions were becoming more common, especially in the Marital Unit of the Tavistock Clinic under the leadership of Henry Dicks. At this point in the history of the FDB, there was considerable ambivalence about the utility and indeed the viability of joint couple sessions.

## Pressure for a joint session

Our attention in our retrospective on the therapy with the "Webbs" now moves to a session with Mr and Mrs Webb *together*—what has become known in our clinical shorthand as a "joint session". Later in her discussion of joint sessions, Lily Pincus compares this joint session very early in the therapy with one where a good foundation was laid for a joint session by the strong link each partner had with each therapist. This suggests something of the hesitation about this very different format for therapy. The model for the FDB had been psychoanalysis, even for what was seen as very much a kind of "applied" analytic work.

Most of the exploration of the use of joint sessions at the time was going on in Henry Dicks' Marital Unit of the Tavistock Clinic, the sister organization to the FDB. Dicks notes that in the early 1950s the joint session (or Joint Interview, "JI", as he was fond of calling it) was seen to be a "risky step". He quotes Michael Balint in a personal communication as describing the JI as an "explosive situation" (Dicks, 1967, p. 197). As a side note, this is interesting, because Michael Balint was the first psychoanalytic consultant to the young FDB, and Enid Eichholz (who became Michael Balint's wife in 1953) was one of the founder members and organizers of the FDB (Ruszczynski, 1993, p. 4). Dicks' Marital Unit forged ahead with the exploration of joint sessions, both for assessment interviews and for on-going therapy, from the early 1950s, first reporting their aims and methods in 1953 (Dicks, 1953).

We shall need to come back to the experiences and ideas of the Dicks' Marital Unit because the joint session has become central in the understanding and practice of psychoanalytic psychotherapy with couples. This methodological issue is related to, but certainly not identical with, the issue of the number of therapists—that is, whether the couple is seen by one therapist or by two co-therapists. This was also something that Dicks and his unit gave a lot of thought to early on, and it has proved to be an on-going issue in the TMSI right up to the present moment.

> After these initial interviews there was a period of anxiety and frustration for both clients and caseworkers. Mr Webb came each week and poured out his complaints about his wife which became wilder and wilder. He was more violent at home and had outbursts in which he hit his wife and smashed china or broke windows. Mrs Webb seemed more and more depressed and began making plans to leave her husband. Both clients pressed for a joint meeting in which some of the practical issues could be thrashed out, and the case workers finally agreed to arrange this. [p. 63]

The description of the joint session with Mr and Mrs Webb gives some idea of why the FDB resisted it, and yet it also gives us some idea of how it functions even when used by therapists who were inexperienced in this format for the analytic process. It undoubtedly added to the anxiety in this session that the therapists seem to have felt coerced into this session earlier than they would have preferred.

Later, we shall see that in the FDB it was felt that each marital partner needed to make a secure relationship with his or her therapist
*before* a session with both was undertaken.

> At the joint meeting both clients were extremely nervous and at first
> found it difficult to say anything. Then Mr Webb turned to his wife's
> caseworker and poured out his troubles to her, making a great
> appeal for her support. He claimed that his wife did not love him
> and was always threatening to leave him, and this was unbearable.
> He said he must have a decision one way or the other. Mrs Webb
> then became very angry and there was some cross-talk between
> husband and wife in which each demanded from the other prom-
> ises of absolute love and no further bad behaviour of any kind. The
> two case workers tried to intervene and to show the clients how
> difficult they both seemed to find it to bear the ups and downs of
> marriage, of alternate love and rejection, kindness and anger, but
> they were not able to listen to remarks of this kind. [pp. 63–64]

From our contemporary perspective, it is interesting to read this
vivid account of one of the very early joint sessions about a decade
after the founding of the FDB. The account is obviously based on
notes made after the session, in contrast to the case reports in Henry
Dicks' account of the work in the Marital Unit of the Tavistock Clinic
which were apparently taken from transcribed tape recordings of
sessions (Dicks, 1967, pp. 267, 328). That is significant here because
so-called process notes, no matter how soon after the session they are
made, are filtered through the emotional experience of the reporting
therapist. Here, what they seemed to have noted, and what seems to
have made the greatest impact on them, is the turning of Mr Webb to
his wife's therapist, Mrs B. He repeats complaints that he has made
to his therapist, Mrs A, and in fact repeats what Mrs Webb in essence
had been saying to her therapist. This suggests that the idea of an
intimate link between Mrs A and Mrs B, as if they were a genuine
couple, albeit a "co-therapist couple", is an idea that does not resonate in Mr Webb's mind or in his internal world.

We can imagine, for example, pointing out to him that he seems to
take no account of the possibility that Mrs B would have heard this
from Mrs A, and wondering with him about the way he turns to his
wife's therapist as if she would not know about his despair. At this
point, we might be wondering about the "internal parental couple"

in Mr Webb's internal world, since he seems to lack confidence in a couple who might together attend to him, keeping him in mind and caring about his interests. It may be, of course, that the fact that the two therapists confer throughout the course of the therapy has not been made clear to the Webbs. If so, this joint encounter might be an ideal opportunity to explore this reality, this psychic reality which is in fact one of the core "boundaries" of co-therapy with couples. More likely, it was not a matter of missing information, but rather evidence of a possible deficit in the internal psychic structure, a deficit that perhaps was shared by the Webbs. If we use the terminology introduced by Teruel and think in terms of the *dominant internal object*, then we might begin to think about a "fractured" internal parental couple, incapable of creative intercourse (Teruel, 1966).

This hypothesis seems supported by the fact that the therapists report their interventions in such a non-individuated, impersonal way. In their previous description of Mrs Webb, they noted that she talked of "the children", "not distinguishing them by name or sex". Here they talk about themselves as "the two caseworkers" and do not distinguish between their interventions, as if what was said could have been said by either—and this following Mr Webb's turning to his wife's therapist, a move that must have had different reverberations in each therapist, to say nothing of the effect on Mrs Webb.

The content of their interventions seems to be what in systemic family therapy is sometimes referred to as "normalization"—that is, trying to put something in a "normal" context. Here the couple's mutual demands for "absolute love" and "no further bad behaviour" is put in the context of the "ups and downs of marriage". This sounds a little like the countertransference "acting-out" that we are so familiar with in our own experience. For example, I have sometimes noted in an initial session with an arguing, contentious couple that I find myself asking how they first met, or what drew them together. The obvious implication is that there must have been some positive attraction, and, almost as a distraction from the current conflict, I invite them to tell me something positive about their relationship. As Diana Daniell suggested to me, underneath this invitation lies our own anxiety about the "first meeting" with this couple. The unconscious message, which the couple often seem to hear, is to tell us something positive not only about "how you first met" but about "how *we* first met"—ambiguously including how I, the therapist, and they, the couple, first met.

Mrs A and Mrs B seem aware of this to some degree because they courageously tell their readers that the couple were "not able to listen to remarks of this kind". Whether it was a kind of acting-out by the therapists or not, it was certainly followed by some dramatic acting-out by the couple.

> Mrs Webb became very upset and said that there were no ups and downs as far as she was concerned, she hated her husband all the time. Then, half weeping, she said she was "absolutely sick of it all" and rushed out of the room and out of the building, although the couple had brought their four-year-old daughter with them and she was playing in another room. [p. 64]

What can one say? Any therapist who has not had one partner in a couple suddenly walk out, has probably not seen many couples. As in analytic work with children, this work with couples is marked by a lot of acting-out of feelings that cannot be thought about—indeed, cannot even be put into words so that it is possible to think about the feelings. As long as the acting-out can be kept within tolerable limits so that it can ultimately be thought about, it can be a valuable aspect of the analytic process—indeed, to some extent it is a necessary part, as Betty Joseph among others has pointed out (Joseph, 1975). We know that both Mr and Mrs Webb are dealing with abandoning internal objects who, so to speak, walk out on each of them. We also know that Mr Webb feels that he is the one to be abandoned, while Mrs Webb seems to identify with the abandoning object, and it is this "all-too-neat" marital fit that is such a dilemma for them. The problem with the "walk-out" in therapy is that the one key person who needs to be able to think about this experience is no longer there to think with us about it.

> Mr Webb made no attempt to follow his wife, but simply said contemptuously: "Now you see what she is like. What can you do with a woman like that?" Mrs B then withdrew (still hoping to have a further word with Mrs Webb), and almost immediately Mr Webb's mood changed. He began to sob, and continued to do so for some time. Mrs A tried to comfort him, and tried also to show him his confused behaviour towards his wife, his great longing for her love and yet his apparent need to see her as hateful and bad. He gradu-

ally pulled himself together and, when able to leave, collected his little daughter, who was inevitably very uneasy about her mother's disappearance. With her, he showed himself as quite a different person, considerate, sensitive and capable. [p. 64]

One can see here why these therapists placed so much emphasis on the hopeful aspect in this relationship—the affectionate attachment of the parents to the children. Apparently, Mrs Webb had acted on her request to bring her "lovely, happy little girl" with her to therapy. Whether this was a common occurrence in the FDB we are not told, but in this joint session it seems to have particular significance. It raises the possibility that we should consider the "walk-out" was an enactment of the splitting that so characterizes the way that Mrs Webb deals with her unbearable internal conflict, the internal mother who deserts her little daughter. Mr Webb, one may suppose, understands this split unconsciously and is able to focus his love and caring on his loved daughter. That is, he not only loves the daughter for herself, but also as she stands for the part of his wife that Mrs Webb feels to be so vulnerable that it must be projected safely outside herself and into her daughter.

What do we imagine leads to this dramatic shift in Mr Webb's mood after his wife's therapist has also left the room? Mrs A's most important role here is not her attempt to comfort him, but, rather, her helping him to see how he colludes with this splitting which dominates their relationship. He seems paralysed by his passivity *vis-à-vis* his abandoning internal object, something that gets acted out in this joint session. Indeed, it reminds one of what I have described as a "Leontean" state of mind, in that, ironically, Mr Webb's need to demonstrate his abandonment takes priority over his capacity to make a claim on the woman he loves. Leontes' delusional jealousy means that his attack seems more active, while Mr Webb appears more passive. What they clearly share, however, is the transferring of the love and attention to the child, Leontes to Mamillius and Mr Webb to his little daughter. In both cases, the mother/wife is experienced as deserting, walking out on, her child/husband.

In the work with the Webbs, the splitting that pervades their relationship now seems to have got into the therapists, lodging itself in their inexperience in *dealing as a couple* with this couple. It is, of course, a difficult situation, even for the most experienced of co-therapists working together in the room as a couple. Nevertheless, the fact that Mrs B enacts a role that might most appropriately belong to the husband means that, in effect, the co-therapists are split. It seems almost inevitable since these two therapists were working within a model of parallel individual therapy and had only reluctantly agreed to this joint session—"joint" not only in that the couple is seen together, but "joint" in that for the first time the therapists are seen together *as co-therapists*—that is, as a couple, and inevitably unconsciously carrying some of the meaning of the *internal parental couple*. We have the advantage, not only of hindsight—which we know means 20/20 vision—but also because we have experience of carrying the unconscious significance of the internal parental couple. Perhaps we should add here that the actual gender of the therapists, which undoubtedly carries some particular meaning, nevertheless does not prohibit the co-therapist couple from having the unconscious significance of the parental couple.

## Therapeutic work with one partner

The joint meeting opened a new phase. Mrs Webb cancelled her next appointment. Mr Webb came to his in a very subdued mood. His wild stories and accusations ceased and he became much more consciously worried about himself. He continued to have outbursts of violence at home, but came to his caseworker childishly and pathetically to confess about these and to beg for her help. She tried hard to make more direct contact with her client's destructiveness and despair, and to help him to recognize his fury with her and with all the women who frustrated him and deprived him, but he remained placatory and anxious, and seemed dull and stupid in the extreme. The only subject in which he was much interested was that of getting his wife back to the Bureau. While he rationalized this by arguing that there was no point in his working at his marital difficulties if she was not doing so too, it was clear that his uneasiness went much deeper than this. [p. 64]

This new phase was critical for the therapy. What was vital was the capacity of the two therapists to maintain their alliance and their availability to the couple. In one sense we might think that there was nothing else they could do, but we all know the temptation to act out our countertransference. It seems clear, however, that Mrs A and Mrs B did not give way to their shock and despair after that dramatic joint session. For example, in this report of the work with Mr Webb we see a recognition that his interest in getting his wife back to the therapy had as much to do with his split-off anger as with what they rightly recognize as his "rationalization" that marital therapy could not continue in her absence. With all the splitting, we could say that it was never clear who was where anyway. If the therapists could hold firm, this "acting-out" of Mrs Webb's absence could be seen as "acting-in" *within* therapy, where it could, eventually, be worked with.

It is also critical to note the effect of this pervasive splitting on Mr Webb. "Stupidity" and "dullness" characterized his presentation from the beginning, despite evidence the therapists had that in other settings, such as his work, he was intelligent. I commented in the previous chapter on Bion's important contribution to our understanding of the analytic process when in his paper "On Arrogance" he called attention to the ability to split off the thinking part of the self, a disastrous splitting of the *ego* which results in a kind of "stupidity" (Bion, 1967).

John Steiner discusses a similar case of splitting in which his patient appeared "stupid":

> Intelligence, the capacity to observe, to make judgements, and to retain contact with reality seemed, in my patient, to lead her to recognize the state of her objects, and to recognize her own impulses, and this appeared to make her afraid of what she would feel and what she would do. She could protect herself by splitting off and projecting these capacities but in the process was seriously disabled. [Steiner, 1993, p. 58]

Although the therapists could not work directly with Mrs Webb in her absence, working to help her husband with his splitting and projection, especially with his split-off capacity to think, would inevitably have an effect on her.

> Mrs A tried to show him that his wife, in walking out on her caseworker and thus expressing her anger with the Bureau and her feeling of being let down, was perhaps expressing these feelings for him too, and that this was what made him so alarmed by her absence. He denied this completely, but, as usual, seemed relieved

that it had been said, and then in a half-frightened, half-provocative manner began to report various critical or sneering remarks that his wife had made about the Bureau. Always Mrs A put these back to him as being partly his own feelings that he was unable to express directly for fear of destroying the relationship that he had made with her. She tried to link this up with the situation within the marriage and to show him his need to drive his wife to do and say things for him. [pp. 64–65]

These persistent interpretations of Mr Webb's split-off anger and hostility hardly need any contemporary comment. They represent a classic example of analytic work in the development of the analytic process. Even the tendency to speak more abstractly about "the Bureau" is eventually brought back to his fear about the relationship with Mrs A herself. It is instructive to note how focusing on the transference to the therapists (sometimes in the form of "the Bureau") allows Mrs A to make a link with similar dynamics in the marital relationship.

After a month, Mrs Webb returned to Mrs B, and for a short time there was a great improvement in the marriage. Mr Webb became much calmer and, for the first time, began to try to talk about his work as well as his marriage and made it clear that he had great difficulties with colleagues and superiors. He was able to talk about his uncertainties of himself as a man and about his own father, whom he saw as loveable but weak and pathetic. He talked about his own children, in particular his son, and expressed considerable anxiety about what he was doing to him. In talking of him he told many stories of the boy's sexual curiosity and anxiety about himself and his body. He talked also of his greed, of his tantrums and jealousy, and yet could see the boy's attempts to make amends for this and to show love for his parents. In this way Mr Webb was gradually able to come to discuss these things in himself. [p. 65]

Although it might seem that talking about his work and about his relationship with his son and with his father was a diversion from the marital therapy, the contemporary reader will no doubt recognize how the splitting and projections that characterize the marital relationship are not limited to that relationship. My experience is that one cannot draw a hard and fast line between couple therapy and individual therapy. Much of what happens in the analytic process with an individual also happens in the analytic process with a couple. Mr Webb obviously used splitting and projection as part of his defensive structure to such an extent that it became "second nature", what we might think of as part of his character structure.

Moreover, we might wonder about the transference relationship to Mrs A in the context of the co-therapist relationship between Mrs A and Mrs B. I have already commented on the issue of the relationship between the co-therapist relationship and the internal parental couple. The fact that neither therapist is male will not preclude the development at some deep level of thoughts and feelings about the father as well as the mother. Whether or not Mrs A ever took this up directly, we suspect that Mr Webb's transference to her included what we might call a *father transference*. He was, perhaps, beginning to have the kind of exploration of his own feelings about his confused sexuality—remember the stories about sexual depravity in others—and his identity as a man that he could never have with the "weak and pathetic" father who was also loveable.

## The impact on the other partner

> Mrs Webb, after her return, seemed relieved that she was able to come back and find Mrs B still there for her. She, too, began to co-operate in interviews and to talk about her husband as a real person with whom she had a relationship and not just a persecutor. She expressed anxiety about her own sexual frigidity, and seemed distressed about her general inability to show warm feelings. She continued to talk of her mother only in idealized terms, always to deny any suggestion of angry feelings about her. In the same way to refute any suggestion of anger or frustration in her relationship with Mrs B. Towards Mrs A she often expressed hostility. During this short period of improvement Mrs Webb had her birthday and received from her husband two loving birthday cards, one from "Your Husband, Alf", and the other from "The Same Bloke Again", which seemed to express some kind of drive on his part to bring to her the contradictory aspects of himself and to have them accepted. Mrs Webb was indeed touched by this, and for the first time for many months responded affectionately to him. [p. 65]

Here we find direct evidence that the good work with Mr Webb about his splitting and projecting unacceptable aspects of himself was having some effect on Mrs Webb and their relationship. We do not know exactly why she felt able to come back to therapy, but it is interesting in the previous excerpt that we are told that "Mrs Webb returned to Mrs B". This is a very personal way of describing her return, and it perhaps reflects some of the countertransference experience of Mrs Webb's "abandonment", a way perhaps of seeing the walk-out as an "acting-in". She now seems to experience her husband "as a real person" and not as full of her projections. Is this a response to his experience of her as more of a real person and not so full of his persecuting projections? When, beginning in chapter eight, we turn to *The Cocktail Party* we encounter T. S. Eliot's dramatic articulation of such a moment, meeting the other almost as a stranger.

We are given a chilling warning, however, that the work is beginning to uncover the core idealization by Mrs Webb of her mother. This rigidity seems at this point lodged in her transference to her therapist, Mrs B, while the positive feelings towards this loved object can only be maintained by splitting off the anger and hostility. Here the transference splitting is dramatically acted out in reference to the two therapists, one good and one bad. On the one hand, this represents a splitting of the internal mother, but in another sense it is also an attack on the internal parental couple. In her history, there were the "good" mother and the "bad" step-mother, a very familiar theme from popular culture and folk tales. It is important to note that the "good" mother is absent from the parental pairing, fracturing the parental couple by her abandonment. The resulting parental couple contains a "bad" step-mother, an impostor, and thus it becomes a "depraved" parental couple which drives out the child (in her view).

Perhaps because the painful internal conflict is now firmly located in the transference relationship with the two therapists, the marital relationship seems to enjoy a period of calm, and even happiness. And, as couples often do, the Webbs give us a delightful concrete metaphor for the working that has been going on in the therapy. The original therapists must have treasured this story as much as we do today: her birthday, and his two cards. At a conscious level, we could imagine that he wanted to underscore his loving birthday greeting, another one from "The Same Bloke Again". Yes, but why? Why the replication, if that is what it was?

Something, we feel, is resonating here in this humorous replication. This man is perhaps becoming aware of being filled up with his wife's intrusive projections, just as it is slowly becoming possible to recognize how he himself projects, intrusively projects, what he cannot bear in himself into his wife and into his therapist. Is this "same bloke" the stranger he is to himself and to his wife? It is one of those moments in therapy we can imagine sometimes being able to explore without having to pin it down to one particular meaning. It is as full of meaning as we and the couple are free to allow it to be.

For example, one question that might have been resonating unconsciously for Mr Webb (and perhaps for Mrs Webb as well) is "why two therapists?" Of course, at one level the answer is so obvious that we might think that the question would never arise. Each of them was in therapy, and hence each had a therapist. But there is another, possibly unasked question, at least consciously. Why two *women*, two of the same, so to speak? One (unconscious) answer was, naturally, because there is a "good" one and a "bad" one—the splitting that we know from the material had been reported in reference to Mrs Webb's feelings towards Mrs B and Mrs A. Perhaps it was some link like this that led the therapists to conclude that Mr Webb was trying to express, unconsciously, some "drive" to bring to his wife "the contradictory aspects of himself".

Still I think there may be another dimension to this theme of what we might describe arithmetically as the "two who are really one"— that is, the reconciliation of the splitting of the loved object into the "good" and the "bad". We might turn it around and talk about the "one who is really two". We have in the back of our minds here the resonance of the parental couple and the arithmetic that constantly puzzles the child. Think, for example, of the account that Ron Britton gives of his analysis with a woman who (as he says he came to understand) could not allow the notion of parental intercourse because she experienced it as a disaster:

> What I felt I needed desperately was a place in my mind that I could step into sideways from which I could look at things. If I tried to force myself into such a position by asserting a description of her in analytic terms, she would become violent, sometimes physically, sometimes by screaming. When it became a little more contained, she could express it in words: she shouted: "Stop that fucking thinking!" I came to realize that these efforts of mine to consult my analytic self were detected by her and experienced as a form of internal intercourse of mine, which corresponded to paren-

tal intercourse. This she felt threatened her existence. [Britton, 1989, p. 88]

Here, the experience of the lone analyst nevertheless conjures up the experience of the "two"—in Britton's reconstruction of the unconscious meaning, the parental couple in intercourse. When the couple is faced with two therapists, two therapists who are linked in a joint enterprise by the bond of their communication during therapy, the co-therapist partnership must inevitably present the couple in therapy with an experience that evokes the unconscious encounter with the almost all-too-concrete meaning of the parental couple in intercourse.

Mr Webb seems at this point far from a direct encounter with the "parental couple", but in his engaging playfulness with "the two of him" offering an expression of love to his wife (and on her "birthday"!) there does seem to be resonating somewhere in the depths the theme of the puzzle of how "two become one". We almost feel that he is working his way towards the thought that if Mrs A and Mrs B could become a real couple (for them), then perhaps he and his wife could as well.

## Thoughts about the experiment with joint sessions

Since it was not customary at that time to see the two marital partners together, Lily Pincus was at pains to offer some further thoughts on that dramatic joint session for her readers, who must have been very curious about what has now become common practice among psychoanalytic psychotherapists.

*As it happens, joint meetings were arranged in the two cases so far discussed [in the Marriage Book] although, in fact, this is not the usual practice at the Bureau.*

*It may be interesting to contrast these two joint meetings. With the Clarkes [the first couple discussed in the Marriage Book] the casework was already well advanced and each client had developed a secure relationship with his [sic] caseworker. With the Webbs, the work had barely begun, and the arrangement was made because it seemed impossible to proceed any further without it. It seems probable that Mr Webb's anxieties were such that he could tolerate*

*further work only if all four people concerned were brought together*
*in actuality—that is if all his splittings and contradictions could be*
*resolved at least momentarily. He had to show his "bad" wife to Mrs*
*A and to try to make contact with Mrs B.*

*For Mrs Webb this meeting proved a very disturbing experience.*
*She said afterwards that she had felt let down and "abandoned" by*
*her own caseworker. She had followed this up by abandoning her*
*husband and child. She did not return to the Bureau for a month—*
*abandoning her worker too.*

*Unlike Mr Clarke, who could not, at first, bear his wife to be a*
*patient, Mr Webb seemed to feel terribly unsafe during this period*
*when his wife was not attending. The contradictions in his behav-*
*iour, and in his conceptions of himself and his wife, occasioned in*
*him such anxiety that he could bear to talk about them only if all*
*were brought together somehow at the Bureau. He could not bring*
*his hate and violence to Mrs A, but he seemed to need his wife to*
*bring them for him. He could not see any good in his wife or give her*
*any affection, but he needed Mrs B to be in contact with the good*
*side of her and to support and protect her from him.* [pp. 65–66]

Because I do not intend to discuss any of the other four cases presented in the Marriage Book, I shall not comment at length on this
contrast between the "Clarkes" and the "Webbs" except to point out
the basic assumption that these therapists seemed to share about the
"experiment" with joint sessions. The idea that each partner in the
couple needs to have a secure relationship with his or her therapist
*before* taking the risk of the four meeting together seems, from our
current perspective anyway, to work against the notion of the co-
therapist partnership. The question of using co-therapists in analytic
therapy with couples is, in any case, not a straightforward one. I will
come back to it briefly in chapter six.

The idea seems to be that it was essential for Mr Webb to be able
to bring together *in actuality* "all his splittings and contradictions" in
relation to the four people so that momentarily, at least, they could
be resolved. We should not imagine that Lily Pincus is saying that
the splitting is actually resolved, but it does raise a question about
the role of what might be called "therapeutic re-enactment". John
Steiner's analysis of the process of resolution of the splitting and
projection by the re-integration of the split-off parts of the self reminds us what a complex intrapsychic process this is (Steiner, 1989).

We know, not only from Steiner's clinical description but also from the story so far with Mr Webb, that the recognition and naming of split-off parts of the self is met with a reduction in anxiety. In fact, that has been a striking aspect of the analytic work with Mr Webb, that he responded to interpretations by Mrs A of, for example, his split-off anger or despair with a reduced anxiety and a more positive, and "rational", engagement with her.

However, we also know that these changes were short-lived, and Mr Webb quickly returns to what must have been a deeply embedded defensive pattern. His internal world seems structured around these projective identifications, so that whether he is dealing with his wife, or his son, or his colleagues, or whomever, the same or similar interactional patterns are soon seen. With that in mind, we must wonder again why the insistence by the couple on a joint session was met by such strong resistance on the part of the two therapists. But perhaps this resistance itself is a clue to what was happening.

It is possible that the two therapists have got caught up in the logic of their own perceptions of the unconscious dynamics, not only in the Webbs' relationship, but, more importantly, in the relationship of each of the Webbs with them. Actually, it is difficult to believe that, in an agency committed to the therapeutic practice of parallel individual sessions for a marital couple, the patients themselves would come up with an alternative way of structuring the therapy. It is possible that Mr Webb's need to "show" his "bad" wife to Mrs A and his need to make a concrete link with his wife's therapist have made this joint session inevitable. But it is also possible, at a time when the other major marital unit in the Tavistock Centre had been experimenting with joint sessions for a number of years, and staff had been moving back and forth between the two units for some time, that recognition of persistent projective identification might have led the therapists themselves to think in terms of "resolving that splitting and projection" *concretely*.

Henry Dicks argued that it was better for the split transferences that can arise with two co-therapists to be lodged in one single therapist (Dicks, 1967, p. 203). And, of course, our practice of using co-therapist partnerships could be seen as a concrete expression of the evoking of transference to the parental couple, which, as Britton and others have stressed, is a central transference dynamic when there is but one therapist. However one decides to work—as a therapist alone or with a co-therapist—it is clear in the work with Mr Webb that the interpretation of his need for his wife to carry his darker, more angry and hostile feelings was central to both the marital relationship and to the transference dynamics with his therapist.

We have not reflected, however, on Mrs Webb's feeling that in the joint session *she* felt abandoned *by her therapist*. When, in that session, Mr Webb made a strong bid to communicate with his wife's therapist, Mrs B, the question of "who is the couple?" became problematic. Did his wife feel that as a desertion, and a desertion by whom? Once again, as she always suspects, "mother" is really interested in someone else. Anna Freud described it first nearly seventy years ago as the "identification with the aggressor" (A. Freud, 1936). Better to be the one who abandons than the one is who is abandoned. This is the kind of thing one would want to explore with Mrs Webb—except, of course, that becomes impossible when she acts out the abandonment, paying Mrs B back in kind.

But, as we know, the story is not at an end.

# CHAPTER FIVE

# Separations
# and the capacity to mourn

In our final reprise here of the work with Mr and Mrs Webb in the 1950s, we return to a familiar theme in the analytic process, that most persistent issue of what therapists provocatively call *breaks*. Even the word itself hints at an unconscious assumption that anything good, desirable, nourishing, and so on should be continuous, without interruption. However, these experiences of disruption are in fact at the heart of the analytic process, precisely because they are moments that mark the therapeutic relationship as a *real* and not a fantasy relationship. Coming to terms with our own finiteness, and the finiteness of the other on whom we depend, is central to emotional development out of narcissism and towards the capacity to be in a relationship, a development that I am talking about as the evolving capacity for marriage. We are reminded of the end of *The Winter's Tale*, where Shakespeare invites the participants in this story of development out of narcissism to reflect on the links between union and separation, between having a part and parturition. As Leontes says to Paulina, the woman who has brought them together:

Lead us from hence, where we may leisurely
Each one demand, and answer to his part
Perform'd in this wide gap of time, since first
We were dissevr'd: hastily lead away.

[V.iii.151–155]

One could say that the story of *The Winter's Tale* is a story of facing reality, in particular the reality of separation. It is also the story not only of every therapy, but also of the process of development in family life, and of the evolving capacity to be in an intimate couple relationship. One way of thinking about this question of parts, being a part, and parting might be in terms of the experience of working through the mourning that is requisite if the projections of parts of the self are ever to be re-integrated in a way that reinforces the strength and flexibility of the personality. There is also the question of the anxieties of being "apart", the feelings of abandonment that can accompany this process of integration. Both come to the fore as we turn to the conclusion of the story of the therapy with the Webbs.

## Working through "abandonment"

The "honeymoon" in the Webb family lasted about four weeks, then Mrs B was due to go away for her summer holiday, and Mrs A's holiday was to follow immediately on Mrs B's return. Both caseworkers feared that the withdrawal of help at this point might undo all the good that had been done so far in this marriage and, after some discussion, they arranged that each should make herself available to see the other's client during the holiday period if Mr and Mrs Webb themselves wanted this. [p. 66]

One has to stop here, if for no other reason than to register the sense of uneasiness any therapist would feel when a clinical case presentation reaches the point introduced by such a phrase as, "then Mrs B was due to go away for her summer holiday". Experience of the difficulty of breaks, whether because they are traumatic—or, indeed, ironically because they are *not*—is critical to the analytic process. We know that the issues of separation are central, and yet we face the reality of interruptions with some dread. It is particularly uncomfortable when it comes to co-therapist partnerships, where the diary seems to rule life as the most unrelenting of autocrats. The diary, of course, is only one of the most irritating markers reminding us of the realities of life, especially our limitations, our multiple and often conflicting loyalties, our need for rest and refreshment, our finitude. The end of a session or, say, the announcement of our summer holiday carries with it the shock of the baby's seeing mother leaving the room, perhaps, it fears, never to return.

Conscious or unconscious anxiety in the countertransference, if not understood and contained by the therapist, can lead to an *acting-out* of that anxiety. I think it all too easy to overlook the fundamental significance of this reality, although it has within its provenance the essential features of the analytic experience. It provides the framework for the experience of the anxieties of dependence which we call the transference—not that we include breaks in the structure of the analytic relationship in order to create that experience, but because limitations mark our human reality.

Consistent adherence to this boundary allows for the possibility of the infantile transference to emerge and for the therapist then to work analytically with it. My experience is that in work with couples there is a tendency to dismiss, or at least to minimize, the significance of the rhythm of the therapy. It is true for both the therapists and the couples that the once-a-week pattern can dull us to the shock of the interruption. One has only to listen carefully to the often not very subtle expressions of the amazement, as more than one couple has said to me, that their week seems to revolve around that session.

We certainly hear about anxiety in reference to the summer holiday interrupting the work with the Webbs, at least the anxiety of the therapists. Their countertransference was marked by a concern that the two summer holiday breaks, which "unfortunately" followed one after the other rather than being simultaneous, were in danger of "undoing all the good work". At the point when it seems that an infantile transference was taking hold, their fear was that the infantile anxieties provoked by the break might overwhelm Mr and Mrs Webb. This anxiety may have been exacerbated by a situation which is all too familiar to those who work with a co-therapist, since it is difficult and sometimes impossible to coordinate timetables. In the work with the Webbs, the difficulty was exacerbated by the fact that

the structure of parallel individual sessions meant that for one therapist to see both partners would introduce a new, and potentially
disturbing, experience. When the therapy proceeds entirely, or
largely, in joint sessions, at least there is a sense that the couple has a
shared relationship with the two therapists.

Some readers might be concerned that offering sessions with the
therapist of the partner to both Mr and Mrs Webb in turn would only
heighten, not contain, anxiety. Only the therapists at the time can
determine how they judge their patients' anxiety, and it may at times
be distinctly different from their own. We shall see in a moment in
the editorial comments that these two therapists, as well as the organization in which the therapy took place, were well aware of the
risks of this arrangement.

> At his first interview after Mrs B's holiday had begun, Mr Webb
> reported a severe domestic upheaval. He said he did not know how
> the row had started, but it had ended in a fight in which he had
> broken a window and blacked his wife's eye. She had gone to the
> police and to her doctor, and was now talking of applying for a
> separation. Mrs A tried to understand with him what had hap-
> pened—perhaps as a result of his anger at the Bureau workers'
> apparent lack of concern for them and his uneasiness now that his
> wife was no longer supported and that he felt that he was not
> sufficiently controlled. He could make little contribution to this
> attempt to understand the situation and seemed very dull and re-
> mote. He could present himself only as a frightened and pathetic
> little boy, wanting forgiveness and love, and wanting to be told that
> all would be well. [pp. 66–67]

We can see why the therapists and the commentator have been laying stress on the "degree of disturbance" in Mr Webb. His capacity
for violent behaviour, especially as directed towards his wife, would
be worrying to any therapist. We have already seen how Mr Webb
uses his wife to express and act out some of his disowned angry and
hostile feelings, experiencing her as an externalization of his abandoning internal object, the mother who could not—or (perhaps in his
mind) would not—feed him. Recent research on couple interaction
has shown that violence by husbands against their wives is linked
with a particular form of the man's insecure attachment to his partner in which any perception that she is abandoning, or about to

abandon, him leads to a violent attack on her (Dutton, Saunders, Starzomski, & Bartholomew, 1994).

In this case, however, it was not the abandonment by Mrs Webb that seems to be the precipitant for Mr Webb's violent attack on her. We have seen something similar in moment-to-moment interactions *in the session* in couple after couple when angry and hostile transference feelings *towards the therapist(s)* are acted out by one marital partner *against the other*. When this happens in the session, and when the therapists are alert to this all-too-common dynamic, it is possible to point it out. In my experience, when this happens it can lead to a reduction in tension as the couples themselves can see that the hostility between them has replaced the hostility they cannot allow themselves to feel for us as their therapists.

Here, the situation is more difficult since the violent behaviour is happening outside the boundary of the therapy. We could say that, in an important sense, part of Mr Webb's therapy is taking place *in the sessions of Mrs Webb with Mrs B*—having split off and projected part of his infantile angry, hostile self into his wife, it is he, as well as his wife, who feels abandoned by Mrs B going off on holiday. The result is that what is left, so to speak, is the "dull and remote" Mr Webb who presents in his own session. Having a *dull and remote* little boy in the room must concern his therapist, Mrs A, who must know that the lively angry man is elsewhere. All she can do is patiently and persistently interpret that splitting and its consequences, to point out how he protects her from the anger that is vented on his wife. It is difficult to say from this distance whether our concern for Mrs Webb's physical safety would lead us to intervene in a more direct way, although one would certainly be worried about it.

After this scene, things calmed down again though there was no further movement towards a better relationship. Mr Webb continued to come to his interviews, but seemed quite unable to make any further attempt to understand himself or his marriage. He came like a little boy, begging for instructions. He seemed to understand almost nothing that was said to him and said again and again: "I don't think I quite follow that." Mrs A accepted his need for support, but tried a little to show him the fear of his anger and destructiveness which lay behind this. He would admit no reaction to his caseworker's approaching holiday, always making admirably reasonable remarks about it. [p. 67]

One of the reasons that I chose this case for an extended discussion is the intuitive way in which the therapists report the process of the therapy, so that anyone who has experience of trying to work analytically with a couple will recognize the familiar, almost predictable developments, frustrations, and discouragements. Mrs A continues her patient analytic work, helping Mr Webb to recognize the fear of his own feelings, especially his anger and destructiveness. He is also a victim of his own destructiveness in that his defensive strategies undermine his adult capacity to think. It is as if he believes, unconsciously, that the only way he, or his loved objects, can survive is if he attacks his own capacity to think. The "tongue-in-cheek" way of describing his "admirably reasonable remarks" about what must feel a psychic disaster for him—the impending abandonment by his therapist—suggests that Mrs A must have used her gentle humour in what is perhaps an ironic way to help him face his most intolerable negative feelings.

> When Mrs A went on holiday and Mrs B returned, Mrs Webb came back to her caseworker very depressed and unhappy again. She said that her husband was as bad as ever and that she was terrified of what would happen during Mrs A's absence. Mrs B spent the whole interview working over with her client this recurrent theme of abandonment and all the anger and fears which surrounded it for both Mr and Mrs Webb. [p. 67]

It is interesting, following the previous comments about Mr Webb's psychic investment in his wife's sessions with her therapist, to see what happens when Mrs B is back and seeing Mrs Webb. Mr Webb now seems to become less violent, contrary to expectations some might have that he would be more upset and volatile now that his own therapist was on holiday. Clearly the splitting and disassociation is powerful. Emotional experiences that belong to the therapy, and therefore belong *in the therapy*, are acted out in the couple relationship. Often, I am aware of some inexplicable intensity of hostility *between* the two partners in the couple which, when I am able to link it with feelings about me and the process of the therapy, then evaporates—and that happens whether or not the couple are able to acknowledge consciously that the anger belongs to the relationship with me.

It is also interesting from our contemporary perspective that we hear so little of the actual content of Mrs B's work with Mrs Webb, in noticeable contrast to the vivid details of Mr Webb's sessions with Mrs A. Again, we might wonder if perhaps some of these therapists were working more analytically, while others were less committed to or clear about the nature of this work—although we must continually remind ourselves how little we can judge accurately from this distance. The only important question is whether thinking about their experiences can help us with our own struggles to understand the analytic process and to find the internal resources to work patiently within the boundaries of the analytic discipline.

## Holiday breaks and the re-integrating of projections

Mr Webb's first interview after Mrs A's return was extremely difficult. He kept his overcoat on (it was early September), turned his chair to face away from Mrs A, and replied to her conventional polite greeting: "How am I? Frightened. I'm always frightened." His caseworker made an attempt to get him to say more and to try to explain himself, but he sat silently, still turned away from her.

Finally she said that he seemed to be frightened at this minute since he had remained wrapped up and was apparently unable to talk to her. She said that she thought he was very angry with her for going away, and, as always, very frightened of his anger which he imagined would harm her, or, at best, destroy her interest in him. She wondered, too, if a little bit of him was wanting to walk out on her, in revenge, and perhaps that was why he had kept his coat on. Mr Webb laughed and relaxed. He denied every word of this, but took off his coat and settled down to tell his caseworker what had happened while she had been away. [pp. 67–68]

It is hardly necessary to comment on this moving scene. It is such an engaging portrait of an easily recognizable interaction. Those who have seen the moving films produced by the Robertsons in the 1950s will also recognize an echo of the moment in one film when a hospitalized child was reunited for the first time with the mother who had "abandoned" him. The scene is still vivid in my mind: the child's chilling look in the direction of his mother, as if she were a stranger, and then his turning away from her despite her loving appeal to him

(Robertson, 1953). Mr Webb, with his overcoat unremoved and his chair turned to face away from his "abandoning" therapist, is that child.

Sometimes, we are desperate for our patients to give conscious assent to our so carefully worked out interpretations. But Mr Webb was, in a sense, quite right when he "denied every word" of what Mrs A had said. His conscious, adult self knew nothing of this frightening, potentially destructive anger of his. Mrs A was addressing his defended adult self, *but* she was communicating with a frightened child within, the abandoned baby in his internal world who only knew overwhelming rage and could not imagine how he, or his loved object, would survive any expression of that rage. Mr Webb had been recognized, and he knew at some level that he had been recognized.

> This whole period of holidays and "abandonment" in the casework seemed to be of immense importance to Mr and Mrs Webb. The experience, for both clients, of feeling utterly let down and furious about it, and of being helped to express this and to understand it a little, seemed to be a very meaningful one. They had managed to make a good relationship, had lived through a crisis occasioned by separation and yet had managed not to destroy it. [p. 68]

Clearly, this has been an important time in the work with this couple. Until there is a genuine encounter with the emotional crisis that attends the breaks in continuity—and for some couples this can take considerable time before they have any real emotional awareness of the impact—the work has hardly begun. In a sense, the therapy with the Webbs is moving quite rapidly in that there is an intense emotional engagement with their therapists. As Donald Meltzer describes the process:

> These two processes, the relief derived from understanding and the shock of separation set in motion the rhythm which is the wave-form, as it were, of the analytic process, recurring at varying frequencies, sessions by session, week by week, term by term and year by year. [Meltzer, 1967, p. 7]

He goes on to make clear the particular role of holiday breaks, which carry the resonance of abandonment—as it certainly did for the Webbs:

Slowly this relatively haphazard movement of the transference
lessens as the setting is erected in its many complex facets and the
rhythm of the analytic process asserts itself. Seldom does it really
settle before the consequences of a holiday break have been dealt
with. It is perhaps the only phase of analysis where experience
counts greatly in relation to time. The tempo of this first phase is
determined to a considerable degree by the technical skill and
clinical judgement of the analyst. [Meltzer, 1967, p. 10]

There can be little doubt about the skill and clinical judgement of
these two therapists working with the Webbs, and it is part of the
pleasure of writing this book that it offers an opportunity to acknowledge those pioneers of analytic therapy with couples. It will
not escape the notice of those who are familiar with Donald
Meltzer's exposition of what he calls the "natural history" of the
analytic process that what he is describing is the *beginning phase* of
the analytic process. At this point, however, in the story of the Webbs
in the Marriage Book they are describing the *conclusion* of the work.
What are we to make of this? Of course, there are many aspects that
one might consider when judging whether we are at the beginning
or at the end of a process. Perhaps most important is the issue of
criteria for termination, which in turn are derived from our view of
the aims of the process

There are many points at which analytic work can be brought to
an end. On the basis of what has been reported in this case study, I
think that if I were working with the Webbs I would tend to think of
myself as at the *beginning* of the work with this couple. Much, of
course, would depend on the couple's view, and sometimes it is a
question of how far they feel they need to go in the process before
feeling that they are ready to end the therapy. Doubtless the ending
process itself is an important part of the experience of therapy, although in my experience couples are less prepared to believe this
than individual patients are. There are differences in therapy with a
couple which distinguish it from therapy with an individual, differences that cluster around the fact that the couple relationship itself
can become, in some ways, an arena for the growth and development
of the two individuals.

Warren Colman has discussed this aspect of marital therapy
in terms of the therapy being a temporary "container", the aim of

which is to help restore the "container" function of the marital relationship.

> It is as though the therapeutic container is "borrowed" over a transitional period and needs to be discarded relatively quickly, before the couple's capacity to use their own relationship in a therapeutic way becomes atrophied or, as sometimes happens, the therapy sessions become the *only* place where that capacity can be exercised. [Colman, 1993, p. 76]

I shall have more to say about the ending process in the final chapter when we consider implications of the endings in Eliot's *The Cocktail Party* and Shakespeare's *Othello*, but for now we return to the conclusion of the work with the Webbs.

> The arrangement that was made, that each could see the other's caseworker, is a rare one at the Bureau, since it might be expected to create jealousies and anxieties which could undermine the therapeutic relationship. In fact, both Mr and Mrs Webb made use of the invitation on one occasion each. These interviews were curiously alike in that they were in a very low key, both clients bringing stories of their suffering and misery, but making no real accusations against the partner and little attempt to bid for support for themselves! Each seemed relieved to establish that the other had a good and supportive relationship at the Bureau, and needed only to be certain that they could both be acceptable to both caseworkers.
>
> Even Mr Webb, whose tendency to persecutory ideas must have made him very suspicious as to what his wife was doing with Mrs B, seemed to have an overriding need to have her protected and seen as good by someone. Only thus could he feel accepted himself. Mrs Webb, who at the time of the joint interview had felt so attacked by everybody and so abandoned by her own caseworker, seemed now only to need to assure herself that she could make contact with her husband's caseworker, and was able to face the partial rejection inherent in the situation. Perhaps, too, some of the division she had made in her childhood between the mother who must be seen as good at all costs, and the "step-mother" who could not be loved at all, made this meeting with "step-mother" of great importance to her. [p. 68]

There seems to be some surprise at how "contained" this couple appeared to be during the disruptive holiday breaks of their two therapists, especially at the one session each had with the other's therapist. Like Mr Webb's "placatory" manner, it faces us with the question of how much their presentation was an expression of their gratitude and their experience of "containment" in Bion's sense and how much it was an expression of compliance. That is one reason why today I might be thinking of this as the *beginning* of the therapy and not the end, wanting to work with how one distinguishes between compliance and cooperation. What the Webbs had experienced in their therapy was clearly important to them, but also something that we could imagine as needing to be worked through again and again, whether in therapy or outside it.

What catches my attention here is the final reference to the struggle of Mrs Webb, about which we have heard so much less than we have heard about Mr Webb's engagement in the analytic process. It is almost as if her therapist has been listening to our discussion and our plea for more, and now she chooses to tell us.

> From this point the character of the work in this case seemed to change. At the next two interviews both Mr and Mrs Webb reported continued scenes and smashings, with the astonishing difference that now Mrs Webb was hitting back and smashing things herself, and that the rows ended with tears and reconciliation. The caseworkers both commented upon the ability of their clients to be loving and reparative after rows, when the hatred had all been shown and there was little left to fear. Mrs B tried to explore with her client the relation between her masochism and her sexual difficulties. She said that her client seemed frightened to think of sex in terms of love, and while unable to allow herself any intercourse with her husband, seemed almost to invite him to beat her. Mrs Webb said that sex had always seemed to her like an attack. Then she began to cry and said that she could remember the violent quarrelling that had gone on between her own parents. She hastily followed this with further insistence upon her love for her mother and said that fortunately her husband had never said bad things about her mother. "If he does, that will be the end, I shall go berserk." Mrs B again tried to show her client her misery about her mother's behaviour and her denial of this feeling. For the first time Mrs Webb was then able to express some of her shame and anger about it. [pp. 68–69]

Here, at last, we come to a core conflict in Mrs Webb. What do we make, for example, of what could stand as a "motto" epitomizing her dilemma: "If he does, that will be the end, I shall go berserk." Could it be that her husband's violent anger, which was often directed *at her*, both disguised and at the same time acted out her own rage at mother? If that were the case, then we can imagine that what would be intolerable for Mrs Webb would be the exposure of that "cloak" for her own rage. That is, if it were to be seen to be directed not at herself as perhaps a kind of punishment for her rage, but at the true object of that rage, *mother*, it would be unbearable. Perhaps like Hermione she has had to turn herself into stone to avoid a rage that she fears could destroy not just her loved object, but, worse, her love *for* the object. However, when a projection of such an unacceptable part of the self can begin to be re-integrated, there can also begin to be a genuine relating in the marriage.

John Steiner's observation about the difference between a model of psychoanalysis that focuses on the resolution of internal conflict and a model that focuses on a re-integration of parts of the self is helpful here. The conflict that he is talking about is not the couple conflict, but rather the internal conflict between opposing impulses in Freud's original psychoanalytic model. But we can see in the work with the Webbs that had the therapists been working classically, they might have taken a different approach. In fact, I think they were working with an implicit model that was very similar to what Steiner describes as the "reintegration model".

> This model [the conflict model], and the aims of treatment which go with it, remain central to psychoanalysis, but carry with them important technical problems since the understanding of conflict involves moral choices which are often very difficult to resolve. . . . I think it is possible to see that the conflict theory takes us only part of the way to understanding this kind of material and that the recognition of projective identification expands the possibilities enormously. The aim of psychoanalysis according to this model [the re-integration model] is to help the patient find an integration and re-acquire parts of herself which were previously lost through projective identification. . . . We are less likely to become caught up in the conflict since the aim is to help the patient re-acquire the means to work through the conflict for himself. [Steiner, 1989, pp. 112, 115]

What happens as the projections begin to be reintegrated is that there seems to be a better balance in the couple relationship. Obviously, we ought not think that the therapists were here celebrating the fact that Mr Webb's violence was now being met by Mrs Webb's "hitting back and smashing things herself". Their point, I believe, is that this couple face what all of us face—the conflicts, moral conflicts, about how we live together in an intimate relationship. Perhaps, however, Mr and Mrs Webb have experienced some reintegration that will allow them more successfully to find the means to deal with those conflicts. Our interest in analytic therapy with couples is not to help them solve conflicts, much as we might be tempted to, but rather to help them understand what prevents them from even engaging in any meaningful way with those conflicts. Reintegrating projections, to use our technical language, does not solve the conflicts in their marriage, it only makes it possible for this couple to set about facing the conflict.

## An assessment of the therapy with the Webbs

One of the most interesting things about working analytically with a couple for someone who has experience of the analytic process with an individual is that one can see how two "templates", as it were, overlay (or should we say under-lay) the same relationship "episodes" with all the emotional complexities. For example, to offer an over-simple picture, Mr Webb's violent outburst directed against his wife can be seen *both* as an expression of *his* rage against his abandoning internal loved object projected into her *and* as an expression of *her* rage against her abandoning internal loved object, only what here is projected is that raging part of herself.

It is possible that what is projected can be either a part of the self in the sense of the "subjective" aspects of the self (for example, feelings) or a part of the self in the sense of the self's internal objects (for example, a loved object). Of course, feelings and objects are closely related, but it is this distinction that allows for one and the same marital dynamic to be an expression of the "script" of the internal world of the two marital partners, *different but "overlaying" scripts*. This picture is closely related to the notions of *shared unconscious phantasy* and *marital fit*, used to account for the nature of the unconscious bond in the intimate couple relationship.

Once a therapist working analytically with an individual has experienced this "overlay" of "templates" in a couple, it becomes possible, indeed imperative, to listen to the material from an individual patient in a new way, a way that is sensitive to the echoes of two different stories. In any case, the story of the Webbs now takes on a new dimension. It is as if finally we have begun to hear that the dynamics in their fraught relationship are the expression of *two* stories, two "scripts" as it were. When we reach this point, the next observation comes as no surprise.

> After this the violence subsided. The couple resumed sexual intercourse after almost a year during which Mrs Webb had completely refused it, and the removal of this frustration, and of the utter rejection and condemnation of his sexuality which it seemed to mean to Mr Webb, helped him very much. They were both able to tolerate the fact that it was not immediately very satisfactory. Mrs Webb began to come to life in the marriage, and the couple started sharing activities and taking the children out together. When they quarrelled it was on a realistic level, as the result of genuine grievances which they had against each other. Mrs Webb seemed to be able to stand up for herself more while, at the same time, doing less to provoke her husband's phantasies. Mr Webb seemed able to see his wife again as a real person and to relate to her as such. He was able to look at some of the projections he had made and understand some of his own behaviour in the marriage—his very great demands, his fury when he was rejected, his terror about this, and also his need to see his wife as bad and dirty just because she was his sexual partner. At this stage he dropped both his servile manner and his pathetic childish stupidity and began to show in his interviews the intelligence and ability that had been so completely hidden before. His appearance changed remarkably and he began to look like a pleasant and capable man. [p. 69]

Given the impressive changes in the way that this couple are now relating, we must assume, I believe, that this paragraph represents not just the *post hoc* assessment of the dynamics in each partner, but more importantly the analytic *work that had gone on*. For example, Mr Webb's ability to look at his projections—his demands, his fury, his terror, and his need to see his wife in a certain way and so on—all must represent analytic work done with him in his sessions. We have only heard, for example, hints about "sexual depravity" (in other people!) and his experience of his wife as "bad". There must have been a lot of work on his view of sexuality in himself and in his loved object to be able to reach the point where he could make a connection between these experiences and emotions and his experience of his wife as "dirty *because* she was his sexual partner".

But what about these changes? They are dramatic, especially in the way each partner can view the other *realistically*. What comes across more clearly is the change in reference to Mr Webb's projection of a persecuting *internal object* into his wife. Perhaps this kind of dynamic is always easier to see and to understand (he experiences his wife, an external object, as if she were his abandoning, rejecting mother, an internal object), while the projections of part of the subjective self (projection of his intelligence or capacity to think into his therapist, for example) are less easy to see and understand. It is perhaps the most dramatic change when we see evidence of the re-integration of his thinking capacity, the "stupidity" which was linked with his subservient and placatory manner.

This report of the changes in the Webbs is a good example of the model of psychoanalysis as aiming to assist the re-integration of parts of the self, in contrast to the model in which the aim is to assist in the resolution of conflict. The resolution of conflict that we see here in this couple is perhaps more an *indirect* result of the analytic work. In fact, conflicts continue, as they must for any couple in that they are two different individuals with different needs and interests, and the improvement is in *their* ability to tackle those conflicts—*and* to live with the less-than-perfect results.

In my clinical experience, this dramatic degree of change does happen, but only after a much longer period of "working through". It is easy, I think, to confuse this with what I call a "plateau", a moment—or better, a period—in the analytic process when there is a distinct period of improvement. This improvement can seem to constitute the basis for termination as both the couple *and* the therapist find themselves understandably pleased by the improvement in the marriage relationship. But this observation is not intended as a retrospective judgement of the work with the Webbs, since I have no doubt in my mind, after spending a lot of time with this case study, that I would put my faith in the clinical judgement of these thoughtful therapists. My observation is intended only to help us think with couples, in a robust way, whether the improvement in their relationship is the beginning or the end of our work together.

> These clients continued to attend weekly for several months, then asked if they could come fortnightly and, later, monthly. By this time it seemed that they had found ways of giving some support and satisfaction to each other and were taking pleasure in their children's development and activities. Their internal tensions seemed to have been partly relieved and it seemed that the much freer and more realistic relationship that they had now established might be able to absorb and contain these anxieties in the future. The pressure might at some time mount up again, but it seemed almost certain in this case that the clients would be able to avail themselves of further help if the situation in the family showed signs of deterioration. [pp. 69–70]

It is nearly time now to leave the Webbs. They have provided us with an experience of the analytic process with a couple, partial and fragmentary as that picture is, and with a number of questions about psychoanalytic technique, especially as applied in the unusual setting with a couple instead of with an individual. It exposes issues that I want to explore further, coming back to this question of ending in the final chapter. Before moving on, however, I want to end with a few excerpts from the final summary of this work in the Marriage Book.

> The work with the Webbs went on for almost the same length of time as that with the Clarkes, but the objective was a far more limited one. Mr Webb's near-delusions and the probable phantasies behind them were not dealt with directly. The work was concentrated entirely on the difficulties which these clients experienced in making and maintaining relationships with one another and with the caseworkers. [p. 71]

It is interesting to see the aim of the work with the Webbs described as "more limited" than the work with another couple in the Marriage Book, the Clarkes, which I am not considering. We need to keep in mind how much these therapists in the Family Discussion Bureau were pioneers, for the most part without a formal analytic training themselves but working under supervision of experienced psychoanalysts. This comment on the work as focused on the couple's difficulties in making and maintaining relationships *with one another and with the caseworkers* seems to me an elegantly simple statement of their openness to working with the transference, to the therapists as well as in the marital relationship. Whatever the limitations of their work in their eyes or ours, it seems to me to have had a solid grounding in the fundamental emphasis of analytic work—that is, working with the transference.

Many readers will have noted that little mention has been made of the work in reference to the children, although it seems clear that the children played an important role as the recipients of projections in the family *system*. It sounds as if there was some *systemic* work, however, that did go on indirectly.

> In the Webb family there were two children who were loved by both parents and who appeared, on the surface, to be remarkably undisturbed. They mediated between their parents and constantly tried to persuade them to "Kiss and Make it up". Both Mr and Mrs Webb seemed to see them as wholly good, and to give them all the love they could not give to one another. The last part of the casework was concerned largely with the clients' relationships with their children, and with some of the confusion of rejection, guilt and reparation in their feelings towards them. As the tensions between the parents eased, the children could give up their "false maturity" and showed more signs of the strain that they had undergone. [pp. 71–72]

Just as analytic work with an individual can keep in mind that this person may be part of an intimate couple relationship in which both partners' unconscious internal dynamics have essential and complementary roles, so in analytic work with a couple the therapists need to have in mind the intimate family relationships and how the children, and their complex unconscious internal dynamics, play an essential and complementary role. The "false maturity" of the Webb children is a counterdynamic to the "pseudo-maturity" of both Mr and Mrs Webb. One has the sense that this case study has been considerably abbreviated, and this reference to the children hints at a dimension of the work which, although important, did not find a place in the account.

Finally I want to note some concluding observations in the Marriage Book about working with what they perceived as such disturbed couples.

It is possible that work with marriages provides a way of helping clients of this degree of instability. While their childishness and violence at home are the focus of the work at the Bureau, in the relationship with their caseworkers they often remain polite, reasonable and co-operative. It seems that neither clients nor caseworkers can risk the degree of regression which might result if these "bad" aspects of themselves were brought directly into it.

. . . Cases of this kind present very great difficulties, especially where there are outbreaks of violence in which the clients themselves are terrified as to what will happen next. It is impossible for caseworkers not to share this terror, and not to wonder whether it would not be better if these people could separate from one another before serious damage is done. On the other hand, the experience at the Bureau may often make a *greater impact upon these clients than upon more sophisticated and more stable ones*, and *if this experience is interpreted* and understood to some extent, there may be considerable permanent gain. Many of the individual difficulties may remain untouched, but if some of the projections within the marriage are withdrawn, both husband and wife can gain the strengthening experience of discovering that their loving feelings are not destroyed by their hate. [pp. 72–73, emphasis added]

This conclusion represents the point of my greatest agreement with and most substantial reservations about the perspective described in the Marriage Book. Where they seem to have reservations about work with very disturbed couples, I would suggest that the more disturbed the couple functioning, the more one needs to consider a disciplined, psychoanalytic approach. That does not mean that all couples who relate in a very disturbed way will be able to engage in the analytic process. But I have found that often an analytic approach is the only one that makes an impact on these disturbed and disturbing couples. However, this is the subject of endless debates I have with my colleagues, and perhaps the question of which couples can benefit from psychoanalytic psychotherapy must be left to individual judgement.

I think that it is important to keep in mind that working analytically with a couple uncovers the "psychotic" dimension of the personality, just as it does with an individual. In my view, the intimate couple relationship itself is a *locus classicus* of infantile transferences, something that is true no matter how well or how badly the couple is functioning. It is not the presence of what could be described as *psychotic moments* that indicates disturbance; indeed, falling in love has been described as a psychotic state. The capacity of the couple relationship to contain those infantile transferences is the mark of emotional health and maturity, while it is the failure or breakdown of that containing capacity that, in part, brings couples to therapy *as a couple*.

That is a question to which we now turn. In order to think about whether or not any given couple can benefit from analytic therapy, we need to think about why anyone would want to engage in the analytic process *as a couple*. Of course, you may say simply that couples do sometimes become desperate when the relationship feels intolerable, and they cannot find a way back to what brought and held them together in better days, so they seek help. And it could then follow that they do not seek out *psychoanalytic* therapy in particular—indeed, that they have little idea what they are in for when they find themselves with a therapist who works analytically. That may occasionally be true in my experience, at least for a short time in my contact with a couple. But at some point early in the assessment, they do become aware that there is a very particular way of thinking and working in this kind of therapy. That is perhaps the main point of assessment: to give the couple a good idea of what it will be like to be in therapy with you so that they can make a reasonably informed judgement as to whether they are prepared to go on. Then the question becomes: why do some couples engage in the analytic process?—*not* why they *do not*, but *why they do*. One does not need an explanation for why couples do *not* engage in this kind of therapy; the reasons are endless. The interesting question is why they do.

# CHAPTER SIX

# That which couples bring to therapy

The therapy with the Webbs has brought into focus some critical questions. For example, when would we encourage people to seek therapy individually and when, if ever, as a couple? Why indeed would one want to engage in the psychoanalytic process *as a couple*?

One of my aims in this book is to convey something of the stark temerity of an invitation to the psychoanalytic experience *in the actual presence of the partner* with whom one shares, potentially anyway, the most intimate of life's experiences. It is possible to imagine that only someone who has experienced psychoanalysis as an analysand can appreciate how forbidding that prospect could be. It is forbidding, I suggest, not only for the couple, but in quite a profound way for the therapist as well. And yet the reality is that couples do seek out psychoanalytic therapy as couples and engage in the analytic process as couples, sometimes for four or five years.

In this chapter, I want to begin to explore the idea that certain forms of narcissistic relating lead to seeking therapy *as a couple*. Or perhaps I should say that a variety of circumstances may mean couples seek out therapy together, but certain forms of narcissistic relating make it possible for some couples to sustain participation in the analytic process as a couple. My query is whether or not *that which couples bring to therapy*, to paraphrase Henri Rey, helps us to make sense of *what brings couples to therapy*.

## In the presence of the other

Unlike the period in which the pioneering therapists in the Family Discussion Bureau and the original Marital Unit of the Tavistock Clinic were working, today there is a strong culture of counselling and therapy in which couples are regularly seen together. However, I think it would be fair to say that there is no comfortable, let alone happy, marriage of psychoanalysis and the practice of seeing couples, despite the fact that a lively but small new professional Society of Psychoanalytical Marital Psychotherapists has come into existence. My personal impression is that there is widespread doubt about the viability of working analytically with couples, although there is some interest in the "application" of psychoanalytic thinking to therapy with families and couples.

Perhaps I should clarify that observation because there is a sense in which the focus in contemporary psychoanalytic theory and practice with individuals is on the intimate couple relationship, the analytic couple. Therapy takes place in the context of that couple relationship, in the transference and countertransference dynamics that constitute the field for investigating the disturbances that make intimate relating difficult or impossible. In a sense, those who seek out psychoanalytic therapy, for whatever reason, are treated *by a relationship*—the intimate relationship of patient and therapist, analysand and analyst.

This, I think, takes us back to the theme with which we began in chapter one, the juxtaposing of the states of *narcissism* and of *marriage*. If by a "capacity for marriage" we understand what in contemporary psychoanalysis might be discussed as a "capacity for object relating", I think it would be a fair generalization to say that this is the focus for much, if not most, psychoanalytic therapy with individuals today. At least that is true in the object relations tradition, although I have a sense reading the literature describing clinical work across different schools of contemporary psychoanalysis that there is a strong emphasis on the capacity of individual patients for genuine emotional intimacy with another person. Another way of formulating this observation would be to say that, for some time now, contemporary psychoanalytic theory and therapy across the various schools have been preoccupied with narcissism, although each defines and approaches narcissism in quite different ways.

This emphasis on narcissism and the vital importance of the analytic relationship as the intimate arena for the emotional work that goes on in therapy also highlights how strange it can feel to contemplate a marriage of the psychoanalytic process and the marital couple. It will be obvious that the kind of intimacy shared by two people in the marital relationship differs in fundamental ways from the intimacy shared by analyst and analysand in the psychoanalytic process. Of course, it is also true that these intimate relationships are alike in some important ways. But I invite readers who have been in analysis or therapy to think now of things that they have shared with their analyst or therapist, particularly those, shall we call them for shorthand, "nightmare" feelings and thoughts. Those are, to some degree anyway, the kind of thoughts and feelings that would have to be couched very carefully were one to express them to a marital partner. The reason is not that necessarily one would want to keep them secret from this person with whom so much is shared. But the aim would be to *communicate* something. That is, there would be a fear, having meant to share something about one's experience, that whatever was said also became a form of *action*, doing something to that other person, not merely communicating something.

This distinction between *communication* and *action* is critical, and it is fundamental not only to understanding a psychoanalytic approach to therapy, but also to understanding reservations about therapy with marital couples. Some thirty years ago, one of the pioneers in therapy with couples, Henry Dicks, concluded: "The dread of treating couples together is generally still prominent" (Dicks, 1967, p. 282). This is still the situation in the contemporary analytic world, and there is good reason for this, I submit, which ought to stand as a cautionary note for all of us who persist in exploring this form of analytic work.

As a further caution, Dicks cites a paper by M. Grotjahn, a family therapist, who observed that Freud did not believe in bringing the couple together in analysis (Dicks, 1967, p. 204; Grotjahn, 1965). Although I have not been able to find the reference in Freud for this quotation, and I even wonder whether it might be Grotjahn's paraphrase, it is worth repeating for the sense of dread it conveys: "Once [Freud] said: If you combine the resistance of your patient with the resistance of your patient's husband (or wife), you are lost; don't do it."

What ever the anxieties of the therapist, I think we must take seriously the patient's fear that talking about one's most intimate, spontaneous wishes, fears, and nightmares, and examining one's most confused, irrational, or unrestrained thoughts, might affect the other person in unpredictable and potentially harmful ways. On the other hand, if each partner in the couple coming to therapy has to censor what is said, how can the analytic process proceed, how can underlying tensions be examined and understood? The aim of the structure of the therapy relationship is to make it possible for an individual to be open and honest in communicating with his or her therapist. One of the most fundamental principles of a psychoanalytic approach to this work is that, insofar as humanly possible, *action is ruled out* as each partner, patient and therapist, analysand and analyst, seek to communicate with each other.

Of course, we might say that as therapists we do want to do something for those who turn to us for help, and in the process do something *to* them. Without turning this chapter into an essay on "aims in psychoanalytic psychotherapy", I think it is important to join with those who have emphasized the dangers of wanting to do something to someone. Any such motivation carries with it significant risks of an appeal to our omnipotent phantasies as therapists. Of course, the couple's wish for help can sometimes result in a projective process in which an omnipotent self is projected by the couple into the therapist so that the therapist is then experienced as a "magical healer", able somehow to produce a solution to their unhappiness. Surely it is vital that we do not join in the couple's conscious fantasies about our omnipotence, and that we monitor as closely as we can our unconscious tendencies to join in with their unconscious phantansies (Caper, 1992, p. 284). But I recognize that this is a complex question, one that is the matter of aims or goals in therapy and can, I think, be safely laid to one side for our purposes here.

What cannot be put to one side is the fact that there is no simple way of ruling out action in psychotherapy *with couples*. What might be intended as a communication from one partner may act on the other partner in ways that may or may not be predictable. Contrary to what we as therapists intend, couples may actually seek out therapy precisely as an arena in which to *do something* to each other. And that may be a benign or a not-so-benign intention. But people seeking therapy may also quite appropriately be very anxious about seeking therapy *as a couple*, even when the couple relationship is the focus of what brings them to therapy, because of the effect that they fear their candour will have on the other.

It is an important question, then, to ask what would lead a couple to seek out therapy together. I think that possible answers to that question—not in the sense of an empirical survey of attitudes, but in terms of attempts to make sense of the dynamics of the relationship that make couple therapy possible and appropriate, as well as tolerable—lead us right back into the tension I have symbolized as "*narcissism ↔ marriage*".

It is interesting to note that increasingly in couples who seek out therapy as a couple, one or even both partners have experience as an individual of the psychoanalytic process. Indeed, in my private practice I regularly have couples where one or both are psychotherapists or psychoanalysts. These couples obviously have some idea of the kind of experience that they might anticipate and have chosen, for whatever reasons, to do something as a couple which they have experienced as individuals. Although occasionally some express a sense of frustration at what they had failed to do in individual therapy, more often it is the success of the individual therapy or analysis of one partner which has altered and unsettled the psychic balance or the unconscious contract at the heart of the couple relationship. In all cases there is a sense that there is something now that they feel they can only accomplish together with the partner.

## The couple's relationship as the patient

As a way of beginning our exploration of the unconscious motivation that leads couples to engage in the analytic process *as a couple*, we might ask the question, paraphrasing the title of Henri Rey's fascinating paper (1988): what do couples bring to therapy? Understanding this may help us to understand what brings couples to therapy *as couples*.

We might, of course, say that couples bring their *relationship* for therapy. In his introductory chapter in *Psychotherapy with Couples*, Stanley Ruszczynski articulates this view that *the relationship is the patient*: "In this sense the patient for the couple psychotherapist is the couple's relationship—the interaction between the two partners—rather than either or both of the individuals" (Ruszczynski, 1993, p. 9). If one is thinking about the focus for the therapist's attention in the session, this is an important observation. It may also represent the way couples picture to themselves their decision to seek out therapy, especially those who have had individual therapy or analysis.

But just because the focus in couple therapy is on the relationship, this does not imply a dividing up of the world of emotions (as if it were really possible)—for example, to concentrate on aspects of one's internal world and internal objects that are seen as relevant to intimate relating with another, excluding what is seen as irrelevant. It is interesting that it is plausible to see the contemporary emphasis on the analytic *relationship* in psychoanalytic practice as a way of saying that it is not adequate to focus in some simple way on instinctual drives (in one school) or on unconscious phantasies (in another school). The arena for understanding is the relationship, the capacity for "object relating", as it is experienced in the transference and countertransference dynamics.

For example, readers will not be surprised to hear that, in a session with a couple, I would not simply acquiesce if a husband or a wife said, "I had a dream but it was not relevant to our marital relationship". Instead, I would be very curious why he or she took that view, curious about the dream, curious about what the partner made of that idea that it was not relevant, and finally curious about why it was mentioned at all. Like most therapists, I would want to explore the thought that the dream was mentioned and described as "irrelevant" precisely to provoke my, and the partner's, curiosity.

In the detailed session-to-session work, it is not clear what saying that "the relationship is the patient" would rule out of court—that is, what individual feelings, thoughts, phantasies, and so on would be seen as inherently irrelevant. We might say that it is like the observation, I think made by Hannah Segal, that "not everything is transference, but everything must be examined for transference". Since what primarily interests me in psychoanalytic therapy is the capacity for "object relating", everything in the session, however "individual" it might seem, is examined for its relevance to that capacity. Therefore, in this sense the focus on the relationship is not what distinguishes couple from individual psychotherapy.

On the one hand, we can imagine, and indeed often encounter, individuals in therapy who are married, or in an intimate relationship, but are preoccupied with issues they neither need, nor feel they want, their partner to be part of in the analytic process in which they explore those issues. In fact, it would seem to be the norm that even when an unhappy marriage is the focus of interest, there is no wish to include the marital partner in the therapy—indeed, the presence of the partner would not, or could not, be tolerated.

On the other hand, this still leaves us puzzling over a question that could be formulated in reference to some people we know: if Leontes were to seek out therapy instead of revenge, can we imagine a circumstance in which he would bring Hermione with him? Or, were Hermione to be looking for help in her distress and grief beyond what Paulina could offer her, can we imagine a state of mind in which she would invite Leontes to seek therapy jointly with her? And what state of mind do we imagine Leontes would need to be in to accept such an invitation?

## The therapists as a couple

In the preceding three chapters, we had an opportunity to get a sense of the pioneering work with couples in the FDB in our examination of the therapy with the couple they called the Webbs. One of the characteristic hallmarks, so to speak, of that organization was the use of two therapists with a couple, one for each partner. We have seen that what made the two therapists a couple was their communication between sessions, sometimes in joint supervision, but always in regular discussions between them about the work. In a sense, this format for therapy with couples can be seen as a natural extension of the model of individual psychoanalytic therapy out of which it evolved.

But once we contemplate a move to a joint session in which the two marital partners are seen together, a similar question arises in reference to the therapist or therapists. That is, are we now considering one therapist seeing a couple, or does the FDB pattern suggest that now the two therapists join together in the session as co-therapists? I have noted that Henry Dicks' remark in the 1960s about a "dread of treating couples together" seems generally to hold true more than thirty years later. But, although Dicks was talking about joint sessions with a couple, he might also have been talking about working with a co-therapist. On the one hand, there clearly is a fascination with this modification of the analytic method by introducing a co-therapist. My experience of talking to groups of therapists about couple psychotherapy is similar to what I have heard others report— that is, that the one question that always arises is the question about the co-therapist relationship.

On the other hand, this fascination is often accompanied by, or complemented by, a corresponding dread. I do not intend to explore this technical question of co-therapists in this book, although it is an important question. What is important, I think, is the sense of the presence of the parental couple in the therapist, since the transference to the parental couple is a central part of the experience of the analytic process. Ronald Britton, in his widely quoted paper on the centrality of Oedipal dynamics, famously noted a patient of his, detecting his internal intercourse with what he described as his "analytic self", shouting "stop that fucking thinking" (Britton, 1989).

Those therapists who have had experience of working analytically in a co-therapist relationship will have a vivid sense of the reality of the transference to the couple, especially when it takes the form of the intolerance of the parental intercourse. I have found this to be an invaluable experience, and I can see how it has increased my capacity in my analytic practice with individuals to notice and attended to this dynamic. In a similar way, most trainee psychotherapists have had the experience of an "internal conversation" with their supervisors during the session, a kind of on-going supervision which Patrick Casement has described as the "internal supervisor" (Casement, 1985). The capacity to tolerate these triangular dynamics, as Britton points out, creates a sense of space, space for thinking.

Dicks talks about it in his usual forthright, down-to-earth fashion as he discusses the innovation of the "joint interview" and its impact on the therapist:

> There was also the need for mutual support of a colleague with whom to share the management of these often highly charged sessions, to exchange roles—one interpreting, the other observing content. . . . It could be followed with immediate conferencing and discussion of the shared experience. From the transference point of view it had the advantage of matching a married couple by another "dyad" who could and did serve as parent figures. . . . There are also obvious advantages for a marital unit having a staff accustomed to work together, sharing concepts and perceptive to each other's trends of thoughts, just as in tennis regular doubles partners are better than scratch pairs. [Dicks, 1967, p. 200]

I think it should also be pointed out that some couple therapists find that they have a preference, once this capacity for the internal parental couple feels secure, for working alone. One advantage can be felt in the integration of what is noticed and attended to by the therapist, as well as in the flow of the therapist's communications with the couple. Interestingly, Dicks also commented on this as a development in the Tavistock Marital Unit as they took the next step of, as he put it, "risking the dreaded triangle situation" (Dicks, 1967, p. 202). He suggests that the senior therapists in the Unit no longer felt the need of an actual partner's presence in the joint session, and he refers to the observation of the American psychoanalyst and family therapist Nathan Ackerman:

> When neurotic family pairs need psychotherapy, the most efficient form of integration of the psycho-therapies would seem to be achieved in the mind of a single therapist. [Ackerman, 1958, p. 268]

What seemed to be most persuasive at that time for Dicks and his colleagues was the analysis of the couple dynamics by G. Teruel in terms of the couple's *shared internal object* (Teruel, 1966). Of the couple in therapy, Dicks suggests: "If they shared such an object, it seemed appropriate to have them share one person in the interview situation" (Dicks, 1967, p. 203). Although I think that Teruel's contribution is important, I find more helpful the idea of a shared internal world in which what is shared often turns out to be a complementarity, a concept I shall be returning to in chapter eleven. Therefore, it is not so clear to me that one therapist is theoretically more appropriate.

My own experience is that questions of the pace, rhythm, and style of communicating with the couple mean that working with a co-therapist has a more jagged quality as the two therapists resonate to each other as well as to the couple dynamics. Seasoned co-therapist pairings themselves often develop a style of their own, and in those cases their familiarity with each other allows them to notice and attend to alterations in their style which are indications of a countertransference experience. In the end, it is perhaps personal preference that takes precedence over theoretical concerns. Of course, as Dicks, the Scharffs (1991), and others have pointed out, there are practical issues that in most cases become the most relevant consideration.

## A retrospective on projective identification

Returning to our exploration of the question of what brings couples to therapy, I want to take us back to a concept that has assumed a critical role in psychoanalytic thinking and therapy in the past half-century since Melanie Klein's pivotal paper, "Notes on Some Schizoid Mechanisms" (Klein, 1946). I am referring, of course, to *projective identification*. Readers will be familiar with the idea that, through a projective process, parts or aspects of the self can be split off and experienced as belonging to the other. From the time when it was first formulated by Melanie Klein, this notion of projective identification has increasingly been a prime focal point of psychoanalytic theory and therapy, helping therapists to understand a range of phenomena.

I think it helpful to remind ourselves of the origin of this concept, which, as Ronald Britton notes, is "conceptually confusing, partly for historical and partly for clinical reasons" (Britton, 1995, p. xiii). What

I want to call attention to is one particular ambiguity inherent in the concept which has important implications for the complex projective and identificatory patterns in a couple relationship. Melanie Klein was originally describing a primitive defence that took the form of phantasied attacks of the infant on the mother. Here I want to re-mind us of the discussion in chapter two, where, in Freud's picture of this early process, the "pleasure-ego" struggles to deal with good and bad sensations by getting rid of the bad through projection, and taking in the good through introjection. Klein is in one sense only expanding on that description on the basis of her close observation of children:

> The other line of attack [after the oral impulse to rob the mother's body of its good contents] derives from the anal and urethral im-pulses and implies expelling dangerous substances (excrements) out of the self and into the mother. Together with these harmful excrements, expelled in hatred, split-off parts of the ego are also projected on to the mother or, as I would rather call it, *into* the mother. These excrements and bad parts of the self are meant not only to injure but also to control and to take possession of the object. In so far as the mother comes to contain the bad parts of the self, she is *not felt to be a separate individual* but is felt to be *the bad self*. [Klein, 1946, p. 8, emphasis added]

In this primitive process, or rather in our reconstruction of that pro-cess, we have the basic ingredient for infantile confusion in the adult couple relationship. It is, of course, important to recognize that this reconstruction is hypothetical, as did Melanie Klein herself. But we should not confuse a picture of the process with the process itself. The picture, reconstructed from the stories that very young children told her, is one of what goes on in the infant's mind—that is, it is a reconstruction of the infant's phantasy about what is happening in-side the infant and what the infant is doing to the mother. In a foot-note, Klein indicates what we might call the "re-constructive" nature of this story:

> The description of such primitive processes suffers from a great handicap, for these phantasies arise at a time when the infant has not yet begun to think in words. In this context, for instance, I am using the expression "to project *into* another person" because this

seems to me the only way of conveying the unconscious process I am trying to describe. [Klein, 1946, p. 8]

What is important, contrary to many of the pointless debates over this issue, is not that parts of the infant can be split off and somehow projected into the mother, but that the infant pictures something like that happening. The relationship between phantasy and reality is not isometric in that a description of the phantasy is a description of the reality. The relationship is much more complex, as Melanie Klein herself realized, despite accusations from friend and foe alike that she was not theoretically sophisticated. For example, two pages earlier in that seminal 1946 paper she notes the difference between the phantasy and the process as well as how they are intimately related:

> The processes I have described are, of course, bound up with the infant's phantasy-life; and the anxieties which stimulate the mechanism of splitting are also of a phantastic nature. It is *in phantasy* that the infant splits the object and the self, but the effect of this phantasy is a very real one, because it leads to feelings and relations (and later on, thought-processes) being in fact cut off from one another. [Klein, 1946, p. 6]

This is critically important in understanding the interpersonal dimension of these deeply unconscious intrapsychic phantasies. It is why in the next chapter I want to give special emphasis to the importance of listening to the couple stories that fill their sessions *as enacted dreams*. The stories are critical if we listen to them, with the third ear so to speak, as expressive of these phantasies, because they lead to, as Klein put it, feelings, relations, and thought processes "being in fact cut off from one another". So, for example, the projection of something inside, an internal object, also involves projecting a part of the self. Hinshelwood points out that, as early as 1930, Klein wrote about one of her child patients:

> ... In thus throwing them [some toys] out of the room he was indicating an expulsion both of the damaged object and of his own sadism. [Klein, 1930, p. 226; quoted in Hinshelwood, 1991, p. 181]

Klein made clear that with the expulsion and projection of an internal object there was also inevitably a splitting of the ego (self) and a projection of it along with the object. Again, this is a phantasy, but the reality in interpersonal relationships is that it leads to acting as if it were true. And that has very real effects on the other person.

We might say that some projections are not particularly intrusive situations, where the recipient of the projection is simply unaware, or even incapable of being aware, of the projection. When I kick the door because it has "aggressively" shut on my hand, the door is affected, but only by the kick. That it is seen by me to be aggressive can have little meaning for it. Some projections, however, are intrusive, as when the recipient of the projection cannot avoid being aware of the projection, being treated by me as possessing whatever it is I have projected. These intrusive projections involve aspects of both my own identity and the identity of the other, both how I identify myself and how I identify the other. Hence, we speak of projective *identification*.

I am particularly interested for our purposes here in a return to Melanie Klein's original formulation. For example, she clearly derives these projective processes from anal and urethral impulses which are felt to be expelling dangerous substances (excrements) out of the self, adding that they were felt to be expelled *into* the mother. We could say that her primary contribution was her clarity in seeing that this process in phantasy was also felt to expel with it parts of the self. It is this insight that has transformed our understanding of the dramatic effect of a projective process that is felt to effect a splitting off of parts of the self that, like other dangerous sensations inside, are felt to be poisoning the self.

For example, we have seen with the Webbs that Mr Webb seemed to need his wife to bring to therapy the angry, hostile part of himself. When that was interpreted to him, he could then expand on critical comments that his wife had made about the FDB and their respective therapists, eventually coming to acknowledge his own displaced anger of which he was so terrified. In this example, we can recognize what I am calling the *subjective* aspects of the self which are projected and experienced in the object. A similar case was reported by Rosenfeld in a paper in which he describes a woman patient of his who was subject to advances from her best friend's husband:

> He tried his best to seduce my patient. At first she had great difficulty in controlling him. The wish to take him away from his wife soon came up as a conscious impulse, but it did not seem that she had any difficulty in coping with this wish directly. Her whole

anxiety turned on whether she could control *his* wishes and arguments. She reported some of his arguments to me, and it was clear
that Denis [her best friend's husband] stood for her own greedy
sexual wishes which she had difficulty with and which she therefore projected on to him. [Rosenfeld 1947, p. 18]

Here we see a subjective aspect of this woman—her sexual wishes,
which are apparently felt to be intolerable and in need of control. By
experiencing them as if they were this other man's sexual wishes and
then by controlling *him*, she creates a situation that she can seem to
manage. She does so, however, at a cost: the loss of awareness of her
own feelings and hence losing a part of herself, though not completely as long as she maintains some proximity with the keeper of
this part of herself. Because we are talking about impulses or wishes,
there can be little difficulty in seeing these as *aspects of the self* that
have been projected into or onto the object.

Of course we only see a portion of the drama in this account, since
Rosenfeld is focused on his patient. The man he calls "Denis" has a
story of his own, his own internal reasons why he plays a part, not
only as a recipient of these projections, but no doubt also experiencing this attempted seduction as a scene expressing some of the dynamics in his own internal world.

It is also important to note that it is not only the intolerable, unwanted parts of the self that can be projected. There are sometimes
positive aspects of the self that, for a variety of reasons, are not felt to
be safe from some internal threat. In a dynamic that can be devastat-
ing to the strength and integrity of the self, good aspects can also
be projected, as Rosenfeld again illustrates with the same patient
discussed above. It takes little imagination to envision how this
dynamic could play itself out in a pattern of mutually interlocking
projections in a couple relationship.

Apart from the projection of impulses which were felt by the patient to be bad, there was also a continuous projection of good
impulses into other people, particularly women friends, who not
only represented good mother-figures, but the good part of herself.
She felt excessively dependent on these friends and could hardly
function without them. [Rosenfeld, 1965, p. 19]

This is one way of understanding the situation with Mr Webb, who,
we might say, seems to have split off and projected his thinking

capacity into his therapist *in the therapy setting*, a thinking capacity that he presumably needed and used to good effect in his professional work-setting, where he had achieved a position of some seniority. This kind of splitting typically occurs in intensely personal, intimate relationships that raise anxieties in a particular way. It is reminiscent of the so-called borderline patient who regresses disastrously in intense personal relationships while maintaining a capacity to function adequately in what are experienced as less stressful situations (Jackson, 1994).

The importance of recognizing and understanding the dynamics of projective identification in the patient's experience is part of the "bread and butter" of our work as therapists for many—if not most—of us today in the psychoanalytic tradition. It is most helpful when I can explore with a patient the process of projective identification when I am the recipient of the projections. But that does not mean that we cannot explore it when a patient describes what we can discover to be projective mechanisms with significant people in his or her life. The presence of *narcissistic object relating* in the form of projective identification in my patient does not suggest to him/her or to me that it is advisable for him/her to invite the partner who is the recipient of those projections into the therapy!

No doubt readers can think of a number of individual patients who spend session after session, often for long periods of time, focused on a particular relationship—for example, with husband, wife, boyfriend, girlfriend. One young man I have seen for nearly four years has spent most of his time struggling in great detail with his precarious relationship with the woman he has lived with, and not lived with, throughout that time. For him any separateness—for example, experimenting with living separately for a time—is tantamount to separation and divorce—not as a "slippery slope", but in the sense Hannah Segal (1955) describes as "symbolic equation". I can sense and sympathize with his girlfriend's frustration in trying to be in a relationship with someone who either has to be "right inside" or is in "outer darkness". This does not preclude my recognizing in his account, say of a particularly difficult weekend, that her anxiety about separateness also contributes to their difficulty in finding anything like a satisfactory way of making a life together.

Although I see couples in therapy, and I recognize how that experience helps me in my work with this young man, I cannot recall

even a passing moment when I wished I were seeing these two people as a couple. Nor do I think that this young man would take
seriously the idea that he should bring his girlfriend to his sessions,
in fact he would, I think, be profoundly shocked by the idea. That
does not mean that he thinks she does not need therapy, only that he
would not want her to intrude into *his* therapy.

Something more than the predominance of projective identification in a couple relationship would lead them, or us, to consider
psychoanalytic couple therapy. What is this "something more"? I
think we need to consider how particular patterns of narcissistic
identifications in the form of intrusive projections and counterprojections can lock a couple in what Mary Morgan has characterized as a
"gridlock" (Morgan, 1995). This gridlock has a particular quality that
we might also describe as *mutual projective identification*, which has
the disturbing consequence of a pattern of interlocking retaliatory
impulses in response to particularly intrusive projections. I want to
explore the possibility that, in part, this insidious pattern of mutual
projective identification is structured around an inability to take in
intrusive projections, which leads to equally intrusive counterprojections.

## "Subjective" and "internal-object" aspects of the self

In this chapter, I am trying to lay the foundation for the exploration
of the idea of an insidious pattern of mutually interlocking intrusive
projections I will describe in chapter eleven. Projective identification
is a central concept, and we have seen how critical it is for understanding of the couple relationship. In fact, it is so important that one
could say that the examination of the dynamics of projective identification has preoccupied much of the psychoanalytic world, particularly in the British tradition. And it has certainly preoccupied the
little part of the psychoanalytic world concerned with therapy with
couples. One criticism that I encountered of the volume I co-edited
with Stanley Ruszczynski (Ruszczynski & Fisher, 1995) expressed
the concern that there was too much attention to the phenomenon of
projective identification and that therefore, as a concept, it was being
required to do too much work.

I do think that we have assumed that because projective identification is such a widespread, even ubiquitous, defence against equally common separation anxieties it accounts for more than it actually does in the couple relationship. For example, by itself it does not help us see why one person seeks therapy as an individual and would never think of doing so in the company of another person, however intimate, while another person does almost the opposite. I think it may help our thinking here to consider the distinction between what we can call the "subjective" and the "internal object" aspects of the self which are split off and intrusively projected.

This distinction, although it appears quite technical, is worth consideration because of its significance for something that obviously has important consequences—the impact of intrusive projections on the other person. It is interesting that the only extensive discussion of this distinction, I believe, is to be found in the work of an Argentinean psychoanalyst, Heinrich Racker, on the nature of the analyst's countertransference experience. The countertransference experience is, to a large extent, one might say, the experience of being on the other end of intrusive projections, of being the recipient of a projective identification. To understand a pattern of mutual projective identification we need to think about this experience of being the recipient of these projections. And to do that we need to think about the distinction between the projection of the subjective and internal-object parts of the self.

I think it is easy then to overlook the dual aspect of what is meant by "parts of the self". These two dimensions are not obvious when we are talking about what I suppose seem clearly aspects of the self—for example, sadism, rage, or anger. Feelings, attitudes, beliefs, and so forth are what we might describe as *subjective* aspects of the self. But that leaves out of the picture what we might call the *internal object* parts of the self.

By this clumsy expression "internal-object-part-of-the-self", I simply mean to call attention to the fact that "internal objects"—the figures that inhabit my internal world such as the internal parental couple—are *internal to the self*. The difficulty is that subjectively we experience our objects, and that must surely include our internal objects, *as objects*, not part of the self. What we need is a picture of the *self*, or perhaps some more precise language, which is able to recognize that the self is made up of both a "subjective" self and the internal objects that together constitute the self as a totality. Not only are my internal objects just that, my internal *objects*, but they are also *my* internal objects. There is a profound sense in which my internal objects are a vital aspect of who I am. Meltzer makes an interesting observation about a shift in the descriptive language used by Melanie Klein:

> Her methods of descriptions moved more and more away from differentiating between ego and id in clinical phenomena in favour of talking of the Self. This was ushered in by the description of splitting processes, in which parts of the self not only embraced Id aspects but also internal object aspects. [Meltzer, 1992, p. 7]

It is seems obvious that when Meltzer here talks about "internal object aspects" of the self he must be referring to the larger sense of self, which for convenience we might refer to as the "phenomenological self". What I want to emphasize is the capacity to "stand outside" one's subjective sense of self to recognize that one's internal objects are also an important aspect of self. Ultimately, it means the capacity to recognize a subjective sense of self which includes both one's relationship to those internal objects and their relationship with each other. It is thus what might be described as a "relational" view of the self.

My aim here is not to explore this issue, an issue of immense complexity, but to focus our attention in considering the experience of projective identification in the couple relationship. We might say that one aim for seeing the couple as a couple might be to help each partner to recognize those projections and to discover how and why those aspects of self are felt to be so intolerable. The process of recognizing those projections and acknowledging them as aspects of the self is the core of what we sometimes describe as "re-owning" or "taking back" the projections, a central aim of the therapeutic work with a couple. It would seem that the process of "re-owning" or "taking back" of projections is one that must include both the subjective and the internal-object aspects of the self.

But in order to re-own both the subjective *and* the internal-object aspects of the self, it is necessary to see the difference in the projection of these different aspects of the self. To do that, I want to turn to an interesting description of what I think is a much more familiar clinical phenomenon than we might have realized until someone like

Henri Rey points it out. When we have seen what, in Rey's arresting phrase, "patients bring to analysis", we may have a perspective on what couples bring to therapy. And, in turn, I think that we may see that in a sense it is the interplay between the subject and object aspects of the self which leads to an impulse to retaliation rather than understanding. And this can result in the most insidious and persistent interlocking projections and counterprojections, which in turn may lead some couples to seek therapy as couples.

## "That which patients bring to analysis"

One of the most common presenting pictures is the couple where *one partner brings the other* as someone who needs "to be sorted out", or at least needs to change in some way. That seems to have been true with the Webbs, although Mrs Webb was anxious and resentful at the prospect of being the "patient" and labelled "mad". In other cases, it could be said that each "brings" the other. Occasionally, the partner who is the "patient" brought *for* therapy will agree that he or she is indeed the one who is the cause of the problem and who therefore needs to change, although both are baffled at how to bring about the change. This view of what is brought for therapy may have a more profound significance than we realize. Perhaps we should take such couples at their word, at least in the sense that their description of the dilemma is likely to contain an important communication to us.

It is commonplace in work with couples to challenge this assumption of the "problem partner", the "patient" who is brought to be changed. Because couple therapists tend to see difficulties as rooted in the interactive processes in the couple, the tendency is to work hard to get them to see how each contributes to the situation. From the point of view of understanding the interactive processes that constitute the couple relationship, it is right that we need to focus on the mutual contributions to what they have together created, no matter how much each might feel it is the other who is responsible. Indeed, this is a cardinal principle of technique in therapy with couples.

Still, I think that it is important not to dismiss this idea of one partner in a couple bringing the other as the "patient", although I do

not mean to ignore the defensive function in which the other is unconsciously felt to carry some split-off *subjective* part of the self. This
idea of the other as the "patient" is not limited, I am suggesting, to
this function of the other carrying unwanted, intolerable feelings
such as anger, envy, and so on. It is worth considering that there
might be a quite different dynamic when what is split off is what we
might think of as an "internal-object-part-of-the-self".

Here I would like to turn to Henri Rey's description in his paper,
"That Which Patients Bring to Analysis" (Rey, 1988), of his experience in psychoanalytic therapy with a group of disturbed patients:

> This group showed very clearly that each member did not bring
> only themselves to treatment, but that they were primarily con-
> cerned, at a borderline conscious–unconscious level, with dam-
> aged inner objects where successful treatment was vital to their
> welfare. They could not do it without help but had kept these inner
> objects going in the hope that help would come some day. . . .
> Those human beings who have sufficiently worked through the
> depressive position and reached a true capacity for reparation are
> in a very different situation from those who have not reached that
> stage. . . . The latter's task is to manage to keep their damaged
> objects alive in the hope of putting them right. [Rey, 1988, pp. 235,
> 236, 237]

Rey's paper is a vivid description of how the patients bring these
damaged internal objects to therapy, having kept them alive but having failed either in their efforts to make some concrete repair or in
their attempts at "pseudo-reparation" like manic reparation. It is
critical to this way of understanding that we recognize the concrete-
ness of the internal objects, that they are experienced as real objects.
He points out that "after all, dream objects, however fantastic, are
felt to be real".

Not only do couples bring internal objects to therapy for repair,
they do so in a very concrete way. Through complex and interlocking processes of mutual projective identification, they bring the damaged internal objects concretely located in the partner. Rey notes that
"the discovery by the patient of his or her real aim is a dramatic
event leading to dramatic changes in the treatment" (Rey, 1988, p.
229).

When I suggested earlier that we might do well to take seriously
one partner's perception that he or she is bringing someone *for*

therapy, some readers might well feel that that fails to acknowledge the importance of our resistance to one partner labelling the other as the *patient*. This is doubtless important even, and perhaps especially, when the partner who is cast in the patient role takes on that role willingly. Still, I want to persist because I think that there is an important psychic reality lying behind this particular kind of couple presentation, a reality that Rey's analysis of the dynamic helps to make clear.

The first psychoanalyst who wrote about this dynamic was Joan Riviere, some sixty years ago, in a well-known and often-cited paper, "A Contribution to the Analysis of the Negative Therapeutic Reaction" (Riviere, 1936). In this paper, Riviere suggests, really for the first time in the psychoanalytic literature, how critical it is in understanding the so-called narcissistic patient to attend to the hidden object relations—that is, the relations with the internal objects. Although Freud's important paper "Mourning and Melancholia" (Freud, 1917e) had introduced the concept of an object internalized and identified with, it was Melanie Klein whose work began to make this important concept central in her evolving revision to psychoanalytic understanding.

Riviere asks the question: why are some patients so resolutely resistant to getting better? Her answer is, in some ways, surprising. What Riviere postulates is that this kind of patient's "negative therapeutic reaction" can be understood as an unconscious anxiety about the damaged internal objects that he cannot repair. This catastrophe means that he cannot risk getting better because it will expose him as responsible for the attacks on his objects, now internalized, and would put his welfare above that of those internal objects.

> Our offer of analysis to make him well and happy is unconsciously a direct seduction, as it were, a betrayal; it means to him an offer to help him abandon his task of curing the others first, to conspire with him to put himself first again, to treat his loved objects as enemies, and neglect them, or even defeat and destroy them instead of helping them. . . . In addition, he does not for a moment believe that any good person really would be willing to help him before all the others who need it so greatly; so his suspicions of the analyst, and of his powers and intentions, are aroused. [Riviere, 1936, pp. 147–148]

Riviere emphasizes that it is imperative to keep in mind that she is referring to *internal* objects:

> I hope that while I have spoken of the patient's unconscious aim of making others well and happy before himself, you will have borne in mind that the others I refer to always are the loved ones *in his inner world*; and these loved ones are also at the same moment the objects of all his hatred, vindictiveness and murderous impulses! [Riviere, 1936, p. 150, italics in original]

We encounter a particularly difficult situation when these internal objects are in turn projected firmly and fixedly into the external characters in the patient's life. This is a situation that we encounter repeatedly in therapy with couples, and in some ways it could be said to characterize the dilemma of most couples who present for therapy *as a couple*. Of course, I think that most of us have seen individual patients who share this sense that we have the wrong person in therapy, that the problems all lie in that other person. Until and unless this dynamic begins to emerge in the transference relationship with us, there is often little way to help such patients see these external objects as an externalization of something going on inside, and therefore accessible to change whether or not they can get their external objects to change. In fact, like the parents of children emerging out of adolescence, these external objects seem remarkably to become wiser and more compassionate as our internal objects mature into greater wisdom and compassion.

But still I think that we have only begun to address this pair of reciprocating questions: what couples bring to therapy and what brings couples to therapy. To explore it more fully we will have to address the phenomenon that Meltzer terms a *mutual projective identification in action*, which seems to give rise to a *folie-à-deux* relationship. This, in turn, requires a fuller understanding of the experience of being the recipient of an intrusive projection and a typology of responses to that kind of projective identification.

First, however, I want to describe in the next chapter a way of thinking about what happens in a session with a couple, a way of listening and observing which opens before us the couple's shared, enacted nightmare. Following that, I want to introduce a story of another couple—in fact, two couples in the familiar triangle of an affair—and their uninvited, unidentified guest who becomes their therapist. I am referring to T. S. Eliot's *The Cocktail Party*, which will occupy our attention for three chapters before we return to this destructive narcissistic phenomenon of a couple relationship marked by mutual projective identification.

# CHAPTER SEVEN

# Couple stories and couple dreams

One question that would illustrate for many the reservations they would have about modifying the psychoanalytic frame work in such a radical way as seeing a couple rather than an individual would be the puzzle about dreams. Whether or not one would still say, as Freud did, that dreams are the royal road to the unconscious, dreams are still for most of us a central feature of the analytic process. Whenever I talk with couple therapists or counsellors about dreams, the consensus is that dreams play little if any role in the work with couples. And it is true, in my own clinical experience, that couples report fewer dreams than do my individual patients. But it is also true that I hear therapists in supervision and in clinical seminars reporting that their increased interest in dreams somehow seems to be complemented by couples increasingly telling them about their dreams.

What is interesting to me now after seeing couples for some years is that when I describe their shared stories as dreams, or sometimes more accurately as nightmares, they join me in that way of thinking about what they are trying so desperately to tell me. And, perhaps surprisingly, they sometimes link the stories with dreams they subsequently have, as if they recognize a quality in these stories that suggests a struggle with the meaning of their shared struggles, conflicts, hopes and disappointments. The symbols that we together begin to see as giving some meaningful shape to their conflicts arise spontaneously as much from their stories as from their dreams.

In this chapter, I want to lay a bit more of the foundation for a way of thinking about the couple's struggle in therapy as an emergence out of narcissism by looking more closely at the process of a session with a couple. In particular, I want to look at how we listen to the stories that couples tell us as *couple dreams*.

## A pictorialized communication of an emotional experience

We have considered at length the importance of the capacity to acknowledge the truth of one's emotional experience. But I think that this is a more complex matter than it might seem. How does one convey what may be beyond what one is aware of consciously. Consider, for example, a remark I have already referred to that Bion made in his Introduction to *Second Thoughts* (Bion, 1967). He was reflecting on something close to the heart of all therapists—the attempt to record the process of a session, an effort in which we want to be able to represent accurately what we have observed. In reprinting papers he had written a decade or two previously, he notes his changed view of the question of a truthful account of what had transpired in the session:

> I do not regard any narrative purporting to be a report of fact, either of what the patient said or of what I said, as worth consideration as a "factual account" of what happened.

He then went on to make two observations about why those papers about his experiences with patients in analysis should not be regarded as "factual accounts":

> In the first place, I do not attribute to memory the significance it is usually given. The fact of involuntary distortions is so well established by psycho-analysis itself that it is absurd to behave as if our reports were somehow exempted from our own findings.

His second point, however, might seem at first sight to be a rather strange observation about memory of what transpired in the session:

> Memory is born of, and only suited to, sensuous experience. As psycho-analysis is concerned with experience that is not sensuous—who supposes that anxiety has shape, colour or smell?—records based on perception of that which is sensible are records only of the psycho-analytically irrelevant.

Bion is not just saying that our memory is faulty, introducing distortions into our account of the session. His conclusion might be read as if he were disparaging memory as inadequate to some ideal "factual" account. However, taking into consideration the thrust of his groundbreaking rethinking of psychoanalysis, I think that he is in fact taking us into a different dimension, a way of thinking that is at once familiar and yet challenges some of our basic assumptions:

> Therefore in any account of a session, no matter how soon it may be made after the event or by what master, memory should not be treated as more than a pictorialized communication of an emotional experience. [Bion 1967, pp. 1–2]

This is an interesting way to describe the result of our attempt faithfully to record what we have observed during the session: a *pictorialized communication of an emotional experience*. Were we to take Bion at his word, we might see such descriptions, our "process recordings", as attempts to picture and thus to communicate something of our emotional experience, although what we consciously aim to record is what we observed happening in the session. It is quite plausible to think of this as a way one might describe a dream—that is, the dream as an unconscious attempt to picture an emotional experience. And the report of the dream could be seen as an attempt to communicate that emotional experience.

It is not as if, at a conscious level, it would be inaccurate to describe the process recording of the session as factual. What sense would it make if we were to try to do anything other than to portray as accurately as we can what we observed and remember of the session? My process recording is my story of what happened. All I can do is to be as faithful as I can to what I remember. Surely Bion is not challenging what we all try to do in that respect. What he is doing is calling our attention to another dimension of this, in one sense straightforward, activity, a dimension that shares something importantly with dreams.

It is an insight that also shares something, I believe, of what the young T. S. Eliot wrote about the relationship between poetry and the personal. As a young poet and critic under the influence of the theory of the *impersonal* of the late-nineteenth-century French literary critic Remy de Gourmont (see Burne, 1966), Eliot seemed to reject what might be described as the emotion of the personal (Eliot, 1920). In fact, ironically he was struggling to find a way to overcome the split between form and meaning, between precision of articulation and expression of intense emotion. In a way, what he was saying has to my ear a remarkable resonance with Bion's attempt to bring emotion to the centre of psychoanalytic thinking.

Eliot has often been seen, especially on the basis of his early theory of the *impersonal* and the "objective correlative", as the advocate of "hard-edged and rigorous classicism" and the opponent of romanticism, with its valuing of the emotional (Vendler, 1980). Others, such as the American poet Randall Jarrell, have taken the opposite view:

> Surely you must have seen that he was one of the most subjective and daemonic poets who have ever lived, the victim and hopeless beneficiary of his own inexorable compulsions, obsessions. From a psychoanalytical point of view he was far and away the most interesting poet of your century. [as quoted in Vendler, 1980, p. 85]

In fact, Eliot's theory of the *impersonal* suggests that the so-called personal poetry, which aims to focus on the poet's emotional experience, almost inevitably concerns itself with what is an "artificial construct". This construct turns out to be what Ronald Bush calls the "conventional self", the self we want to see or wish to be, what we in our psychoanalytic language might call the "pseudo-mature", the "as-if", the "false-self" personality (Bush, 1984, pp. 41–52). Eliot instead wished to peer into the "depths of feeling" but recognized how difficult it is to do that directly. Poetry, like dreams and the process of symbol formation, seeks to articulate what can carry emotional meaning:

> Why, for all of us, out of all that we have heard, seen, felt, in a lifetime, do certain images recur, charged with emotion, rather than others? The song of one bird, the leap of one fish, at a particu-

lar place and time, the scent of one flower, an old woman on a German mountain path, six ruffians seen through an open window playing cards at night at a small French railway junction where there was a water-mill: such memories may have symbolic value, but of what we cannot tell, for they come to represent the depths of feeling into which we cannot peer. [Eliot, 1933, pp. 146–148]

We might say that the poet who seeks the depth of emotion explores, paradoxically, not the "self-I-am-conscious-of", but, rather, detailed observations of the object-world of the self. In our objects, we discover the depths of our emotional life, the depths of the domain of meaning—objects in the world described by physics, chemistry, and biology such as the song of a bird, the scent of a flower. These elements of what we call the *external world* become symbols, carriers of meaning, in what we call the *internal world*. Conversely, the disjunction, "the internal world *or* the external world", fails to recognize that *the internal world is the meaning of the external world*.

Donald Meltzer summarizes Bion's contribution in respect of his view of the centrality of emotion in the psychoanalytic orientation, to which he contributed so much:

[Bion's] work places emotion at the very heart of meaning. What Bion says in effect (and this is almost diametrically opposed to Freud's attitude towards emotion) is that the emotional experience of the intimate relationship has to be thought about and understood if the mind is to grow and develop. In a sense the emotion *is* the meaning of the experience and everything that is evolved in the mind through alpha function: e.g., dreaming, verbalizing dreams, painting pictures, writing music, performing scientific functions—all of these are *representations* of the meaning, but that *the meaning itself is* the emotion. [Meltzer, 1981, p. 182]

What we could add to that list, perhaps under the heading of "scientific function", would be "process recordings". The meaning itself is the emotion.

From the point of view of understanding what happens during the session in a similar way, I am suggesting, we can consider the many stories with which couples fill their sessions also as pictorialized communications of their emotional experiences. It is a way of listening to these couple stories as what we might think of as couple dreams.

## Couple stories as pictorialized communications of emotional experiences

I want to emphasize that we can regard the descriptions couples bring, especially in their conflicting accounts of what has happened between them, not as "factual accounts" but as their attempts to communicate an emotional experience. I think that we ignore the "dream" meaning of these stories at the risk of missing the urgent unconscious communications from the couples, desperate because they have no way to speak to us more directly. Let me hasten to add that I do not mean that these accounts or stories are fictional. They are offered as factual accounts, and I think that there is no reason to assume anything other than what we would insist for ourselves in our attempts to be truthful in our recording of what we believe transpired in any given session.

The point here is not that memories, and hence the accounts the couple bring, are full of what Bion called "involuntary distortions", although that is obviously important. Sometimes it is possible to help couples become interested in these "distortions", although usually one person becomes interested in the *other's* distortions. The issue invariably then centres around the question of whether the distortions were really "involuntary" or whether they were deliberate attempts to rewrite history.

One has a very different experience, however, if these *stories* are thought of not as "factual accounts" but as attempts to communicate emotional experiences. Actually, I have found that this perspective is something that makes sense to most couples. They are quick to realize that their arguing and fighting over conflicting factual accounts is a way of expressing their difficulty in tolerating the reality of the other's emotional experience, especially when either it differs from what they expect or want it to be, or it has an unwanted impact on them. It is almost as if they are aware of the significance of the stories they want to tell us precisely because they are, in Bion's phrase, pictorialized communications of emotional experiences.

The greater difficulty with this perspective, I think, is for the therapist, and that is for the same reason. That is, to acknowledge these stories as not just factual accounts, but as attempts to picture and communicate emotional experiences exposes the therapist to their emotional impact. We might say that the fight within the couple results from the reality that they cannot escape what we might call the "transference" implications of the accounts that each offer as the truth. He cannot tolerate her version of what happened over the weekend just because it makes him feel guilty, and he believes that it was designed to do precisely that. Arguing that her version is totally wrong is a nearly undisguised attempt to convey that he cannot bear the impact of her emotional experience. It is just such an experience, I suggest, that the therapist is unconsciously trying to avoid in resisting hearing any of these stories as communications of emotional experiences.

But when we try to shift our focus to the emotional experience, two things tend to stop us in our tracks. One is the difficulty of thinking about our emotional experience. The second is intimately related to it: the difficulty—I would almost say the impossibility—of feeling that we are able adequately to communicate our emotional experience. The poverty of our vocabulary, the inadequacy of our syntax. We make do, but in our heart of hearts the words feel hollow in the face of the nuances of emotion which we hardly know how to represent to ourselves, let alone to communicate to the other. As therapists, we sometimes feel, although do not know how or to whom we can acknowledge, that we need to have the voice of a poet to speak adequately to our patients of their emotional experience that they seek to communicate to us, and the soul of a poet to listen to their stories as pictorialized communications of emotional experiences.

How do we listen to the stories that couples bring to us? If we fail to take these stories seriously as the couple tell them, these "factual accounts", we are in danger of not hearing them at all. It was said, I believe, of the composer Schumann (although I have heard it told of other composers) that after he had played a new composition for a group of friends, someone asked him what it meant. He thought a moment, then he sat down and played the piece again.

Sometimes we are too keen as therapists to translate what we hear from our patients into a language more familiar to us, more under our control without giving ourselves time to listen to the music of what we are hearing. And when, having listened to one of the stories that couples tell us, we say to them, "what you're really saying is . . .", they often—and quite rightly, I think—*play it again.*

Perhaps at this point we should look at one of these couple stories. What follows is the kind of story that the reader will recognize as a "common or garden variety" from our day-to-day work with couples.

Mrs J began the session saying that she would not be here next week. Their daughter had rung; she was pregnant and, because of complications, the doctor was suggesting complete bed rest. The mood in the room was tense; it was as if they could not voice their apprehensive anticipation of a grandchild. Mr J was silent, while Mrs J said in a flustered way that she had not really had a chance to assimilate it all. There had been a message, and Mrs J had known immediately what it meant.

There followed some tense exchanges about Mrs J booking a flight without checking with Mr J whether he supported her going, her complaint about his being distant since her recent visit to her parents and now going off to look after their daughter. It was difficult to make sense of their uneasy, desultory complaints about the other. Finally, Mrs J told a story about a strange experience as they were driving home from his having met her at the station on Monday. The story was not easy to follow, and what I shall relate is a summary achieved after much effort to hear what each was saying. In some ways it was not an unusual story, but I invite you to listen to it as more than just a "factual account".

She began by explaining that Mr J is always out on Wednesday evenings, a meeting or something, while on Thursday evenings she attends a course. The previous Thursday, just before she went away for the weekend to see her parents, there had been a request for the course to meet this week on Wednesday. She had forgotten to mention it to Mr J before she went away, and anyway she assumed he would be out on Wednesday evening as usual, so it didn't matter. When she mentioned this change in arrangements to him on Monday, telling him that she was not going to be out on Thursday evening but on Wednesday—at this point it all became confused.

She was now not sure what she heard Mr J say. At first she had thought he said he had made a special arrangement to be home on Wednesday instead of going out so they could be together, perhaps as a way of welcoming her home. But that is impossible since he has a meeting on Wednesdays. But then, when he became hostile, she understood that he had arranged for a business colleague to visit him at home on Thursday evening when she would be out anyway. Now that was spoiled, since she was unexpectedly going to be home.

It is easy to imagine how this story played out in hurt feelings, misunderstanding, and a disappointment with the other that made it feel impossible to acknowledge the other's feelings, let alone to see any humour in it. It was a caricature of the O. Henry humorous short story *The Gift of the Magi* (1906). It is a story about a man who at Christmas hocked his only possession of value, the pocket watch that had been his father's and his grandfather's, to buy a set of combs for his wife's long lovely hair, the set for which she had for ages longed. She meanwhile had cut and sold her long hair to buy him a fob chain for his treasured pocket watch. That was a story where there was a poignant misunderstanding that only deepened love. But in the story Mr and Mrs J told in this session, one could feel only the pain, the hurt and despair. And this was what had "contaminated", to use Mr J's word, the experience of their daughter's message about her threatened, yet hopeful, pregnancy.

In a sense, it is a conflation of the two stories we heard in *The Winter's Tale*, the parental and the grandparental. Hermione's pregnancy threatened the couple in ways that neither could explore with the other. And it was only when the next generation in the person of the lost daughter Perdita and Florizel, the son of the split-off Oedipal threat, Polixenes, come together that it is possible for all of them to begin to integrate the threat and the hope of pregnancy. Mr and Mrs J unconsciously share both the hope and the threat of coming together to create something both beyond themselves and yet intimately part of themselves.

The reader will perhaps be somewhat ahead of where I was at this point in the therapy with this couple. What seems clear now in retrospect is also, I think, what made it difficult for me at the time to listen to this story as an unconscious communication to me about their emotional experience in therapy with me. This was a couple where both of them had extensive experience of therapy, and they were both earnest in their attempt to make sense of what was destroying their relationship at a time when they both had high but, it must be said, conflicting hopes for this time of their life together. They were earnest, and they had a therapist who was also earnest. But that only made the missing each other the more poignant. Not completely— we did not miss each other completely. But that is the point, one point at least, of their story. I was blissfully unaware, at least consciously oblivious, to the communication about what was happening in our relationship. It would have been helpful to them had I been able simply to acknowledge how not only did they miss each other, but also that it was possible for me to miss what they were trying to say about their relationship with me.

It was reminiscent of many couples where one partner has been dissatisfied for years but masochistically never manages to communicate directly about that dissatisfaction, and the other partner wakes up one day in shock to find the marriage at an end. Only here the couple was me, the blind and deaf therapist, and the other a couple in distress because I was not hearing what they were communicating. The fact that we as therapists are drawn to this profession suggests that we are seeking to repair our own damaged internal objects. And to the extent that that is so, the appeal to our omnipotence is powerful. Heinrich Racker, in his helpful study of countertransference, pulls no punches—and I do not think his language obviates the point, since "therapist" or "counsellor" and "client" and "wanting to help" and "doing the client harm" will do as well as substitutes at the appropriate places:

> These communications begin, one might say, with the plate on the front door that says "Psychoanalyst" or "Doctor". What motive (in terms of the unconscious) would the analyst have for wanting to cure if it were not he who made the patient ill? In this way the patient is already, simply by being a patient, the creditor, the accuser, the "superego" of the analyst; and the analyst is his debtor. [Racker, 1968, p. 146]

Our wish to "help" can draw us into the dramatic accounts, the urgency of which puts pressure on us to act. In the face of this pressure to "do something", I think that trying to listen to the "factual accounts", the stories with which couples fill their sessions, *as dreams*, helps us to hear what they are trying to communicate, because, in a sense, this is the only way that they can communicate these emotional experiences. These emotions are too complex for even a poet to speak of directly.

## The couple story and the couple dream

At the heart of the matter of the couple story is the urgent need to find a symbolic form for that experience in order to be able to think about it—indeed to be *able to think it*—as well as to be able to communicate it in the intimacy of a relationship. The "place" *par excellence* for the formation of the symbols that make it possible to image our most private experience is that psychic space that we call *dreams*. It is true that Freud saw "dream-work" primarily as defensive, functioning to distort unwelcome thoughts through condensation, displacement, and so forth, with the result that these now-disguised unwelcome thoughts escape an internal unconscious censor to become dreams that we can remember and think about.

It is not so much that one rejects Freud's description of "dream-work" as defensive, as that our interest has expanded from the process of disguising unwelcome thoughts to include trying to understand what happens in the process of dream-thinking. Bion and Meltzer in particular have prompted us to see dreaming as the place, the state of mind, where we *think about the meaning* of our experience. It is, potentially at least, where the meaning of our experience is given symbolic form.

Bion's creative understanding of the psychoanalytic process has led to a new understanding of the human mind, an understanding of the mind in which being able to think one's emotional experience is itself the means by which the mind grows and develops. In effect, Bion suggests that if you do not "digest" your experiences, you will poison and destroy your mind (Meltzer 1978a, *II*, p. 50). This alimentary metaphor of "digesting" needs to be correlated with our observation of how we make sense of our experience. We only have to look at our dreams to see this process of symbol formation in action. What we do in essence is tell ourselves—and each other—*stories*. Our dreams *are* stories, or fragments of stories, peopled by all sorts of characters, or fragments of characters.

I mean here "stories" in the widest sense, a sense that can include the plays of Becket and Pinter, or indeed Eliot's never completed *Sweeney Agonistes* (1926/1932), "stories" without story-lines, able to create what Eliot describes as "an unmistakable tone". This is particularly important when, as is so often true in therapy with couples, the emotions seem out of proportion to the situation in which they arise. Eliot characterizes the role of the artist in relationship to the expression of emotion, what we are calling *pictorialized communication of an emotional experience*, particularly when that emotion seems more intense than the situation seems to call for:

> The intense feeling, ecstatic or terrible, without an object or exceeding its object, is something every person of sensibility has known; it is doubtless a subject of study for pathologists. It often occurs in adolescence: the ordinary person puts these feelings to sleep, or trims down his feelings to fit the business world; the artist keeps them alive by his ability to intensify the world to his emotions. [Eliot, 1919, p. 49]

I would only modify Eliot's point by noting that in the conflicts of intimate relationships these feelings, so often "put to sleep" or "trimmed down" in those whose emotional lives seem otherwise limited and pedestrian, are reawakened with remarkable intensity. These conflicts give rise to vivid though despairing "stories", sometimes as enigmatic as a Becket or Pinter play. Of course, we are not alone in our private story-making and story-telling world. We exist in circles of stories, myths, and world-historical characters in the wider religious and sociopolitical cultures from which the stories in our family cultures derive and in which those family cultures live. But, in the end, we each must find the particular myth that makes sense of our emotional experience—"myth" being, after all, the Greek word for story.

I think therapists risk falling into what we might call a "translator's fallacy", or perhaps I should say an "omnipotent translator's fallacy". The jargon with which we try to articulate the complex emotional experiences that we encounter in our consulting-rooms is useful only as a kind of shorthand for ourselves. But it can never replace the rich symbolic imagery of the dream language in which our patients speak to us. If we in effect ask them what their stories mean, they might—if we are fortunate—simply "play it again". Mr and Mrs J certainly did.

A couple of weeks later, when Mrs J had returned from looking after their pregnant daughter, they were in a desperate mood. Although the reports were good and the pregnancy was still viable, there was no sign of joy or hope. Instead, Mr J said finally in tears that he could no longer go on. It was just too painful.

What followed was another story, this time about "not quite meeting" when he went to pick her up at the airport. He had spent all day in anticipation, polishing the car and arriving very early for her flight. He had gone up to the observation platform to watch her plane land. The flight was due at a quarter past six, and at a quarter to six a plane of the distinctive airline she travelled on touched down—but that couldn't be it. Some time later, when no other plane from that airline had arrived, he got anxious and went down to the waiting area to see what was wrong.

Of course, her flight had arrived early. But he was not there to meet her as promised. She had a coffee, waited, and then decided that she couldn't wait "til the cows come home" and made to find her own way home, anxious that something terrible had happened to him. I don't need to finish the story except to say they could not talk about it, each so angry and shaken that they had hardly spoken until coming to the session that day.

In a sense, it is the same story. And yet in an important sense, it is a different story. One could wonder with them how these muddles and confusions arise and why they fill them with such despair. They were "factual accounts" which I could help them to understand, and I did, or I tried. But in another sense these were, I suggest, *shared unconscious phantasies*.

The point is—again, as I see it in retrospect—that it was indeed a shared unconscious phantasy, shared not just between this couple, but also between them and their therapist. Once again we missed each other, and this time he made it clear that he felt that the pain was becoming too much for him. His unilateral announcement a few weeks before Easter that he was not returning after the holiday break came as an incomprehensible shock to me, both because he had had long experience of psychoanalytic therapy and because he felt that the only way the decision could genuinely be his was if he made it on his own. He insisted that Mrs J could make her own decision, seemingly oblivious that he was preempting something for both his wife and his therapist.

In the session in which he announced his intention to leave, Mr J also spoke of Sophocles' *Oedipus at Colonus*, having said something that reminded him of the play. He had never known why he liked that play, but now he did. It seemed to him that Oedipus was right in his feeling justified at the end that he was not guilty. This was before I read John Steiner's paper in which he interprets the play as the retreat of Oedipus into omnipotent denial of the emotional reality of what had happened (Steiner, 1993, pp. 116–130). What I remember of Mr J's comment was the sweeping rejection of any sense of guilt or remorse and my feeling that he was unreachable. It was a mirror, I think, of their unconscious sense of my being unreachable.

In order for the relationship to give birth to something new and alive—that is, either their marital relationship or our therapy relationship—there would have had to be adequate intercourse. Intercourse would mean taking seriously the differences, not acquiescing to avoid frightening conflict as they both felt they had always done. They must have touched something in my internal world of the fear of challenge, difference, and confrontation, and I in turn had become another edition of their unreachable internal object. The only options unconsciously open to them were either to acquiesce or to withdraw.

## Shared unconscious phantasy

I think the term "unconscious phantasy" has a ring of the mysterious about it, the unknown unknowable. Perhaps it would help us to be able to make more use of this concept in our clinical thinking if we can bring it more into the world of our everyday experience, where I think it belongs. It is a term we could say ultimately is derived from the way that Melanie Klein was able to listen to the stories children told. Donald Meltzer points out that this way of listening enables us to see unconscious phantasies as transactions actually taking place in the internal world, and this perspective in turn has transformed our view of dreams:

> Dreams [now] have to be seen as pictures of *dream life* that is going on all the time, awake or asleep. We may call these transactions "dreams" when we are asleep, and "unconscious phantasies" when we are awake. [Meltzer, 1983, p. 38]

He went on, in his book *Dream-Life*:

> I would agree with Bion that dreaming *is* thinking, that dream life can be viewed as a place to which we can go in our sleep, when we turn our attention fully to this internal world. The creative process of dreaming generates the meaning that can then be deployed to life and relationships in the outside world. This means, in a sense, that all of our external relationships have a certain transference quality, that they derive meaning from what exists in our internal world. [Meltzer, 1983, p. 46]

Meltzer then goes on to talk about "shared unconscious phantasy":

> Sometimes [our external experiences] derive an adult meaning so that through our identification with our internal objects the adult part of our personality is able to meet other people on an adult level through communal phantasy, a kind of congruence of internal objects. It is this congruence of internal objects that brings people together and it is living in different worlds that drives them apart so that they cannot communicate with one another. [Meltzer, 1983, p. 46]

This description of Meltzer's is critical for our understanding of the dynamics of the intimate adult couple relationship. One could almost say that it is one of the central themes of this book. In order to begin to appreciate its radical importance, consider this description of the analytic experience. Meltzer suggests that at its best the analyst shares his or her own internal objects with the patient, that the transference is to the analyst's internal objects (Meltzer, 1995, p. 144). If this is a model for understanding what we can think of as transference in the marital couple relationship, then one can also begin to appreciate the intense intimacy that arises when there are mutual, interactive and often very intrusive projections on a spiralling trajectory through the history of the marriage.

Here, however, Mr and Mrs J presented me with a paradox. Their *shared* stories—their *shared unconscious phantasies*, if you like—were about living in *different* worlds. What held them together was a story about never being able to be together, to share the same emotional world. Mr J was in tears, sobbing and hardly able to get out his words while telling us the airport story. When I tried to explore Mrs J's apparent indifference to his distress, she finally blurted out that she knew how bad he felt, but if she attended to his grief, *who would be there to attend to hers*! Once again we hear about the despair in the face of an unreachable internal object.

It was the promise and threat of the birth of a child that precipitated this crisis. The two of them seem to have been able to be "playmates" together, but when there is a child—in this case, the child of their child—they seem to be faced with an emotional reality that challenged their capacity for creative intercourse. Had I been able to take up Mr J's story about *Oedipus at Colonus*, I might have discovered something of the fear of what kind of child would come of such an intercourse as that of Oedipus and Jocasta, a daughter who was also a sister. Or, with Mrs J, the fear that such an intercourse might be with a husband who was also a son and thus would give birth to children who were also grandchildren.

What Mr and Mrs J shared in this situation, paradoxically, was a state of mind dominated by the loneliness of *not being able to share*. Sometimes I think that we look too hard for *shared unconscious phantasies* because we have not learned to listen to the stories that are right there before us. The "archetypal" story for Mr and Mrs J was a story that they recounted early in therapy, repeating it a number of times, "playing it again", so to speak. After a special evening out at a large concert hall, he had gone to try to find a taxicab. Somehow he ended up in one doorway and she in an adjacent one. Every time he looked out for her or for a taxicab, she was back in her doorway; and every time she looked out for him, he was back in his doorway. They saw this story for what it was—a picture of their shared internal world, a symbol of their shared internal dilemma. If we have ears to hear and eyes to see, this is what a *shared unconscious phantasy* looks and sounds like—a waking "dream", a living "nightmare"—until they can find someone who hears and sees it with them, not someone in yet another doorway.

# CHAPTER EIGHT

# The uninvited guest

aving become engrossed in an exploration of some rather technical and theoretical considerations, it is perhaps time to pause for a moment and look at another example of therapy with a couple as we did with the "Webbs" from the Marriage Book. This time I want to turn to what is perhaps the earliest recorded description of a couple therapy session. It is possible, in a sense, to identify the exact date and place for this first couple session—the 22nd of August 1949 in Edinburgh. In a way, of course, it is frivolous to link the serious therapy with often desperate couples, which we have been exploring in this book, with the portrait of a couple in T. S. Eliot's *The Cocktail Party* who are brought together for a "therapeutic" session with a mysterious figure whom Stephen Spender described as "an *eminence grise* of the psycho-analytical world" (Spender, 1975, p. 203). The consulting-room is one thing, the theatre another, worlds apart. And yet . . . are they? Perhaps I can appeal to the reader's generosity to indulge me this link for a moment before judging how serious or how frivolous is my use of Eliot's comic poetic drama.

From the perspective of contemporary psychoanalytic therapy with couples, it is an uncanny experience to enter the world of T. S. Eliot's *The Cocktail Party*. Ever since I began to take it seriously, my interest in its portrait of a marriage and in its author and his own marriage has grown into fascination. In this and the next two chapters, I want to look at this play of Eliot's, neither as an amateur literary critic nor amateur biographer of this complex poet, but as a story of a couple, two couples in fact, their troubled relationships, and the intervention in that relationship by someone, the *uninvited guest*. The fact that it is fiction gives us a certain liberty to allow these vivid characters to dramatize for us dynamics familiar to all therapists. And the fact that it resonates profoundly with Eliot's own life gives it an edge that opens up unexpected insights.

I suggest that in *The Cocktail Party* we have a "story", a *poetic drama* in Eliot's description, which, I am suggesting, can be listened to (and watched) as a *pictorialized communication of an emotional experience*. It is particularly interesting to keep in mind Eliot's intention as a poet to learn to write what he calls "poetic drama" in distinction to "prose drama", although he himself admits with regards to *The Cocktail Party* that it is "perhaps an open question whether there is any poetry in the play at all" (Eliot, 1951, p. 144).

I am assuming, although this assumption is not essential to the idiosyncratic picture of *The Cocktail Party* I want to paint, that poetry is *par excellence* the attempt to communicate an emotional experience. Although I am suggesting that there is an autobiographical "undertow" in this play, as indeed there is in all of Eliot's *poetic drama*, it is not the "factual account" of T. S. Eliot's life that is central here. What is "autobiographical" is the emotional experience that he is struggling to communicate in his six poetic dramas. We might say that each "poetic drama" is a "dream" of the poet, and in my view the plays taken together are a series of "dreams" in which Eliot *unconsciously* seeks to express in symbolic form his experience of intimate relationships. Why he wanted, or perhaps even needed, to portray his most private, intimate agonies on the stage, and seemed particularly anxious to be seen to be successful in a creative form that Helen Gardner says was "against the bent of his genius", are fascinating questions (quoted in Gordon, 1988, p. 177). I want to come back to the issue of the autobiographical in a moment.

In Eliot's plays, as well as in his early poetry, one can hear and enjoy his keen ear for rhythm and sounds—for example, the echoes in *The Waste Land* of the ragtime of the Mississippi river town of Saint Louis where he was born: "O O O O that Shakespeherian Rag—/ it's so elegant / So intelligent" (Eliot, 1922, pp. 128–130, cf. Sigg, 1994). One can also hear just how keen Eliot's ear is for the dialogue of couples. That is, especially his ear for the hostile, bitter exchanges of couples locked in relationships that seem so empty and yet impermeable to anything benign.

Take, for example, Eliot's nightmare image in the section "A Game of Chess" in *The Waste Land*, which biographers like Lyndall Gordon make clear is drawn from the early years of the young Eliots' marriage (Gordon, 1977, pp. 95–97, 111): ". . . Under the firelight, under the brush, her hair / Spread out in fiery points / Glowed into words, then would be savagely still". Couples may describe their relationship as "a game of chess", but Eliot offers us, just as couples do, not a description, but an experience of hell.

I should say that I shall be describing some of the scenes in *The Cocktail Party* and occasionally using Eliot's own words. References will be by page number to the version currently in print as most editions do not contain line numbering. I will quote Eliot as much as possible since he captures with a poet's ear the cadence and tone of what therapists will recognize as the most ordinary of couple exchanges. Readers should not need to have the text of the play before them, although I find as I reread this play that it is in Eliot's use of language that these couples have come alive for me.

## The guests at the cocktail party

The play opens with the eponymous cocktail party, as it ends with another cocktail party about to begin. Edward has tried to put off the party that his wife Lavinia had arranged, having come in that afternoon to find her gone. As he later tells the Unidentified Guest, he doesn't know where she's gone (Eliot, 1950, p. 30, Act I, Scene 1, lines 213–217 [subsequent references will be presented in the form: p. 30, I.1.213–217]). The only people Edward couldn't put off were four guests who themselves form two "couples" of sorts.

Julia and Alex are two characters who veer between the roles of "comic disturbers", to use Martin Browne's term (e.g. Julia's intrusive searches, first for her umbrella and then her spectacles, p. 29, I.1.201–202; Alex and his "special gift" of "concocting a toothsome meal out of nothing", p. 46, I.1.498) and the roles of "guardians" in league with the doctor, Sir Henry Harcourt-Reilly, the Unidentified Guest (Browne, 1966, pp. 13ff.). In this latter role, they facilitate the facing of psychic reality which alone can be the basis for transformation and emotional growth, and yet they never lose their irritating, but endearing, qualities of the story-telling "fools" in the opening scene. They open the play wrangling as if they were a long-married couple.

And we meet the second pair of characters at the party, Peter and Celia, who are linked though not a couple. They share an interest in films and creative writing, Peter having written a novel and Celia poetry, but both are searching for something. In a style reminiscent of a "comedy of errors", Peter confides to Edward his infatuation with Celia, while the audience is about to find out that Celia has had a long-standing secret relationship with Edward. And then much later we, along with Edward, are shocked to discover that all along Peter had been having an affair with Edward's wife Lavinia, the (absent) hostess of the cocktail party.

Finally, there is the enigmatic, unidentified guest. Perhaps I should say something about the accidental, or should I say the unconscious, process that led to the expression that became the title of this chapter and later of this book. When rediscovering the play some ten years after first seeing it performed on the stage in London, I was struck by its engaging and provocative portrayal of a session with a couple in the Act II. The figure of the doctor, Sir Henry Harcourt-Reilly, had become in my mind the *uninvited guest*, and I realized only in subsequent readings that in fact he is characterized as the *unidentified guest* during the first act of the play.

Nevertheless, it is clear in the play that Reilly is indeed an *uninvited guest*. Eliot later claimed that one of the "points of departure" for this play about a couple relationship was Euripides' play *Alcestis*, a drama about a couple and an uninvited guest, Heracles (Eliot, 1959, p. 103). In this image, Eliot has illuminated an essential aspect of the relationship between the couple and the therapist. As we shall see in our exploration of this play, there is a sense in which Reilly as "therapist" was invited by both wife and husband, separately and unknown to the other, into their troubled relationship. But there is also a sense in which Reilly was, and remained, *the uninvited guest* similar to our experience as therapists, invited for a time into the most private intimacy of couples and individuals, and yet both we and our patients finding a dimension in which we *become* "uninvited guests". We call it the transference, the name for patients' experience of encountering figures, in the person of the therapist, that they had not anticipated meeting.

In the first scene, the husband, Edward, has said only a few words to the unidentified guest after the cocktail party when suddenly he spills out the news that his wife has just left him. Already we hear something of why the play seems to suggest an image of a therapist as the "uninvited guest". Edward protests to this stranger that, although he initiated the conversation, it was not what he expected. He had, as he put it, only wanted to relieve his mind by telling someone what he had been concealing. His guest responds:

> . . . all you wanted was the luxury
> Of an intimate disclosure to a stranger.
> Let me, therefore, remain the stranger.
> But let me tell you, that to approach the stranger
> Is to invite the unexpected, release a new force,
> Or let the genie out of the bottle.
> It is to start a train of events
> Beyond your control. . . .
> > [Eliot, 1950, p. 33, I.1.262–269]

Indeed, in the context of the psychoanalytic encounter, to approach the *stranger*—the therapist—is to *invite the unexpected*, to start a train of events beyond the control of either the couple or the therapist. For example, the thing that Edward tries to keep secret from everyone, and can hardly admit to himself, he blurts out to a stranger.

This is perhaps one of the most common reasons that couples themselves give for seeking out psychotherapeutic help. As we saw with Mrs Webb when she was so easily able to tell Mrs B about her most private agony in the story of her deserting mother, it does seem true that it is possible to be more candid with a stranger. The only thing that is striking about this human tendency is how often the same couples will complain to their therapist: "We do not know anything about you!" Our patients may complain that they do not know us, but often what they are complaining of is that they know us all too well but cannot integrate what they know because it leaves them vulnerable in an intimate relationship. Edna O'Shaughnessy describes this in a young patient, "Leon":

> In one of his rare spontaneous remarks he said too loftily, "I know all your little habits. I know the way your watch on your arm slips around. I know the way your shoe slips off." These two selected observations are accurate. I thought their meaning was that he knew how my watch—that is, his mother's eye—had the habit of slipping round him and not really seeing him. And he also knew his father's habit of not staying in himself and slipping off, i.e., projecting himself into and getting too close and involved with Leon. But Leon did not want these "little habits" to be transference phenomena with a dimension of meaning such as my watch to be linked to an eye. *He cut the links* between his inner world and his analysis, which he stripped of meaning, and *he wanted me to accept and to adopt his disconnections*. . . . [O'Shaughnessy, 1989, pp. 133–134, my emphasis]

Edward, too, quickly finds that he is uncomfortable with what the Unidentified Guest says to him when he challenges Edward's unthinking assumption, his conventional reaction, that he wants Lavinia back. He thought that he was only seeking an evacuation of strange, unnerving emotions, wanting to relieve himself, to relieve his mind of what he has been concealing. But when the stranger takes him seriously, Edward is taken aback, suggesting that the Unidentified Guest's "speculations" are offensive (p. 33, I.1.250–260). What seems to offend him most is the observation that wanting his wife back may be more an expression of embarrassment and inconvenience at her unexplained disappearance.

As a therapist, I would be encouraged by Edward's angry response. He is being more candid here than his conventional self might usually allow, and that suggests that the Unidentified Guest has touched a chord with his "speculations". Of course, in terms of the play we soon discover that Edward is right and that the Unidentified Guest does know more than Edward had suspected. But that is irrelevant since that is *not* the basis of what he has said to Edward. But is the Unidentified Guest "speculating", or is there something else going on?

What, after all, is the basis for what we say to our patients? Michel Gribinski explores the role of "guessing" in the psychoanalytic process, noting Freud's use of the term *zu erraten*—which is variously translated in the *Standard Edition* as "to detect", "to divine", "to discover", "to make out", as well as "to guess"—and links it with Freud's discussion of "re-construction" in analysis (Gribinski, 1994). He suggests that these varying translations, or "mis-translations", have inhibited our articulation of the centrality of *guessing* in our work. Certainly, Strachey in his translation seems to have preferred to think that Freud meant that analysts were "detecting" or "discovering" than to think that he meant they were *guessing*!

But perhaps there is something related to, but different from, either "guessing" or "detecting" which involves both careful observation and the use of the therapist's analytic *imagination*. What needs to be emphasized is the reality that the patient can only be known from outside, and in this sense the therapist always remains the stranger—unless, of course, one succumbs to the unconscious intrusive projections that in phantasy give the illusion (or delusion) of being inside the other. With this in mind, we might do well to be cautious when the Unidentified Guest responds that he "knows" Edward as well as he "knows" Edward's wife. Throughout the play, this Uninvited Guest can be read as pompously omniscient, the epitome of the omnipotent analyst. One person who knew Bion said of the character, Sir Henry Harcourt-Reilly, as a therapist: Bion at his worst! Perhaps. No doubt Reilly can be read that way. And played that way on the stage.

But I am inviting the reader to join me in allowing these characters to take on the qualities we associate with dream figures. Sir Henry, or Reilly as Eliot usually denotes him, is sometimes in this play an analyst's, and sometimes a patient's, caricature of a psychoanalyst.

## Inviting the unexpected

I want to take us back to that provocative speech of Reilly's where he seems to suggest to Edward that "to approach the stranger / Is to invite the unexpected, release a new force, / Or let the genie out of the bottle" (p. 33, I.1.265–267). Why is it that Reilly decides to remain the stranger? In a sense, the thrust of the theme of this book is that the emergence from narcissism is the emergence into a relationship in which the other is, in essence, a stranger. It is precisely this being an other accessible only by invitation that tends sometimes, I suggest, to provoke intrusive attempts to penetrate to the inside, the interior, of the other. But for the other to remain the stranger is to start a train of events beyond the control of either.

The play now takes us into the specifics of the unhappy relationship between Edward and Lavinia, an unhappiness largely unrecognized by Edward himself. He is one of those husbands who is surprised to discover that his attempts to be "accommodating", as he would think of it, are experienced by the wife as infuriating passivity. Later, when he next meets Lavinia, his wife, she is surprised to find that he seems to be recovering his voice, his passivity apparently beginning to dissolve a little: "I may not have known what life I wanted / But it wasn't the life you chose for me" (p. 95, I.3.332–333). In amazement, Lavinia muses: "who could have taught you to answer back like that?" This is a couple for whom confronting each other, recognising differences, is a developmental achievement. But we pick up the story as Edward is forced by Lavinia's absence to think about their relationship.

Edward hesitates as the Unidentified Guest asks if he was about to protest that he loves his wife. He responds that they took each other for granted, so why speak of love. They were used to each other (p. 34, I.1.285–288). But there is more to it than that. The Unidentified Guest suddenly takes us into another realm, not just the bored marriage where expectations have died, but facing Edward (and us) with an unexpected dimension of the loss of his wife, what he calls "a loss of personality". It is that state of existing in which you have lost touch with the person you thought you were.

The Unidentified Guest suggests to this bewildered husband that it is like suddenly being reduced to the status of an object, the kind of thing that happens to us at the unexpected extra step on the stairs when you come down with a jolt, or the experience on the operating table when you are only an object to the surgeon. It is always happening, he observes, "because one is an object as well as a person" (p. 34, I.1.296–302). But what Edward is discovering, or rather being shocked into facing, is the reality that in the supposed intimacy of marriage there was no genuine relating of two persons. Might we even suppose that sometimes marital breakdown, like mental breakdown, could be an unconscious attempt to find a way out of the narcissistic nightmare in which one is trapped.

To face himself, Edward is told that must be prepared to be the "fool" he is, to learn to survive humiliation. Edward seems now to understand something of what is being said to him. And he realizes that even though he saw his wife at breakfast, he now can no longer remember what she is like. He *must* get her back! But why? Because he suddenly realizes: "I must find out who she is, to find out who I am" (p. 37, I.1.356). Technically we might say that he has projected parts of himself into her, so that without her he literally cannot find out who he is. But Eliot needed no technical concepts to describe what is an all-too-familiar dynamic in marriage.

Couples who seek psychoanalytic therapy are not always able to articulate their dilemma in the way that Edward does here. At least Edward seems shocked into an awareness of what we could describe as his narcissism, and he seems suddenly able to listen to the uncomfortable words of this stranger. To be told that he has lost touch with the person he thought he was is to be faced with his "false self". Eliot portrays Edward as locating something essential in this process in his partner. To find out who he is, he must find out who she is. To face the truth of his own emotional reality, he has to face the truth of hers. For some individuals, this can mean that they need to seek out therapy *together* as a couple.

In constructing this poetic drama, Eliot recognizes the interactive dynamics—what I am calling the *folie-à-deux* aspect of the relationship. However, there are two overlapping couple stories, the husband and wife, Edward and Lavinia, and the husband and lover, Edward and Celia. We will see in the next two chapters that Lavinia is well able to speak for herself, but, in terms of understanding something of the woman's internal world, it is really with Celia that we are given an entrée into what is going on in her mind. That may be for dramatic reasons. That is, the dynamics of the play may call for Celia to become the voice of passion, while Lavinia is left with the voice of one who is left to "make the best of a bad job".

There is a sometimes disturbing autobiographical directness in this play, and, because I feel the personal so powerfully in what Eliot writes, I want to share with the reader something of the link between the personal and the fictional. In fact, it is plausible to say that the entirety of Eliot's poetic drama taken together can be read as a "serial autobiography" written for the stage. The first of the six chapters of the "autobiography" is the early, shocking but incomplete *Sweeney Agonistes* (1926/1932), then his best-known play, *Murder in the Cathedral* (1935, originally titled *Fear in the Way*), his poignant picture of mother in *The Family Reunion* (1939), the story of his Leontean struggle about legitimacy and children in *The Confidential Clerk* (1954), and finally his "Oedipus-at-Colonus" self-portrait (complete with the main character's Antigone and a moving dedication by the author to his own Antigone) in *The Elder Statesman* (1969).

Limiting myself to the aims of this book in the remainder of this chapter, however, I want briefly to describe some of the literary and personal background to this unusually vivid picture in *The Cocktail Party* of couples needing and seeking therapy. What I have tried to do here, and in the other biographical references in the next two chapters, is to note the points that seemed to echo through the dialogue of the play.

## Tom and Vivienne

Anyone who has read the biographical studies of Eliot by Peter Ackroyd and Lyndall Gordon will be painfully aware how much the poet's profound understanding of the most painful of couple dynamics was rooted in his own personal life. Over and over again, lines in *The Cocktail Party* resonate with Eliot's own experience with Vivienne Haigh-Wood from the time soon after he married her in 1915 until her death in Northumberland House, a private mental hospital in Finsbury Park, North London, in 1947 (Ackroyd, 1984; Gordon, 1977, 1988). Although Eliot initiated a formal separation from Vivienne in 1933 (much against her will), ostensibly ending a marriage that he described as "a Dostoyevsky novel written by Middleton Murry", her presence haunted him not only during the nine years of her compulsory confinement, but for most of the decade following her death. In his inability to break from Vivienne emotionally, she indeed had a "permanent advantage" over him.

At the beginning of that relationship, Vivienne was described as an "adventurous and vivacious" young woman, for Eliot a "revelation of sexual and emotional life" whom Aldous Huxley described as "an incarnate provocation". Ackroyd suggests that "in these first months, her own impulsiveness and gaiety were adopted by Eliot so that he seemed much more vivacious than in fact he was" (Ackroyd, 1984, p. 63). Bertrand Russell wrote in 1915, just a month after their marriage:

> She is light, a little vulgar, adventurous, full of life—an artist I think he said, but I should have thought her an actress. He is exquisite and listless; she says she married him to stimulate him, but finds she can't do it. Obviously he married her in order to be stimulated. I think she will soon be tired of him. She refuses to go to America to see his people, for fear of submarines. He is ashamed of his marriage, and very grateful if one is kind to her. He is the Miss Sands type of American. [quoted in Bush, 1984, p. 54]

By 1920, Vivienne's chronic illnesses—the list is almost endless—and her ominous fluctuating moods were matched by Eliot's ill health, physically and emotionally, leading to breakdown for both of them in 1921 (cf. Gordon, 1977, pp. 72–81, 104ff., who gives a vividly documented account of those early years). It was during his treatment for that breakdown in Switzerland that Eliot completed *The Waste Land*. Valerie, Eliot's second wife, quotes a private paper written by him in the 1960s, just over a decade after *The Cocktail Party*. It gives us some idea of his retrospective view of those early years:

> To explain my sudden marriage to Vivienne Haigh-Wood would require a good many words, and yet the explanation would probably remain unintelligible. I was still, as I came to believe a year later, in love with Miss Hale. I cannot however make that assertion with any confidence: it may have been merely my reaction against my misery with Vivienne and desire to revert to an earlier situation. I was very immature for my age, very timid, very inexperienced. . . . I think that all I wanted of Vivienne was a flirtation or a mild affair: I was too shy and unpractised to achieve either with anybody. I believe that I came to persuade myself that I was in love with her simply because I wanted to burn my boats and commit myself to staying in England. And she persuaded herself (also under the influence of Pound) that she would save the poet by keeping him in England.

> To her the marriage brought no happiness . . . to me, it brought
> the state of mind out of which came *The Waste Land*. [Eliot, 1988, p.
> xvii]

There is, I have been suggesting, a fascinating story yet to be told of
the interplay of Eliot's life and his creative work, with special reference to his plays. The plays are more autobiographical than most
critics have appreciated, with the notable exception of Lyndall
Gordon (1977, 1988), although she discusses the plays only briefly.
Gordon's two books, along with Ronald Bush's *T. S. Eliot: A Study in
Character and Style* (Bush, 1984), are to my mind the best studies of
the links between Eliot's life and his poetry and poetic dramas and
their interplay. The only literary critical study I am aware of that
draws significantly on a psychoanalytic understanding is Tony
Pinkney's *Women in the Poetry of T. S. Eliot* (1984).

Having in mind the biographical echoes in the lines of *The Waste
Land*, especially the section "The Chess Game", one listens to the
dialogues in *The Cocktail Party*, for example, in a new way. It gives
some idea of why Eliot has such a keen ear for the dilemmas of
intimate relationships.

## The curriculum vitae of this "therapist"

In thinking about *The Cocktail Party*, we would do well to have in
mind some things about the origin of the Uninvited Guest, if only to
help us decide to what extent to allow this caricature to affect our
image of ourselves as therapists. It is difficult to decide how firmly
Stephen Spender had his tongue in his cheek when he called Sir
Henry Harcourt-Reilly "an *eminence grise* of the psycho-analytical
world." Perhaps it is not irrelevant that he also described Reilly as a
"high class creep" (Spender, 1975, pp. 203–204).

As I have already said, Eliot has suggested that he was prompted
to write this play by the question posed for him in Euripides' play
*Alcestis*. In Euripides' version of an obscure earlier myth, Apollo has
persuaded the Fates to prolong the life of Admetus the king, provided that he can find someone who will die in his stead. A large
portion of the play is taken up with the remonstrations of Admetus

against his mother and especially his father, both of whom refuse to die in their son's place.

In the end, Alcestis, the wife of Admetus, agrees to die in her husband's place. Before her body has been buried, Heracles, son of Zeus, arrives unexpectedly on another of his heroic labours. Richard Lattimore in his introduction to the translation of Euripides' play, emphasizes Admetus' obsession about the right treatment of guests, the principle of xenia where strangers are to be received hospitably as friends (Lattimore, 1955, pp. 3–4). Because of this principle of xenia, Heracles is entertained properly and not told of Alcestis' death because that would spoil his enjoyment. The picture of Heracles' drunken singing apparently gave Eliot the basis, or so he claimed after the fact, for the song "The One-Eyed Riley" sung by the Unidentified Guest. I suspect that there is more to it, especially as Eliot's original title for the play was "One-Eyed Riley", but that will have to be left for another time.

When Heracles discovers the story of the death of Alcestis, he descends to the Underworld to wrestle with Death to bring her back alive to Admetus. Eliot says that he was intrigued: "the question arose in my mind, what would the life of Admetus and Alcestis be, after she'd come back from the dead; I mean if there'd been a break like that, it couldn't go on just as before" (Eliot, 1959, p. 103). And he wrote this play in the year and a half following the death of Vivienne. What he did not mention was that Admetus' virtue was rewarded, not just for his hospitable treatment of the stranger, the uninvited guest. The reward was for his refusal to welcome the woman offered to him as a replacement for his dead wife (who, of course, unknown to him at that point was Alcestis), remaining loyal to the wife who had sacrificed herself for him. Admetus is a strange contradiction, selfishly bullying the father and mother who would not die for him, yet loyal to his wife who did.

We can imagine that Eliot pictured this king as a selfish, narcissistic figure, while the queen seems in the very few hints in Euripides' play to be an entirely sympathetic figure. While the former could be said of Edward in The Cocktail Party, the latter could not be said of Lavinia. We will see in chapter ten that Eliot insisted she be played as fierce. And we know that, from the beginning, young Tom Eliot found his wife Vivienne to be just that. There was apparently little time in the eighteen years of their marriage which they spent together that there was even a brief interlude of peace. Early on, Bertrand Russell said that he wanted to help them in their troubles "until I discovered that their troubles were what they enjoyed" (quoted in Ackroyd, 1984, p. 67). Therapists who work with warring couples will know both just how true, and how false, that description is.

Not only was Vivienne in almost constant treatment for her somatic and emotional complaints, Eliot too in the early 1920s was, as Trosman describes him, "exhausted, depressed, anxious, hypochondriacal and dreaded a psychotic disintegration" (Trosman, 1974, p. 295). At the point that he was completing The Waste Land in 1921, he was in treatment with a Dr Roger Vittoz, a psychiatrist in Lausanne, whom Ackroyd describes as a "pre-Freudian analyst" (Ackroyd, 1984, pp. 115–116; cf. Trosman, 1974, and Bush, 1984, pp. 68–70).

Eliot later (sometime before 1925) asked Leonard Woolf to recommend a doctor with psychoanalytic knowledge for himself, saying that Vivienne was suffering a nervous rather than a mental breakdown, because of her fear that he would leave her, and that it was he, not she, who needed treatment. Woolf referred him to a Sir Henry Head, although all that is known of this encounter is that Eliot found him "not modern enough" (Gordon, 1988, pp. 58–59). As an interesting aside, it might be noted that this same Dr Henry Head appears as one of the actual historical figures in Pat Barker's The Regeneration Trilogy of the First World War, in particular in The Eye in the Door (Barker, 1993).

In 1927, Tom and Vivienne Eliot were in treatment together at a spa near Geneva, although it was even less psychoanalytically oriented than had been Eliot's individual therapy with Vittoz. Sencourt (who was a fellow patient with the Eliots at the spa) reports that "the doctors on the whole deprecated drugs and avoided psycho-analysis". He goes on to describe their "hydrotherapy", an approach in which the couple were treated with a form of douche écossaise: alternating gushes of hot and icy cold water were played on the naked body (Sencourt, 1971, p. 124; Trosman, 1974, p. 296).

None of this experience, it seems to me, gives us much insight into how Eliot paints such a striking picture of both the dynamics of a disturbed couple relationship and the nature of a therapeutic intervention into that relationship. Sir Henry Harcourt-Reilly's curriculum *vitae* does not tell us what we want to know, so the only alternative is to look more closely at his actual style of working.

## Tom and Emily and the ghost of Vivienne

One of the strengths of Lyndall Gordon's two-volume biography is the sensitive way in which she explores the links between Eliot's life and work. She is the only biographer to describe in any detail his long relationship with Emily Hale, his first love. He had an ambiguous relationship with her originally in Boston as a graduate student at Harvard University, just a few years before he precipitantly married in London in 1915. The young Eliot had married Vivienne having known her for only a month or so at Oxford. It was a marriage much against the wishes of his family in America. It is not clear when Eliot resumed the relationship with Emily Hale, but it was probably not until he in effect separated from Vivienne. It was expected by many of those who knew Eliot that he would marry Emily when he was finally free of Vivienne (Gordon, 1988, pp. 146–190).

One interesting detail pointed out by Gordon was that Eliot had seen Emily on stage in Vermont in 1946 acting in Noel Coward's *Blithe Spirit*. This play, by the writer who was master of the drawing-room comedy format that Eliot uses in *The Cocktail Party*, concerns a man, the ghost of whose dead first wife comes back to haunt him and his new wife. There is more than a little irony, and perhaps considerable stimulus to his imagination, in the fact that Eliot saw on stage in *Blithe Spirit* a "first wife driven with tyrannical passion, agitated, hysterical, and howling like a banshee" acted on the stage by the woman who was expecting that *he* would marry *her* (Gordon, 1988, p. 168).

Celia's description of Edward in the play echoes the language of *The Hollow Men*, in which we hear of "dried voices whose whispers are as meaningless as wind in dry glass, or rats' feet over broken glass in our dry cellar" (Eliot, 1925). It is difficult not to think that this also echoes something of Eliot's own personal despair. If so, it gives us an idea of just how personal *The Cocktail Party* is, especially since we know that Emily Hale believed that he used *The Cocktail Party* to convey a "hidden message" to her (Gordon, 1988, pp. 168–

175). After spending much time with this play and Eliot's biographies, I am inclined to accept her view as quite plausible.

I think that the reader or playgoer who knows something of the tension in the relationship between Tom Eliot and Emily Hale in the time between the death of Vivienne in January 1947 and the summer of 1949 when Eliot finished the play will find the story of Celia and Edward electric with that tension. For example, when Eliot visited Harvard in the spring of 1947, soon after Vivienne's death, to receive an honorary doctorate and to visit his dying elder brother Henry (who died twelve days after Eliot arrived), there was an unintended meeting with Emily Hale. Lyndall Gordon describes it vividly:

> Henry's widow, Theresa, invited Emily to her apartment, meaning with all good will to bring her together with Eliot on the assumption that they would wish to marry. But when Eliot arrived he turned on Theresa in a white fury which she remembered to the last months of her life. [Gordon, 1988, p. 169]

We have no record of exactly what transpired between Tom and Emily at that fraught meeting just over three months after the death of his wife Vivienne, but Gordon speculates, quite plausibly I think, that we have a good idea of the substance of it from *The Cocktail Party*: "The confrontation of Edward and Celia in the second scene of the play seems to correspond so exactly with Emily Hale's account of her exchange with Eliot in June 1947 that the dialogue may recreate the substance of their very words" (Gordon, 1988, p. 173). In fact, in August 1947 Emily Hale wrote to a friend about this meeting:

> Tom's wife died last winter very suddenly. I supposed he would then feel free to marry me as I believed he always intended to do. But such proves not to be the case. We met privately two or three times to try to sift the situation as thoroughly as possible—he loves me—I believe that wholly—but apparently not in the way usual to men less gifted, i.e., with complete love thro' a married relationship. I have not completely given up hope that he may yet recover from this—to me—abnormal reaction, but on the other hand I cannot allow myself to hold on to anything so delicately uncertain. [quoted in Gordon, 1988, p. 170]

The scene between Edward and Celia contains some of the play's most poignant lines in recognition of the illusion that can masquerade as love between two people. The unmasking of such illusions provides some of the most disturbing but most important moments in the analytic process with couples. Celia faces this with courage, and it is interesting that Eliot himself observed (retrospectively, and thus to be taken with some caution) that although the play revolves around Edward and Lavinia, Celia became the play's most important character. If Lyndall Gordon is right, his relationships with both Vivienne and Emily may have been, in a sense, the point of the play.

> Those two people [Edward and Lavinia] were the centre of the thing when I started and the other characters only developed out of it. The character of Celia, who came to be really the most important character in the play, was originally an appendage to a domestic situation. [Eliot, 1959, p. 103]

It is interesting to note that in an interview in April 1950, soon after the original Edinburgh production had moved to the Henry Miller Theatre in New York, Eliot is reported to have said that "he did not intend to portray one [character] as more important than the others" (Jones, 1960, p. 124). We might understand these characters in terms of the dynamic figures of his troubled internal world. Perhaps rather than rely too much on Eliot in interview, we should listen to his more considered view in a lecture in 1953 entitled *The Three Voices of Poetry*. It is a particularly clear picture of the relationship between the author (the "self"?) and the author's characters (the "internal objects"?):

> It seems to me that what happens, when an author creates a vital character, is a sort of give-and-take. The author may put into that character, besides his other attributes, some trait of his own, some strength or weakness, some tendency to violence or to indecision, some eccentricity even, that he has found in himself. Something perhaps never realised in his own life, something of which those who know him best may be unaware, something not restricted in transmission to characters of the same temperament, the same age, and least of all the same sex. Some bit of himself that the author gives to a character may be the germ of life from which that character starts. On the other hand, a character which succeeds in interesting its author may elicit from the author latent potentialities of his own being. I believe that the author imparts something of himself to his characters, but *I also believe he is influenced by the charac-*

*ters he creates*. It would be only too easy to lose oneself in a maze of speculation about the process by which an imaginary character can become as real for us as people we have known. [Eliot, 1953, pp. 11–12, emphasis added]

I have little doubt that one of the reasons that *The Cocktail Party* has such a bite when it comes to portraying the tensions and dilemmas of a couple relationship lies in the fact that it is intensely autobiographical. Eliot said that the author is influenced by the characters he creates, especially as they bring into view his *internal objects*. This gives to the characters a life and intensity that allows us a greater intimacy with this troubled poet than he himself may have anticipated. Perhaps somehow Eliot could see that, like Edward, his struggle to conceive of the possibility of a genuinely fulfilling marriage for himself meant having to emerge from a state of mind in which marriage was equivalent to torture. Such a marriage is a hell, not as Sartre suggested where "hell is other people", but where "hell is oneself, the others merely projections" (p. 99, I.3.417–419).

Eliot's own view of the "birth" of *The Cocktail Party* suggests that he was, not surprisingly, in a rather mixed state of mind between the time he conceived of the idea of the play sometime after death of his first wife in January 1947 and its first production at the Edinburgh Festival at the end of August 1949. Not only was he disturbed by the death of Vivienne while still confined under a mental health order and troubled by the expectations of Emily Hale and others that he would marry her, he also felt a new surge of creative energy. In a letter to Martin Browne, his director and theatrical confident, dated 25 January 1948, he wrote:

> I certainly expect the play to be born this year. I do not know how long it will be before it learns how to walk, to say nothing of an acrobatic turn worthy of the theatre. Knowing how slowly I work and the amount of time it is likely to take up to get up a head of steam with an engine which has been out of action for so long, I know the thought of working to a date for this summer would throw me into a panic. I should be quite happy with the prospect of spring 1949, and if, as I hope, I can break the back of the newborn infant during the summer, I should be able to do the polishing work even while at Princeton. [Coghill, 1974, p. 189]

Even with a poet and critic as obsessionally careful as Eliot, I think we would want to be cautious about reading much into what is probably only a mixed metaphor in correspondence not intended for publication. On the other hand, this play contains so much painful resonance with his own personal struggles in his intimate relationships that perhaps he did sometimes want to "break the back" of this "new-born infant". No doubt it is best to be restrained here regarding our assumptions about a human being whose struggles, it seems to me, were all too public. It is appropriate to follow Eliot himself and agree that, as we have just heard him say, it is "only too easy to lose oneself in a maze of speculation about the process by which an imaginary character can become as real for us as people we have known". But I think that we can, with reasonable confidence, say something about *Edward's* and *Lavinia's* and *Celia's* struggles to emerge from—to give it its proper name—*narcissism* towards a genuine possibility of love and marriage, or, should we say, towards the possibility of a genuine marriage.

# CHAPTER NINE

# Hell is oneself,
# the others merely projections

One of the most interesting remarks reported to have been made by T. S. Eliot about *The Cocktail Party* is that it constitutes his rejoinder to Jean-Paul Sartre's biting judgement that *hell is other people*. An interesting thought. In an earlier version of Eliot's play, he puts the following often-quoted lament in the mouth of Edward:

> What is hell? Hell is oneself,
> Hell is alone, the other figures in it
> One's own projections.

> [I.3.417–419]

Martin Browne, director of all of T. S. Eliot's plays (except the unfinished *Sweeney Agonistes*), who, as he put it, assisted at the birth of each, claimed that Eliot said during rehearsal of *The Cocktail Party* that it contained his rejoinder to Sartre's 1944 *Huis Clos* (Browne, 1969, p. 233). That may be, and we have only Browne's account for what Eliot said. However, I think that it is just as plausible to read *The Cocktail Party* as Eliot's *exegesis* of Sartre's forlorn thesis, although it is likely that if it is an interpretation of Sartre it was an unconscious one. Eliot, whether consciously or not, had a remarkable insight into what it means for someone to experience other-people-as-hell.

The Cocktail Party is, in the language I have been exploring in this book, a vivid portrayal of "narcissistic object relating". The characters are struggling to escape, to find a way to take hold of the handle of the door that can lead them out of that prison, that claustrophobic world, in which others are "merely projections". Could it be that the kind of world that Sartre is describing, a world where there is "no exit" (Huis Clos), is a world in which the "others" are in fact one's own inner demons? If so, I think Eliot's reading would be a profoundly interesting interpretation of Sartre's existentialist despair. Locked in that prison of narcissism, it seems impossible to believe that there is anything to, or for which, one might escape. How might it be possible that one is not alone?

## "Only since this morning / I have met myself"

When Edward acknowledges to Celia that the Unidentified Guest has told him that he will bring Lavinia back because he has asked him to, Celia reacts with horror that this Unidentified Guest must be the Devil: "How did he persuade you to want her back?" She goes on to suggest he must be that "mad", "on the edge of a nervous breakdown", and urges him to see a "very great doctor" by the name of Reilly. She is desperate to hear Edward say that he does not want Lavinia back, that he means to gain his freedom, and that everything is all right between them. This leads Edward to voice what he has discovered in his encounter with the Unidentified Guest: that he has never been in love with his wife. Poignantly, he says to Celia that, if he has ever been in love, he was never in love with anyone but her. And perhaps he still is! We will see in a moment just how personal that declaration may have been for the poet himself.

Edward's process of emergence from narcissism, one might say, begins with his self-discovery as "a middle-aged man". He was, perhaps for the first time, beginning to face, if not yet fully to acknowledge, "the inevitability of time and ultimately death" (Money-Kyrle, 1971). Of course the author of these lines himself had just turned sixty and had just found himself free from a woman he had sought to leave for nearly thirty years. However, he would not *feel* free—sufficiently free, at least, to marry again—for another ten years. Edward does not really believe that Celia can understand his despair, although in this speech it is not at all difficult for many of us to identify with this man discovering his own mortality:

> . . . Only since this morning
> I have met myself as a middle-aged man
> Beginning to know what it is to feel old.
> That is the worst moment, when you feel that you have lost
> The desire for all that was most desirable,
> Before you are contented with what you can desire;
> Before you know what is left to be desired;
> And you go on wishing that you could desire
> What desire has left behind.
>
> [pp. 67–68, I.2.228–236]

It is also true that Edward is discovering what many married men and women discover about their affairs: that the affair was a way to create and preserve an illusion that one still has what in reality has been lost, or that in fact one never had. The affair, being secret and forbidden, confuses the excitement of secrecy with a sense of being emotionally alive. It is an illusion that is unmasked when the forbidden becomes a genuine possibility. In Celia's own dawning recognition that she wants something more than an illusion, reality soon begins to seem more like a dream. Her sense of humiliation at wanting this world as well as her dream world perceptively reflects Eliot's own awareness of the anguish of emerging from a state in which the other, the lover, is discovered to be a fiction of one's projections.

A more hopeful way of construing Celia's experience, perhaps closer to what one imagines to be Emily Hale's perspective, might be found in what Donald Meltzer has described as a "ripening into love". Perhaps she is becoming aware of her aspiration that now the "falling in love", that state of almost unbearable yearnings and expectations, will develop into something more, that it will ripen. Not only is Edward awakening to the reality of time with the inevitable regrets and remorse, Celia too is finding that she has been locked in a dream-world. I think that Meltzer's description of the organic process of "ripening" is worth quoting here because it paints such a vivid contrast with the sense of timelessness that can mark a narcissistic state of mind:

> I myself think of it in terms of the metaphor of the natural process of fertilization and ripening. In the case of fruits, of course, many are pollinated and few ripen. I have no idea what the factors are that determine this. But one can see it happening: they fertilize in clusters, and then, of the cluster, one or two ripen. Grapes are quite different. Grapes are fertilized and almost all ripen, with the exception of a few that remain tiny little green things. In nature there are different processes. I think the usual process amongst people of our culture who are capable of falling in love is that they fall in love many times before one ripens. In order to ripen, one can see that it requires a fairly high degree of reciprocity, as it does with the baby. [Meltzer, 1995, p. 134]

It is just this reciprocity that has been missing between Edward and Celia. They are only just now beginning to be honest with each other, and hence only just beginning to be able to be honest with themselves. Throughout the play, this is the central dynamic as the characters begin to learn how to be honest with each other, and thus with themselves, to learn the meaning of sincerity. One could say that one thesis that this book is exploring is the idea that the heart of the analytic process is the uncovering of the many ways that one hides from the truth of one's own emotional reality, as well as that of the other.

Celia says that it is "humiliating", this wanting both the dream and reality. But why humiliating? Perhaps there is a sense in which her "wanting", her desire, is contaminated with omnipotence. We can imagine her saying to herself: "Everything would be just as I want it to be, if only it weren't for her." As long as she can ignore this inconvenient "if only", her dream feels to her like the "real reality". What is humiliating is to discover not that Edward can humiliate her by rejecting her, but that she is not omnipotent after all. It is like Edward's dawning recognition that he is not, as he had surely unconsciously assumed, immortal and had limitless time. Reciprocity, I think, means facing the reality of the other, and with it the loss of omnipotence.

## Feeding on the ruin of loveliness

In the scene that we have been considering in which Celia and
Edward begin to emerge from their shared illusion, it is the absence
of Lavinia that has brought them face to face with themselves. Their
shared fantasy was a belief in the *if only* reality of their relationship—that is, if only it were not for Lavinia, or whatever. I can imagine that it might be tempting in staging *The Cocktail Party* to
under-emphasize the sense of shock at Lavinia's unexplained absence, playing the scene only for the humour of the bewildered and
embarrassed husband anxiously trying to cover for it.

Even if we ignore the autobiographical significance of this scene,
there is a sense of genuine urgency that at last Edward and Celia face
the possibility that their relationship could come out into the open
and ripen, so to speak, into the something more that Celia now allows herself to contemplate. There hovers in the background the
question of children, an intercourse between two people that includes the potential of the unknown, the next generation. It is in the
air throughout the play, but mainly in negative, bitter, and cynical
asides about "making the best of a bad job", as when Eliot has Reilly
describe for Celia those couples who have "ceased to regret" losing
the vision they once had:

> Two people who know they do not understand each other,
> Breeding children whom they do not understand
> And who will never understand them.
>
> [p. 137, II.651–653]

This sort of cynicism fuels the defensive denigration in one of the
most striking speeches in this play. Edward is trying to respond to
Celia's wanting to understand him, and it is possible to believe that
she sincerely does want to understand. She is beginning to face herself and her illusions and thus is able, for the first time, to see Edward
as he is and not as she wanted to see him. She does not loathe him,
she says, but can he really be happy with Lavinia? Edward's response is to denigrate his marriage in the most cruel terms:

> No—not happy: or, if there is any happiness
> Only the happiness of knowing
> That the misery does not feed on the ruin of loveliness,
> That the tedium is not the residue of ecstasy.
>
> [p. 68, I.2.244–247]

Is Edward trying to soften the cruelty of his rejection of Celia? Or does he really believe, as we hear from so many couples when despair has taken hold, that there really was no ecstasy of "falling in love", no original loveliness in the "loved" one? If so, then there can be no regrets. We might say that to avoid the despair of the ruin of loveliness, Edward was willing to deny that there was anything to spoil. Such manoeuvres to evade the reality of despair are among the most unbearably cruel moments that we as therapists have to witness.

What I am suggesting is that it is a fiction that, in at least some of the troubled relationships we see in our consulting-rooms, there never was an original "being in love", no irresistible beauty in the other at the beginning. I think that if one probes deeply enough it is possible to find traces of that original love object, and that falling-in-love, which resonate in the bitter disappointment of what has become intolerable. I do not mean that literally all couples who seek out therapy ought to stay together until they rediscover what brought them together. In those cases where there really seems to be no shared basis for wanting to be together, I believe that there is a story of constructing a shared defence against the agony of the beauty that was found originally in the loved one.

We are touching here on one of the most complex and fascinating debates in contemporary psychoanalysis. I am referring to the question of whether there is an experience of the encounter with the beauty of the world in the form of the infant's encounter with the beauty of the mother, which is prior, logically as well as historically, to the two fundamental "positions" described by Melanie Klein, the paranoid–schizoid and the depressive. Donald Meltzer has posed and explored this question of the role of the original aesthetic object and the infant's experience of and response to the impact of the encounter with the mother's beauty. For the reader who is interested, I would suggest the reading of the "autumnal beech leaves" dream and the "copper beech" dream with which Meltzer opens the first, and defining, chapter of The Apprehension of Beauty (Meltzer, 1988, pp. 2–4). In these two dreams, we hear of two patients at a point in life not dissimilar to that of Edward. But their view is very different on the defining question of whether "misery feeds on the ruin of loveliness", or whether "tedium is the residue of ecstasy".

The paranoid–schizoid defences that we have been exploring in this book—the denial, the splitting, the intrusive projections of unwanted parts of the self—are all needed in the face of something unbearable. Meltzer's analysis points to the earliest pain of the aesthetic conflict, the conflicts and anxieties generated by the *present* object prior to those generated by the *absent* object. It is a point of view that I think we find echoed in Eliot's early poetry, and I suggest that we hear it here in Edward's affirmation-by-negation of the "ruin of loveliness".

In that sense, what unconsciously Eliot is telling us through Edward's voice is true (forget the *not*): that the misery is always feeding "on the ruin of loveliness" and the tedium is always "the residue of ecstasy". At least, I am inviting the reader to explore that hypothesis with the most miserable and most tedious of couples he or she sees in therapy. One sees a rather different world when one assumes that paranoid and schizoid defences are defences against a depressive reality.

## "He was only a projection"

As Celia begins to understand and face the disappointing reality of her narcissistic retreat into a dream world in her affair with Edward, she also begins to be able to see him as a real person and not just the man of her dreams and projections. Emerging from that narcissistic state of mind, she is suddenly aware how dramatically her objects seem to change. It is an experience that happens over and over in our consulting-rooms. As one partner starts to be honest with himself or herself, there is an amazement that it seems, inexplicably, that the other partner has started to be honest as well. In fact, it is a reasonably reliable rule-of-thumb that the person complaining of the other's dishonesty has not yet begun to appreciate what honesty will entail.

Celia responds by describing what is left of the man she thought she loved when the illusion disappeared in a speech resonant with Kafka's nightmare in his short story *Metamorphosis* (Kafka, 1933). She does not awake as an insect, but as one who awakes to see a face, the contours of which she has known and loved, and it is as if she had unwrapped a mummy. The voice she had loved became the noise of an insect, the "dry, endless, meaningless, inhuman" sound he might have made by scraping his legs together. She looks at him and sees only a beetle the size of a man with nothing more inside than what comes out when you tread on a beetle (p. 69, I.2.263–280).

Reading the accounts of Vivienne (especially that of Lyndall Gordon) and her own unpublished writings, one might feel that, like the language and images of "The Game of Chess" in *The Waste Land*, we are listening here to what Eliot himself listened to in the dark days of the earlier years of their marriage. It sounds less to me like an attack than a desperate cry of one who has lost the reality of one she (or he) has loved, or whom she (or he) desperately wanted to be able to love. It is the language as well of "The Hollow Men", with its images of dried voices, quiet and meaningless as wind in dry grass, or rats' feet over broken glass in our dry cellar (Eliot, 1925).

Edward responds to her as if she only gives voice to what he already feels: "Perhaps that is what I am / Tread on me, if you like" (p. 69, I.2.280–281). There is a quality in this exchange which can make one feel that this is not tit-for-tat retaliation, so familiar in warring couples, but rather something more like a process of mutual acknowledgement of the reality of what has transpired between them. But Celia is not bitter, nor does she need to retaliate against one whom she now sees is not the person she thought she knew and loved:

> The man I saw before, he was only a projection—
> I see that now—of something that I wanted—
> No, not *wanted*—something I aspired to—
> Something that I desperately wanted to exist.
>
> [pp. 69–70, I.2.285–288]

Had Celia been able to go no farther than to see Edward as this "beetle-the-size-of-a-man" who makes meaningless sounds as grasshoppers do by scraping his legs together, her biting words might have sounded like the ones we hear in therapy with couples when disillusionment has set in. But there seems to be a process under way, a process of painful self-discovery that allows Celia to be honest, not attacking: "Edward, I see that I was simply making use of you. / And I ask you to forgive me" (p. 70, I.2.290–291). The Edward she is addressing is a person she has never really seen before. It is one of the most familiar experiences in psychoanalytic therapy with couples, at least when the process has taken hold. There is a surprise, even shock, when each looks at the other in amazement, seeing someone they have never seen before, someone no longer filled with, coloured by, their intrusive projections.

As we have already noted, psychoanalytic therapy can be viewed as a process that requires mourning in order to lead to the reintegration of lost parts of the self alienated in projective identification. If we take Celia's forgiveness of Edward to be sincere, which is a plausible enough view, then we must assume, I think, that Celia is in a state of mourning as she owns her projection of something into Edward.

Edward and Celia are alone together only briefly once more, at the beginning of Scene 3 of Act I when the guests find that they have all been mysteriously summoned the next day to meet the returning Lavinia. Nervously Edward says, "We can't sit here in silence", to which Celia replies, laughingly, that he looks like a little boy who's been sent for to the headmaster's study. Edward cannot see the humorous side of it. He cannot see that she is not laughing *at* him, that she has come at last to see him as a human being and is inviting him to join her in this liberating, although terribly painful, experience (p. 78, I.3.86–92).

But Edward is not there yet, in fact, he is a long way away from Celia's state of mind and roughly responds: "I wish I could. I wish I understood anything. / I'm completely in the dark" (pp. 78–79, I.3.93–94). From this point, the trajectory of the play appears to divide: on the one hand, we have what appears to be central, the story of the destiny of Edward and Lavinia's marriage, and, on the other, the story of Celia's choice between two ways.


## "The world I live in seems all a delusion"

Before we return to Edward and Lavinia's story of their shared attempt to face the reality of their marriage, I want to follow this apparent sub-plot of Celia's choice a little further, in anticipation of the two stories coming together in the final chapter. At the end, we shall see that there do seem to be only two alternatives, at least in Eliot's view. Either there is the "making the best of a bad job", in which two people make the necessary compromises to make a relationship possible. Or there is an ecstasy that brings inward fulfilment such as Celia finds in her martyrdom, which translated into a relationship seems to end in what we might term "Othello's solution". It is the burden of *The Cocktail Party*—indeed, of the poetic dramas of Eliot taken as a whole—that these two ways cannot be brought together, not with integrity.

We see that, with the collapse of her illusions as she emerges from her narcissistic state of mind, Celia finds that her world has become meaningless She cannot imagine an alternative, and therefore she takes two "symptoms" to her therapist, who happens, of course, to be the same Sir Henry Harcourt-Reilly. As she describes what is wrong, we see immediately why she has no need for couple therapy now, if indeed she ever did. I do not mean that she has no need for therapy as a couple—for example, with Edward—because their relationship was an affair and not a marriage. In the sense that I have been using the term "marriage", theirs was as much, and as little, a marriage as any of the narcissistic relationships that we see in therapy. No, I mean that when we consider her description of her symptoms we see that her internal objects, whether her good or her damaged internal objects, are not now insistently located in a particular other, as perhaps they once had been located in Edward. In that sense, her "couple therapy", albeit as a individual with this strange "therapist", has already come to an end.

Celia now describes her growing awareness that her crisis is not the end of the relationship with Edward, but rather that trauma has revealed to her something about her relationship with *everybody*. She is shocked to find that she feels everyone is alone, people making noises and thinking they are talking, making faces and thinking they understand each other. Is this a delusion, she asks this "therapist" (pp. 130–131, II.505–531).

Part of the humour of this scene on the stage is that we soon see that this "delusional" view of the world appears to be Reilly's view of marriage, at least the "making-the-best-of-a-bad-job" variety. That it is not the end of the matter is linked with Celia's second symptom. She is plagued by a sense of sin, which with the collapse of her illusions seems to make no sense at all. Why should one worry about hurting someone if the other is just a bundle of one's own projections? Celia humorously dismisses this sense of sin in a caricature of Eliot's own Unitarian upbringing as either "bad form" or "kinky", kinky meaning that it is a curious psychological aberration. She is simply left alone and yet feeling guilty. Her picture is poignantly simple as she comes to see Edward as a child who has wandered into a forest, playing with an imaginary playmate, suddenly discovering that he is only a child, lost, and desperate to go home (p. 135, II.609–612).

Reilly's response is to suggest that her compassion may already be a clue towards finding her own way out of the forest (p. 135, II.613–614). Perhaps too it reflects what Eliot hoped to find in writing this play, a play full, I think, of compassion for not only Emily Hale, but also—and perhaps more importantly—for Vivienne. It was with her illusions and delusions, as well as his own, that he had been struggling since they married and had now, with her death, to try to come to terms.

Celia is in a process of discovery, and, although in the couple story in the rest of this and the next chapter she plays little part, she is vital to the meaning of *The Cocktail Party* because I think that she represents an insight into important internal processes. That is, she is about to say to Reilly that it would be dishonest for her "to try to make a life with *any*body" since she is incapable of the kind of love that is needed. It is a recognition, or at least the beginning of it, that the story of the capacity for a loving intimate relationship is a story in the first instance of one's internal world and the relationship with one's internal objects.

And her last major speech before Reilly sends her off to his sanatorium, "to work out her salvation", is a vivid picture of this stage of her struggle to emerge from narcissism. It is a stage in which she is still confused both about the intimate link between love and suffering and between desire and fulfilment. It was written by someone who could not yet imagine an integration of the passion of the soul with sexual passion. One might wonder whether or not she gives voice to what is going on unconsciously in the minds of Edward and Lavinia.

Celia's not being afraid of being hurt again is itself an expression of despair since she believes nothing can hurt or heal. Perhaps the ecstasy of love was real, although those who experience it may have no reality. She imagines the ecstasy and intimacy of love as a dream in which one is exalted by the intensity of love, "in the spirit" Eliot adds. In this dream there is delight *without desire* because the desire has been fulfilled in the loving. When she says that this dream is a state that one does not know when awake, Eliot draws us towards a picture of the unending bliss of Narcissus gazing at that beautiful youth, a bliss shattered only when waking he reaches in desire to possess that which he loves. Celia's conclusion is a disturbing image of narcissistic longing:

> . . . But what, or whom I loved,
> Or what in me was loving, I do not know.
> And if all that is meaningless, I want to be cured
> Of craving for something I cannot find
> And the shame of never finding it.
>
> [p. 136, II.631–634]

## Edward and Lavinia: two strangers meet

At the beginning of the third scene of the Act I, Edward is faced with the return of his wife Lavinia, although he tells the Unidentified Guest that he is tempted to change his mind (about wanting her back) just to show this irritating stranger that actually he is free— another Sartrean theme, the possibility of freedom. But as Reilly tells him again, Edward is not free. It is just because he is not free that he has sought out this "therapist". Edward's freedom is now Reilly's affair (pp. 114–115, II.212–214)!

Again it is possible to hear Reilly here as unbearably pompous and omnipotent. But it is also possible, I suggest, to see this scene as Eliot's dramatic, and humorous, portrayal of what is in fact a complex process in which the analyst or therapist takes on the cloak of the transference. If so, Reilly might be reminding Edward of the emotional reality of his relationship with his therapist.

I am suggesting that we could paraphrase Reilly's comment along lines something like this: "It is through this analytic process that you will have a chance of freedom, Mr Chamberlayne." Reilly, like all analytic therapists, is only an agent of that process, albeit an essential agent given its interpersonal nature. After all, Reilly does make a candid admission to Julia (*his* "guardian"?) about his doubts concerning what he had just said to Celia at the end of Act II: "And when I say to one like her / Work out your salvation with diligence, I do not understand / What I myself am saying." Julia's deflating, humorous response is salutary for any therapist: "You must accept your limitations" (pp. 144–145, II.781–784).

The main thing that the Unidentified Guest has to say to Edward at the beginning of this scene concerns how Edward was to greet Lavinia when she returns "from the dead". Here is Eliot's most obvious reference to Euripides' *Alcestis*, and immediately Edward objects to this "somewhat dramatic figure of speech"—after all, Lavinia only left him the day before! In fact, as we shall soon see, Lavinia herself later describes her hope that as a result of her "dying to him" he might be able "to find his way back".

The Unidentified Guest suggests that Edward is to meet his returning wife "as a stranger": "We must also remember / That at every meeting we are meeting a stranger" (p. 74, I.3.29–30). But how, Edward protests to the Uninvited Guest, can he meet his wife of five years as a "stranger"? We are all too ready to believe that we know ourselves and those with whom we are most intimate. And in some sense of course we do. But mostly what we know are the masks we wear and impose on others against the surprises that we fear in meeting the strangers we have only glimpsed.

Both Edward and Lavinia puzzle over what to say since they have agreed neither to ask questions nor give to give explanations. Lavinia, at least, seems to have understood a first principle of the analytic process: candour. She greets Edward with the observation: "We have wasted such a lot of time lying." Lying, yes to each other, and, as they are gradually coming to understand, to themselves as well. But is this an *insight*, developed in the time she has been away, or is it an attack when she goes on to say: "I see that I've taken you much too seriously / And now I can see how absurd you are" (p. 92, I.3.269–270).

Although this sounds cruel, Edward responds not as someone wounded but as someone who recognizes the seriousness of what she had said. He wonders only how she came to this "serious conclusion" in just "thirty-two hours". She responds that it is indeed an important discovery to find that you have spent five years of your life with a man who has no sense of humour. Her "always giving in" to him has had the effect of her losing her own sense of humour (p. 92, I.3.273–278).

A therapist listening to this exchange will recognize the dilemma that the couples" "dialogue" takes place at many levels. With one ear, we hear spontaneous thoughts that seem to be part of journey of self-discovery. At the same moment, the words seem designed to cut and wound. Therapists, too, find that voicing their thoughts to one partner can affect the other in unforeseen and unintended ways. Communication and action, saying something to the other and *doing* something to the other, become confused, entangled. Even the attempt to point this out, to communicate this, to the couple may itself be drawn back into the "acting-out" in the session. One of the interesting things about the dialogue that Eliot has created is that it illustrates this dilemma so accurately.

I will not quote all of this painfully vivid exchange, except to note the point at which Edward cries: "Well, I tried to be accommodating. But, in the future, / I shall behave, I assure you, very differently." They are on the edge of something new. Edward has arrived at the point, as he puts it, "At which humiliation ceases to humiliate / You get to the point at which you cease to feel / And then you speak your mind" (p. 96, I.3.344–346).

I think that humiliation is a common experience for couples as the analytic process really gets under way, as one discovers something about oneself *in the presence of the other*. When Edward talks about "the point at which you cease to feel", I think we might understand him to be referring to the inhibitions of the "acquired self", the self under the constraints of the conventions that is mistaken as being the "true self". To have those conventional restraints questioned, to face what one actually feels, and to be able to articulate those feelings without regard for the consequence is to begin to be able to "speak one's mind". Perhaps it is only when "humiliation ceases to humiliate" that one can bear being honest with the other and with oneself.

## Now we can at least fight with each other

When Edward responds to Lavinia that changing comes from becoming able to see oneself through the eyes of an other, he evidences his growing awareness of the intimate link between one's capacity to see oneself and one's capacity to be aware of how one is seen—by real people, not one's projections. There is a persistent humour in these exchanges which suggests that, were it actually a picture of a therapeutic process, what is happening has a genuine, not sentimental, quality. We might even think of it as a *process* of what Freud called "working through": not a matter of sudden revelation and instant transformation, but a painfully slow process of struggling towards the emotional reality of the other in an intimate relationship.

The couple's perception of what is happening between them in this scene is that here they are back in the trap again. Except, as Edward points out, with one important difference—they can fight each other instead of each taking his corner of the cage (p. 97, I.3.363–378). Now that Edward and Lavinia can engage each other, although at the moment only to fight, they are moving towards the possibility of a real relationship. In a sense, it still feels like a "trap", but they can now speak candidly to each other about their different experiences of not being understood. Their capacity to define their different corners is better than the denial by which they cushioned themselves from any genuine encounter.

They have reached the point, for example, where they can ask the question that all couples ultimately want to ask each other (and I mean ask honestly, for most will have found by this time how to talk about this question in ways that are dishonest): Edward puts the question directly—"I've often wondered why you married me." It is a painful exchange as Lavinia responds that, although he was quite attractive, he always seemed to be trying to persuade himself that he was in love. It is striking that years later Eliot used the very same language to describe his own feelings about his marrying Vivienne: "I believe that *I came to persuade myself* that I was in love with her" (Eliot, 1988, p. xvii, emphasis added).

Lavinia's description of why she disappeared is, in some ways, shocking as it articulates both Eliot's version of Euripides' *Alcestis* and a version, no doubt quite unconscious, of his picture of both Vivienne's hospitalization and finally her death.

> . . . I thought that if I died
> To you, I who had been only a ghost to you,
> You might be able to find the road back
> To a time when you were real—for you must have been real
> At some time or other, before you ever knew me:
> Perhaps only when you were a child.
>
> [pp. 98–99, I.3.400–405]

But Edward cannot accept this "sacrifice". In this he is portrayed as quite different to the king Admetus in the *Alcestis*, who not only accepted his wife's sacrifice but remained loyal to her. If we should read this as Eliot's gloss on Euripides' play, it would suggest that the husband's "loyalty" is actually more like being frozen by his wife's defining him as selfish. Certainly Edward is suspicious that this is but another of Lavinia's subtle attempts to define him as he struggles, surprisingly, against his own temptation to passivity:

> I don't want you to make yourself responsible for me:
> It's only another kind of contempt.
> And I do not want you to explain me to myself.
> You're still trying to invent a personality for me
> Which will only keep me away from myself.
>
> [p. 99, I.3.406–410]

These angry words suggest why couples, even when they seem to be on their way to working their way out of the "trap" of an empty relationship, feel that they need to find help from someone outside. The two share a deep unconscious fear of what the acknowledgement of emotional reality will entail, and I have often seen one partner "rescue" the other, who is about to emerge into a depressive awareness, by drawing him or her back into a fight.

Since withdrawing projections means a process of mourning, there is a sometimes overwhelming sense of despair not just that one cannot bear it, but that the other cannot. Certainly there is a shared fear that mutual withdrawal of mutual projections will mean a shared mourning. And that, for most couples, feels intolerable.

Edward now makes the speech in which Eliot defines hell as oneself, imprisoned in a narcissistic "claustrum":

> There was a door
> And I could not open it. I could not touch the handle.
> Why could I not walk out of my prison?
> What is hell? Hell is oneself,
> Hell is alone, the other figures in it
> Merely projections. There is nothing to escape from
> And nothing to escape to. One is always alone.
>
> [p. 99, I.3.414–420]

In *The Family Reunion* (1939), the play that Eliot was writing between the time of his formal separation from Vivienne in 1933 and the time he agreed to her involuntary incarceration in a mental hospital in 1938, and also in the poem *Burnt Norton*, the first of the *Four Quartets*, published in 1935, Eliot speaks of love as a door, a door into a rose-garden into which he can only peer. Here the door in *The Cocktail Party* is shut, and Edward cannot even put his hand to the handle, echoes of that *Burnt Norton*.

In the play, however, Eliot counterbalances the haunting image of the door that cannot be opened with a humorous counterpoint. Perhaps to prevent the audience sinking into some premature sentimental dream, Lavinia wakes us with a shock—the shock of the familiar—as if we really were listening in a session to one of our couples. Lavinia cannot bear her husband's image of hell as being alone, the others only projections. That is, she cannot bear to be merely the image in Narcissus' pool, and she exclaims, Edward, can you bear for a moment to think about me (p. 99, I.3.421–423)! But Edward is not listening. He can give voice only to his total despair.

> O God, O God, if I could return to yesterday
> Before I thought that I had made a decision.
> What devil left the door on the latch
> For these doubts to enter? And then you came back, you
> The angel of destruction—just as I felt sure.
> In a moment, at your touch, there is nothing but ruin.
> O God, what have I done? The python. The octopus.
> Must I become after all what you would make me?
> [p. 101, I.3.454–461]

Is this the question—one version of it, at least—that brings couples to seek therapy *as couples*? Must I become what you would make of me? It is a shared question, the question of a sadomasochistic *folie à deux* in which somehow each feels defined by the other. Both Edward and Lavinia feel it. But I do not think that that alone makes them ready to seek therapy together. That only comes with the question that is the defining moment at the end of the couple therapy session, the moment when Lavinia turns to Edward and says, "Edward! / What can we do?" (p. 124, II.400). But first we must get to the beginning of that session.

# CHAPTER TEN

# Making the best of a bad job

At the end of the last chapter Edward cries: "Must I become after all what you would make me?" In the grip of his inner demons projected into the hell he calls his marriage, he can see no way out. In order to feel his hopelessness we need to see through his eyes the demons he saw. It is possible to play *The Cocktail Party*, I think, as such a tame drawing-room comedy that the audience misses a moment when it is possible to look into hell itself. Irene Worth, who played Celia in the original Edinburgh production of *The Cocktail Party*, reported that there was only one time that Eliot intervened during the rehearsals. It was in the rehearsal of the scene when Edward and Lavinia were quarrelling:

> Eliot bolted up to the stage looking quite unsettled. "The wife", he insisted, "must be fierce. *Much more fierce.* The audience must understand that she is impossible." [quoted in Ackroyd, 1984, p. 294]

What do we imagine provoked this outburst? About whom was Eliot thinking? Lyndall Gordon, in her sensitive study of the characters in the story of the poet's life, suggests one reason Eliot found it impossible to visit Vivienne for the whole of the seventeen years of her incarceration in a mental hospital: "Eliot never visited Vivienne in the asylum, not, I imagine, out of callousness, but because he must have feared the compelling power of her strong Welsh shriek" (Gordon, 1988, p. 148). Gordon does not document this suggestion, leaving us to imagine that it might have been the result of her intimate study of this couple *plus* perhaps evidence like this well-documented outburst at the rehearsal for *The Cocktail Party*.

In the next chapter, I want to return to my review of the psychoanalytic theory relevant to our understanding of the couple and therapy with a couple, particularly to look at the picture of the sado-masochistic *folie-à-deux* relationship. The related concept that Donald Meltzer termed "mutual projective identification in action" will help us to make some sense of the complex dynamics of this kind of *folie à deux*. But in this chapter I want to complete a picture of what I think this *folie à deux* looks like in the flesh, so to speak. In fact, it turns out to be an all-too-familiar picture to therapists who have worked with couples, in part, I think, because it is largely these couples who make their way to our consulting-rooms.

## Edward, his therapist, and psychoanalysis

At the beginning of the Act II, the audience is alerted to what will clearly be an unusual encounter by details of all of Reilly's machinations about arrangements for the comings and goings. We are about to hear in lively detail the "process recording" of the first couple psychotherapy session.

Once Edward has recovered from the shock of discovering that the great doctor to whom he has been referred is none other than the Unidentified Guest, he insists that he is on the edge of a nervous breakdown. After all, two people have recently told him just that. Reilly responds that "nervous breakdown" is a term he never uses, although Edward persists that his is a *very unusual case*. "All cases are unique, and very similar to others", Reilly retorts (p. 109, II.106). Indeed, one of the fascinating things about *The Cocktail Party* is that it has the ring of authenticity that makes us sure its author must have first-hand experience of it, and yet it is that very particularity that gives it the feel of the universal.

The heart of the matter, Edward suggests, is that he "has ceased to believe in [his] own personality", which Reilly agrees is "serious" and "very prevalent indeed". At this point, Edward begins to talk about his childhood, as if he expected that this is what people like this "great doctor" expect. Donald Meltzer has described such expectations as what he calls the "pre-formed transference", the common experience these days that "everyone knows" what psychoanalysts are interested in (Meltzer, 1995, pp. 188–189). Reilly promptly interrupts with a most contemporary view, worthy, I submit, of any respectable psychoanalytic therapist!

> I always begin from the immediate situation
> And then go back as far as I find necessary.
> You see, your memories of childhood—
> I mean, in your present state of mind—
> Would be largely fictitious; and as for your dreams,
> You would produce amazing dreams, to oblige me.
> I could make you dream any kind of dream I suggested,
> And it would only go to flatter your vanity
> With the temporary stimulus of feeling interesting.
>
> [II.119–127]

It is one of the first principles of analytic therapy that we begin, as Reilly says, "from the immediate situation". Why? Whatever "Reilly" (or Eliot) meant, our interest is in what is emotionally alive at the moment of our encounter with our patients. Of course, we assume that the past is alive at any given moment, that what the patient may be suffering is the "living in the past", in some unresolved internal dilemma that may be replayed over and over again in current relationships. But explicitly to invite the patient to tell us about that past is often to invite a retreat from what is emotionally alive. What may instead be presented is the well-rehearsed story with which the patient has become accustomed to consoling himself or herself.

I say "often" to emphasize that we are thinking now about general principles, and it is important to say that there may be occasions when we choose to ask about something in the patient's history. But when we do, we may find, as we saw in chapter four with Mrs B's encounter with Mrs Webb, that this only invites a compliant, frequently deadly, rehearsal of history *for the therapist's benefit*, as Mrs Webb seemed to think.

When, however, we begin with the immediate emotional situation, as Mrs A did when she commented as forthrightly as she could, on Mr Webb's unconscious anxieties, paradoxically the patients make their own links with their history almost *as if they had been asked*. But here the "therapist" boldly suggests that in his patient's current state of mind his "memories of childhood" would be "largely fictitious". That is, the memories he would consciously call to mind would be shaped by his conscious desire to convey what he understands of his present dilemma, his "theories" of how that dilemma relates to his early childhood experiences.

Betty Joseph talks about this problem of the patient who offers an almost irresistible invitation to attend to "interesting" material, leaving the analyst in danger of being "able to understand the material but not the patient." For example, she describes one such patient:

> I find I listen to but almost do not believe what she is telling me, as if she were confabulating history, inventing boyfriends, or details about boyfriends, or stories that she tells me that people have told her. Yet I do not think that she is consciously lying, but my countertransference is very uncomfortable. My suspicion is—and only time will or may show whether I am right—that this patient as an infant or young child had no real belief in her world, in her emotional surroundings, as if deep sincerity was lacking between her and her parents—whom I suspect at depth she saw through. And this mixture of disbelief and pretence in real relationships is what she is living out with me in the transference. [Joseph, 1983, p. 144]

It is just this lack of belief in a real emotional world that Edward describes throughout *The Cocktail Party*. The sense of "therapeutic alliance" with such a patient, Betty Joseph suggests, can turn out to be inimical to a genuine alliance, just as what seems to be understanding can turn out to be actually anti-understanding:

> Many of these patients tend to respond quickly to interpretations or to discuss in a very sensible way previous interpretations, using such expressions as "do you mean", referring to previous dreams and the like and seeming eminently co-operative and helpful. One finds oneself in a situation that looks exactly like an on-going

analysis with understanding, apparent contact, appreciation, and even reported improvements. And yet, one has a feeling of hollow-ness. If one considers one's countertransference it may seem all a bit too easy, pleasant and unconflicted. . . . [Joseph, 1975, p. 76]

Or, as Reilly points out to Edward, such a caricature of the analytic process "would only go to flatter your vanity / With the temporary stimulus of feeling interesting"—and, we should add, mindful of Betty Joseph's warnings, make the analyst pleased to have such an "interesting", responsive patient. It is a persistent temptation for us as therapists to become drawn into the patient's wish to be "special", but in the end it is our responsibility to be aware of this kind of seduction through a continuous monitoring of our countertransfer-ence. I should note that my reading of Reilly here is at variance with the common reaction to his representation of the analytic process. Even one of the most psychoanalytically sophisticated literary critics of Eliot's work, Tony Pinkney, concludes:

The play itself attempts to rule out a psychoanalytical interpreta-tion by having Reilly, who is both psychotherapist and religious director, dismiss psychoanalysis as mere buttress of the patient's vanity. [Pinkney, 1984, p. 129]

Another prominent critic, Hugh Kenner, suggests that this interpre-tation was common at the time of the play's first London perform-ances. One wonders who Kenner is referring to (he gives no reference) when he points out that after *The Cocktail Party* moved to the West End: "Certain members of the psychiatric profession even complained to the press that their mode of operation was being mis-represented" (Kenner, 1959, p. 289). No doubt it depends on how one reads or sees this play whether one is inclined to feel offended by the ambiguities of Reilly, the character Stephen Spender called a "high class creep" and a contemporary analyst described as "Bion at his worst".

One can only assume that these critics, even one as familiar with psychoanalysis as Pinkney, are unaware of contemporary psycho-analytic thinking. I think my reading of the play finds support in the way that Reilly continues the discussion of this common trap into which patient and therapist are all too often drawn. Protesting that he is obsessed by the thought of his own insignificance, Edward seems readily to understand Reilly when he points out that he could make him feel important and he would then imagine it a marvellous cure (pp. 110–111, II.128–138).

We might describe post-Bion psychoanalysis as "reality therapy" in that the aim is not to feel better but rather to be able to acknowledge one's emotional reality, both in the sense of recognising what one is feeling and in increasingly being able to tolerate difficult feelings, positive as well as negative. The "endless struggle to think well" of oneself, as Reilly puts it, is premised on an inability to imagine the possibility of forgiveness, either forgiving or, what is more unimaginable, being forgiven.

One can imagine Eliot himself reflecting in these lines, no doubt unconsciously, his own experience of being persecuted by guilt in reference to his relationship with his first wife. If that were the case, it would be particularly so in the period immediately following her death, although, as I have already noted, he had not seen her (as far as we know) in the seventeen years preceding her death. I believe— although this is not the place properly to explore this idea—that Eliot worked out his own salvation, as Reilly puts it, through a self-analysis both in his poetry and in his poetic drama. For some unconscious reason, he seemed to need to do this in public, for the most part without his audience being aware. One might imagine him finding some secret satisfaction in thinking that what he was doing *on the stage* for all to see was in reality private, a private confessional, so to speak, in public. It is similar—in mood, at least—to his telling an interviewer about the pleasure he took in the fact that no one had recognized the link between *The Cocktail Party* and the *Alcestis* of Euripides (Eliot, 1959, p. 103).

## "I cannot live with her and I cannot live without her"

Having got these preliminaries out of the way, Reilly now invites Edward to talk about what has happened since he and Lavinia were reunited. Edward gives voice to the dilemma so often heard in therapy with couples: I cannot live with her and I cannot live without her. The question is, why not? What is there about the nature of their relating that makes them feel so trapped? Edward protests that fifteen minutes alone again with his wife and he found himself subject to the roles that he felt she "imposed" on him. That he is describing an experience we conceptualize as intrusive projection or projective identification is suggested by his feeling of something imposed on him by the *obstinate, unconscious, sub-human strength* "some women have" (pp. 111–112, II.150–151).

Were we listening to Lavinia at this moment, we would no doubt hear that the "obstinate, unconscious, sub-human strength" is typically male. Nevertheless, it might be worth considering that there is a gender element intrinsic in this dynamic in that the basis of projective identification undoubtedly lies in the mother–infant relationship, although again this description would do as well for the mother's experience of her infant as for the infant's experience of its mother. The reference to the infant–mother relationship gives particular poignancy to Edward's protest about how he experiences his wife in their "adult" couple relationship:

> Without her, it was vacancy.
> When I thought she had left me, I began to dissolve,
> To cease to exist. That is what she has done to me!
> I cannot live with her—that is now intolerable;
> I cannot live without her, for she has made me incapable
> Of having any existence of my own.
>
> [p. 112, II.151–156]

But how much can Edward, or Eliot for that matter, see that this is also what he described to Celia: that "obstinate, the tougher self; who does not speak / Who never talks, who cannot argue; / And who in some men may be the *daimon, the genius* . . ." (p. 68, I.2.255–257)— projected into the other! Is it what ties Edward to this *other*, this other *with* whom one cannot live, this other *without* whom one cannot live—it makes him incapable of having any existence of his own. But it also, in Eliot's case, gave rise to his greatest creation, *The Waste Land*. Vivienne does seem to have been his *daimon*, his "obstinate, tougher self" who could not speak!

We could say that Edward cannot live without Lavinia because she carries something of his essential self, something I think Eliot himself understood, perhaps primarily unconsciously, about his relationship with Vivienne. When Lavinia has gone, Edward can then become aware of his inner emptiness which he has filled with the conventional roles that he blames on her. Reilly does not take this up—and again we are not aiming to second-guess this "colleague"— but we might imagine exploring with Edward how it is that he finds himself in a state of mind in which Lavinia can "impose" these roles on him. In these apparent sadomasochist relationships, it is characteristically the masochistic partner who calls the tune, not the sadistic one (Meltzer, 1995).

Edward's poignant conclusion is that he has "ceased to believe in his own personality". When he complains that he doubts that this perplexing therapist has heard a word of what he has been saying, Reilly responds that in fact he learns a great deal by observing him. That is, he lets him talk as long as he pleases, and presumably about whatever he please, and then takes note of what he does *not* say (p. 112, II.163–166). It would border on the perverse to suggest that we therapists are not interested in what our patients say, only in what they do not say. However, it is true that when we listen with our "evenly hovering attention", what often strikes us is what the patient cannot or will not say.

In fact, at this moment I think that what Edward goes on to say *is* important, because we see the transference beginning to come into full view. Just as he has handed over responsibility for his life to his wife, claiming to be the victim of her "obstinate, unconscious, sub-human strength", so now he begins to relate to his therapist in a remarkably similar way, protesting that coming to see Reilly was the last decision of which he was capable. This sounds as if Edward had listened to what Reilly has said to him about freedom, his lack of it, and why he has come to the "right sort of doctor" whose affair it is to "give him his freedom" (p. 113, II.173–176). But, having in mind the admonitions of, for example, Betty Joseph, we might wonder about the speed and ease with which Edward has taken up this uncomfortable point and has made it his own. Although he may sound like a thoughtful, responsive patient, what he conveys is his distortion of what Reilly has been trying to say to him.

Edward's conclusion is that he "cannot take any further responsibility", that he is in his therapist's hands—as if to say, you said it was your affair, so over to you. It is what Lavinia has been complaining about: Edward's inability to see the difference between listening to the other and passivity, between being responsive to the other and handing over all responsibility to the other. This is not *relating*—this is a collapse of relating into a narcissistic world in which there is only one person. This passivity is parasitic, and Reilly simply brushes aside the invitation into Edward's narcissistic world.

What is more important is Reilly's insistence that sometimes, before he can treat a patient like Edward, he needs more information than the patient himself (or herself) can tell him. This can be understood in terms of what the patient can *consciously* tell us, in the way that we need dreams and associations to be able to hear what the patient is consciously unaware of and therefore cannot tell us directly. Edward is not prepared for what he is about to hear from Reilly:

> ... it is often the case that my patients
> Are only pieces of a total situation
> Which I have to explore. The single patient
> Who is ill by himself, is rather the exception.
>
> [p. 114, II.193–196]

Edward, to the contrary, wants to be sent to a sanatorium, a "place of healing", and in his mind this means being alone, as if he did believe that "hell is other people". But what if he were right that "hell is oneself, the others merely projections"? In his comments on this speech in the play, Raymond Williams points out that not only is the "cure" the cure of the delusions and dishonesties of Edward and Lavinia, it is "a cure *within* society" (Williams, 1968, p. 214). Yes, within society at large and within the society of the couple. Williams is a critic with a sharp eye for the social context of the poets and dramatists, but the context of this scene soon makes plain that the "society" with which Eliot is immediately concerned is the *couple*. Nevertheless, I agree with the thrust of Williams' point, which we might express by saying, again with reference to Winnicott, there is no such thing as an individual.

## Bringing the couple to therapy together

We come at last to what is, I think, a remarkable description of a therapy session with a couple. We have already seen that Eliot's imagination has created a figure in Reilly who has a plausible affinity with some aspects of contemporary psychoanalysis. When Reilly decides that his patients are "only pieces of a total situation", and then proceeds to devise a scheme for seeing two of these patients together, he adds a new meaning to the concept of "the total situation" used by analysts such as Melanie Klein and Betty Joseph. Clearly, we have to allow ourselves, and Eliot, some literary license for the way that Reilly sets about bringing this couple together. But as I said at the beginning of chapter six, I want to hold on to the, often ignored, temerity of our inviting a patient into the analytic experience in the actual presence of the marital partner.

Eliot manages to convey this sense of temerity in us as serious professionals in a disarmingly humorous way. Reilly suddenly shocks Edward by saying that he recently had another patient whose situation was much the same as his and therefore he had to accept a rather unusual procedure. Reilly announces that he proposes to introduce Edward to the other patient (p. 114, II.197–200)!

Edward's outrage at this proposal is such engaging theatre that it might distract us from what is, in fact, a very serious question for therapists who are prepared to entertain the idea of the analytic process *with a couple*. Should we not take Edward's reaction with the gravity it deserves? Analytic therapists who only have experience with individual patients will perhaps appreciate this more than those of us who have become accustomed to working with couples. If the reader needs any further encouragement to feel Edward's outrage here, I suggest imagining your reaction had your analyst made such a proposal to you in the middle of your analysis! Would you not have protested, with Edward, that you considered this very unprofessional conduct? (p. 114, II.201–203).

To repeat the point, those of us who have been seeing couples in psychoanalytic psychotherapy may, I think, have become insensitive to the radical nature of what we are attempting to do. In his perceptive comments on this play, Raymond Williams spoke of Eliot's use of language, his words that "have often a network of tentacular roots, reaching down to the deepest terrors and desires" (Williams, 1968). That, it seems to me, also captures something of the psychoanalytic session. To invite an opening up of the "deepest terrors and desires" is unnerving enough in the safety of the analytic relationship between the individual patient and therapist. To invite a couple into the analytic process may literally be to invite the unexpected, to release a new force, to let the genie out of the bottle. It is indeed to start a train of events that is beyond our control (p. 33, I.1.266–269).

But Reilly appears unrepentant, insisting that is the only way in which it could be discussed. But why? This point in *The Cocktail Party* is one place where we must distinguish between the fiction of the play and the realities of the clinical setting. What I want to suggest is that, technically, Reilly's intervention, if we were to take it at face value, is unethical. Moreover, it is so unilateral as to suggest that it reflects the *therapist's* acting-out of his own omnipotence.

But I am not proposing that we read this play as a *factual* account of psychoanalytic therapy with a couple, but as way to portray a psychological reality about the process of seeking therapy either as an individual or as a couple. The difference with a couple is that the splitting can be between the partners as well as internal to them—the splitting between the self who will under no circumstances seek out a therapist, and the self who is desperate for help. It would perhaps be much too much like real life had Eliot portrayed either Edward or Lavinia as wanting couple therapy but having to persuade, or even manipulate, the other to get him or her to therapy.

The emotional reality commonly for couples in therapy is that, in a real sense, neither of them wants to be there. It is as if they join unconsciously in saying to the therapist: all right you got us here, now what! It is the counterpart to the feeling in the therapist of being the "uninvited guest" in the privacy of the couple's intimate moments. Again, and I have felt this more than once, it is as if the couple turns to the therapist to say: and who invited you! I would say that, perhaps contrary to first impressions on an initial reading, Eliot has got this scene just about right as it plays *unconsciously* between the couple and the therapist.

In the "couple session" in *The Cocktail Party* we see Reilly persistently facing both Edward and Lavinia with the realities that they, both individually and as a couple, have become adept at evading and avoiding. Reilly's assumption seems to be that, in the words of Raymond Williams, "health lies in the acceptance of reality" (Williams, 1968, p. 215). And here, of course, the critical reality is the psychic reality of the internal world, the world of the emotions.

What is striking about the couple aspect of this for Edward and Lavinia is that their therapist has made the judgement that for them to be able to face themselves, their illusions and deceptions, it is necessary for each to face the reality of the other.

## Incapable of loving or of being loved

Having insisted that his therapist send him to a sanatorium because he cannot be in the same world as his wife, and now having been told he is to be introduced to another patient, Edward is adamant that he will not discuss his case before some other patient. Whatever the reader thinks at this point, the time has arrived to see the couple. Lavinia enters and is as shocked as Edward. While she was prepared to talk *about* her husband, she was no more prepared to meet him than he was to meet with her (p. 115, II.305–307).

Therapists with experience of analytic work with couples may enjoy the humour of *The Cocktail Party*, but always, I think, with an uneasy sense of the implied trauma that underlies the exchanges between Edward and Lavinia. For example, in the exposé of the affairs of Edward with Celia and Lavinia with Peter, when challenged as to how he knew of these "secrets" Reilly protests that he has his own "method of collecting information" and cannot reveal it as it is "a matter of professional etiquette". Lavinia, who has just exclaimed that she "did not come here to be insulted", now responds that she has "not noticed much professional etiquette" in Reilly's behaviour. Within the play, the audience is led to believe that his information was "all obtained from outside sources", but if we stand *outside* the play for a moment, we might come to a rather different view of the matter.

If we imagine the play as a portrayal of the author's internal world—and we have already heard Eliot talk about the sources of the writer's characters, as well as the influence of the characters *on* the writer—then we can imagine what these "outside sources" might be. Remembering Meltzer's description of the "gathering of the transference" as something like the "gathering of the clan", it is as though the various characters of the internal world begin to appear in the life of the therapy (Meltzer, 1967). Perhaps we can now candidly reveal what Reilly declined to discuss—that is, our own "method of collecting information" as therapists. It comes from the patient's internal world, with its cast of characters revealed to us in the *transference* and its essential correlate, our *countertransference*! As we make ourselves available to the "gathering of the clan", we hear from all these essential "informants", the many internal objects, as they come to life in the analytic process in the transference.

We can now see in Edward's inability to consummate the relationship with his mistress, Celia, how he encounters himself as someone who has lost, or perhaps never had, the capacity for loving. Lavinia responds bitterly: "My husband has never been in love with anybody." Reilly suggests that Edward's own realization that he has never been in love with anyone has made him suspect that he is incapable of loving.

> To men of a certain type
> The suspicion that they are incapable of loving
> Is as disturbing to their self-esteem
> As, in cruder men, the fear of impotence.
>
> [p. 122, II.352–355]

Reilly has touched here on an important distinction between self-esteem as we might think of it in the paranoid–schizoid and in the depressive positions. In the former, it has to do with power or its lack, impotence. Being potent means that one esteems oneself. In the latter, it has to do with concern for the object, for the other, and is marked by a capacity for loving. It is reminiscent of Bion's discussion of "arrogance": "In the personality where life instincts predominate, pride becomes self-respect, where death instincts predominate, pride becomes arrogance" (Bion, 1967, p. 86).

From a couple point of view, it is interesting to see Reilly link what we might think of in our language as a shared unconscious phantasy. However, here he helps us to see a form of a shared phantasy in which the sharing is complementary rather than identical. We might say that a symmetrical shared phantasy is based on what is identical, not on what is complementary. Edward's despair is only one side of this couple's dilemma, as Reilly is quick to point out to Lavinia. She discovers a different form of despair as she begins to face the reality that Peter, her young lover, felt something for Celia, Edward's lover, that he never felt for her.

For Lavinia, this meant facing the fear that, wanting to be loved, perhaps no one *could* love her (p. 123, II.370–374). These deeply held beliefs constitute the psychic reality, the internal world of this unhappy couple. Reilly names their shared unconscious phantasy of a "shared" isolation with painful clarity. What they share in common is the same isolation—he that he is a man incapable of loving, and she that she is a woman no man can love. Lavinia responds that what they have in common seems just enough to make them loathe one another. The shared despair is so great that it must remain unacknowledged lest neither survive. But Reilly offers an alternative interpretation:

> See it rather as the bond which holds you together.
> While still in a state of unenlightenment,
> *You* could always say: "he could not love any woman;"
> *You* could always say: "no man could love her."
> You could accuse each other of your own faults,
> And so could avoid understanding each other.
> Now, you have only to reverse the propositions
> And put them together.
>
> [p. 123, II.384–91]

In the past, Lavinia could always console herself that her husband could not love any woman. And Edward could always console himself that no one could love his wife. Put that way round, it is a relationship of perfect, and tragic complementarity, a shared illusion—or perhaps even a shared delusion? Eliot, the dramatic poet, now puts in Reilly's mouth one of the clearest summaries of projective identification in the couple relationship: *you could accuse each other of your own faults, and so could avoid understanding each other.*

Reilly concludes with his humorous version of what we describe as the "owning of the projections": "Now, you have only to reverse the propositions / And put them together." Only! Sometimes the intrusive projections are so entrenched in the couple relationship that they, and we as their therapists, might wonder, with Lavinia, "Is that possible?"

## Reconciliation to the human condition: two ways?

Edward and Lavinia's "therapy session" with Sir Henry Harcourt-Reilly seems to reach its denouement with her despairing cry: "It seems to me that what we have in common / Might be just enough to make us loathe one another." Reilly's response, however, suggests that this is, rather, a *bond* that holds them together *"while still in a state of unenlightment"*. The conscious experience of mutual loathing which we so often see in couples when they come to us in desperation, unable or unwilling to part, but seemingly held together in what feels like mutual contempt, has an unconscious dynamic that we conceptualize as intrusive projections. In the next chapter, we will take this conceptualization forward with the idea of mutual projective identification in action as the basis of a sado-masochistic *folie à deux*. But here I want to consider what happens when couples begin to recognize and acknowledge these dynamics, the process Reilly refers to rather quaintly as "enlightenment"?

For example, consider what I suggest *is* the denouement of this "session". It comes immediately after Reilly has suggested that Edward and Lavinia have *only* to re-own these projections that have dominated their relationship. This is *not* to be accomplished by a "retreat to a sanatorium" somewhere, they imagine, away from the "hell" they want to escape. Such an "escape" would have been a disaster in their present state of mind. It is this state of mind from which Edward and Lavinia need to be freed.

In a sense, the denouement of the couple therapy comes, almost unnoticed, just at this point in the drama of Edward and Lavinia's marriage when Lavinia cries, "Then what can we do when we can go neither back nor forward? Edward! What can we do?" (p. 124, II.3.398–400). Lavinia's cry is not addressed to their "therapist", nor really to herself. It is a cry *addressed to Edward*. And it is a cry, not an attack, not a narcissistic plea to someone who is "only a projection". Her use of Edward's name, standing alone in a sentence on its own, is a direct appeal to him, and to him alone. At this moment, we can believe that at last this desperate couple are at a point where it becomes possible to address the other *as an other*, to be in a relationship. It is such a poignant moment, as it often is in the consulting-room, when we see before us the difference between "object relating" and "narcissism". Or perhaps we should stick with the clear and direct way that Eliot's director of *The Cocktail Party* put it:

> This is the beginning of spiritual health. One of Eliot's recurrent themes is the danger we all run of making use of people by seeing them as "projections" of our own desires; no true relationship can exist unless we see them as they are, "as a human being". [Browne, 1966, p. 42]

In case we might have missed the significance of Lavinia's cry, Reilly makes it clear as he says to Lavinia, "You have answered your own question, though you do not know the meaning of what you have said" (p. 124, II.400–401). In the first draft of the play, Eliot has Reilly go on to add: "You said 'What shall *we* do?' The common action / In the commonplace life" (Browne, 1966, p. 31). We are close now to the central dramatic conflict that forms the core of *The Cocktail Party*: the possibility—or the lack of it—for intimacy. Intimacy, I suggest, means both being *ordinary* in an *ordinary* real world *and* yet sharing in a relationship the experience of which is transcendent with a meaning that is a symbolic expression of the most profound depths of meaning. But the possibility of intimacy rests in the capacity to recognize the other *as an other*, a genuine other.

A couple I saw recently with a co-therapist had been engaged in a series of bitter attacks on the other. Each felt, like Edward and Lavinia, that the other failed to understand them and failed to appreciate how that made each feel victimized by the other. "I am not number one in your life" was the complaint each reiterated endlessly in their different ways. At the end of the session, she finally erupted: "You're not trapped in this relationship", and after an ominous pause she growled, "And neither am I!" There was a profound sense of shock as she put into words a moment of recognition, the realization of the possibility that either of them could walk out of the marriage. And not only could, but at that moment she was actually doing so. It was a chilling moment in which I felt paralysed. Since it was at the very end of the session, there was no opportunity for either of us as their therapists to act out what felt to be an irresistible impulse to try to say something that could counteract the finality of her words.

After the session, I talked to my co-therapist about this scene in *The Cocktail Party*. Intellectually, I could see that this was in fact a moment in which a relationship was beginning to be possible. But emotionally it did not feel like that. We both felt deeply shocked by the intensity of moment. We should not, however, have been surprised that they came back to the next session remarkably more open to hearing something of the other's point of view. It then began to feel that Reilly was right. This "Lavinia" did not know the significance of what she had said—or did she? Did she unconsciously understand that, until both realized "in their gut" that neither was trapped in this relationship, there was no possibility of a genuine relationship, no possibility for intimacy?

But for Eliot in *The Cocktail Party*, this is not the end of the story. Edward's response gives us the phrase that for many commentators on the play suggests the poet's own cynicism about marriage, indeed his rejection of the mundane life in contrast to an other-worldly spirituality: "Lavinia, we must make the best of a bad job / That is what he means." Are we to understand that Reilly is agreeing with what seems to be a pessimistic view of the option open to the couple? After all, Reilly did say to Edward, "The best of a bad job is all any of us make of it—except of course, the saints (p. 124, II.3.403–407).

Eliot in *The Cocktail Party* seems to present us with two alternative options to the central dilemma of the play and, I suggest, to the poet's own personal dilemma: the possibility or the impossibility of authentic intimacy. The traditional interpretation of the play focuses on Reilly's discussion with Celia in Act II where he juxtaposes two ways, I would say two kinds of relationships, between which she can choose. One, as we discover in Act III, Eliot pictures as the ecstasy of martyrdom, an assumption that I want to explore in the last chapter. The other seems to be the humdrum life of the couple, "the best of a bad job", what Reilly describes as being reconciled to the human condition.

Reilly's speech starts reasonably enough and we might think that he is describing the ordinariness of marriage. We can all recognize it. Maintaining the common routine, learning to avoid excessive expectation, becoming tolerant of ourselves and others. But then Eliot adds an edge of what sounds less like realism and more like cynicism as Reilly says of these couples that they

> Are contented with the morning that separates
> And with the evening that brings together
> For casual talk before the fire
> Two people who know they do not understand each other,
> Breeding children whom they do not understand
> And who will never understand them.
>
> [p. 137, II.647–652]

This does certainly appear to take us towards a cynical view, not only of the couple relationship, but of family life and the relationship between the generations. If confirmation were needed, one would only have to read Tom Eliot's last letter from London to his father in St Louis at the end of 1918, two months before his father's death (Eliot, 1988, pp. 246–249). In the next few years, desperate that his father had died with no real idea about the value of the career path his son had chosen, Eliot's relationship with his mother became even more fraught. If, in one sense, *The Waste Land* was an outcome of his unhappy marriage with Vivienne, it could also be said that it reflects the despair that his parents would never comprehend what had become so important to him—his poetry—although his mother was a published poet herself. Her first visit to England in the summer seemed to have contributed to his breakdown that autumn and the treatment in Switzerland during which he completed the writing of the poem that was to give him a central place as one of the twentieth century's most influential poet, *The Waste Land*. This success only heightened the sense of alienation from that parental couple—"breeding children whom they do not understand and who will never understand them".

But does it matter for us as therapists what Eliot thought about marriage and parenthood? In fact, we might ask: does it matter what marital psychotherapists themselves believe about the institution of marriage? The answer to this question is more complex than it might first appear. We have now reached an area that takes us to the outer limits of psychoanalysis, and it also brings us back to our starting point. That is, to a view of *marriage* as the capacity for mature, intimate relating. The question I want to puzzle over in the final chapter is whether Eliot's "making the best of a bad job" is to be understood in terms of his cynicism about the possibility of an ultimately meaningful relationship, or as the painful awareness of the ambivalence at the heart of what Klein called the depressive position. The question, does it matter?, inevitably raises the question of the role of values in psychoanalysis.

I hope that, with the introduction of this question of values linked with the dynamic that I am picturing as *narcissism ↔ marriage*, it has become clearer why we need to face this issue of Eliot's struggle, his two ways, and I want to do that in the final chapter in the context of termination and the aim of psychoanalytic therapy. We shall want to think back to that final scene in Act II where the dialogue between Reilly and Celia gives us the clearest insight into the views that shaped this play, views on the nature of human intimacy, indeed of the possibility of intimacy. In a sense one could say that conceptually that is the final, defining moment of the play.

However, in a theatrical sense the denouement of *The Cocktail Party* comes in the Act III, which was in fact added almost as an "after-thought" (Eliot originally called it an "epilogue") to the original version of the play (Browne, 1966, pp. 9, 25). Here we find the main characters of the original "cocktail party" gathered after some years. The mundane conversation builds in a desultory way towards the announcement of what has happened in the intervening time to Celia. This story of Celia presents us with what is usually seen as the "other" of Eliot's "two ways". Are there two ways, or is this a picture of the two paradoxical dimensions of human intimacy? This is a question that I want to consider using Shakespeare's *Othello* as a version of Eliot's "two ways".

# CHAPTER ELEVEN

# A sado-masochistic *folie à deux*

In this penultimate chapter, I want to return to the theoretical
structure that underpins the view of psychoanalytic therapy with
couples that I have been describing as a struggle to emerge from
narcissism towards marriage. By this point in the story, I hope the
reader can entertain an understanding of narcissism in which the
expression *narcissistic object relating* does not appear to be the oxy-
moron it might be in a different theoretical framework. That is, I am
assuming a view of narcissism which sees it not as an object-less
state, but rather as a way of relating. My aim in inviting the reader
on a journey through *The Winter's Tale*, the case study of the Webbs,
and *The Cocktail Party* has been to discover how plausible it is to see
in them portrayals of narcissistic object relating. When we turn in
the final chapter to the picture that Shakespeare paints in his play
*Othello*, we come, I suggest, to what might be described as the portrayal of the apotheosis of narcissistic relating. But before we look
more closely at that most disturbing of interlocking couple stories,
Othello and Desdemona, and Othello and Iago, I want to consider
some more of the complexity of forms of narcissistic relating.

In the retrospective on narcissism in this chapter, I want to turn first to the myth that gives narcissism its name: the myth of Echo and Narcissus. This myth is an intriguing portrait of a familiar dilemma, inviting us back and back again to wonder about how it is that the choice of a beloved, what is pictured as a falling-in-love, turns out to be something more like an identification, a being-the-same-as. The myth voices the uncomfortable truth that the wanting to be together contains a wanting to-be-the-same, and we recoil from what seems in the myth to be a caricature of that longing.

And yet this myth of Narcissus portrays something that echoes through our own personal experiences, as well as in what we experience in our consulting-rooms. For example, our poets articulate for us what I think we would all recognize as a common wish, a wish for the two to be identical, to be equal in the sense of being the same. Consider, for example, Eliot's poetic dedication of his last play, *The Elder Statesman*, to his second wife, Valerie, with whom he appears to have found contentment and happiness which for him had previously been so elusive. Eliot says that he dedicates this play to the person:

> To whom I owe the leaping delight
> That quickens my senses in our waking time
> And the rhythm that governs the repose of our sleeping time,
>     The breathing in unison
> Of lovers . . .
> Who think the same thoughts without need of speech
> And babble the same speech without need of meaning.
>
> [Eliot, 1969, p. 7]

I hasten to point out, especially since the poet here has inevitably taken us into his private life, that I do not mean to suggest that this experience of "oneness", so characteristic of moments of passion, is inherently problematic. What I wish to emphasize is the *dialectic* of that oneness with the moment of awakening to the reality of the separation, the otherness, which is less an antithesis than a necessary complement to the oneness. Or, as I have been suggesting, these two states can be pictured in an oscillating tension symbolized, following Bion, as *"narcissism ↔ marriage"*. Perhaps, at first glance, one might have thought that, in this formula, oneness was antithetical to marriage. However, marriage must recognize and make room for the awakening to the reality that, although two may *think the same thoughts, breathing in unison*, they are—and will remain—two separate human beings.

It is not the state of identification or oneness that is problematic but the rigidity that cannot also allow for the reality of difference, and thus it attacks and undermines that reality in a variety of ways. Marriage, as I am conceptualizing it, is the state of object relating that can tolerate the tensions of the oscillation between oneness and separation. Narcissism would then take the form either of the phantasy of the fusion of two people, or of the phantasy of the absolute isolation of the individual which results from experiencing separation as abandonment.

The exploration in this chapter will take us from a brief consideration of the Narcissus myth itself to some reflections on a kind of identification which is more like mimicry or imitation. It has been pictured as a "being stuck to the other", and consequently described as *adhesive identification*. And then I want to expand on the notion of intrusive projection as a kind of identification, an idea that has been the pivot for much of psychoanalytic thinking about disturbed couple relations. Complex permutations of these forms of narcissistic relating lead to the most disturbed couple patterns in which two people can neither live with each other nor live without each other. Finally, I want to look at the living in a kind of hell which has the quality of what Donald Meltzer terms a "claustrum" as well as at what can be described as sado-masochistic *folie-à-deux* relationships.

These disturbing patterns, as I am trying to make clear in this book, give some idea why psychoanalytic therapy with couples can be such a formidable enterprise. And yet they also suggest why some couples in particular may respond to a psychoanalytic approach concerned with challenging and unravelling these interlocking narcissistic defences. A psychoanalytic understanding allows us to appreciate how intransigent these patterns can become because they reflect a universal desire and persistent struggle to achieve intimacy. When, by way of illustration, I turn in the final chapter to Othello's version of Eliot's two ways, we will come face-to-face with an unbearably tragic picture of "two-becoming-one", a story that throughout bears the cruel marks of a turning to a sado-masochistic, *folie-à-deux*, solution to the longing for a "breathing in unison".

## Narcissus: a longing for the other and a hatred of separation

I want to begin with an interesting observation that Freud's conception of a period of primary narcissism in "Mourning and Melancholia" offers us (Freud, 1917e). It is a picture in which *"identification with* objects is almost indistinguishable from *the choice of* an object" (Meltzer, 1978a, *I*, 80, emphasis added). We do not need to take a detour into the history of psychoanalysis in order to be struck by the idea of a state in which it is difficult to distinguish between choosing someone and identifying with someone.

Freud said he borrowed the term "narcissism" from Havelock Ellis's discussion of the myth of Narcissus and Echo, although he credits Paul Näcke with coining this term (Freud, 1905d, p. 218). Subsequently the word has found a place in the vocabulary of this century far beyond the technical meaning that it has in psychoanalytic theory. It will be instructive to return for a moment to the myth of Narcissus itself. I am calling it a "myth", although it is interesting to note that Robert Graves suggested that it was a "sentimental fable" rather than what he called a "true myth", because, as he pointed out, it lacked a connection with public ritual (Graves, 1955, p. 12).

What is at stake here is whether or not we find in this story an articulation of something fundamental to human experience. The link with public ritual is significant because, one might say, ritual marks the existence of something genuinely shared. This was particularly the case in pre-modern societies, which were less susceptible to sentimental manipulation than is our media-dominated age. It is possible that this myth is in fact one of the most fundamental pictures of the human dilemma and in that sense is universally shared. As such, it has taken on a critical importance in contemporary psychoanalytic clinical theory, particularly in the object relations tradition influenced by Bion, and it is seen to complement the emphasis by classical psychoanalysis on the centrality of the Oedipus myth. In fact the two myths, I believe, are intimately related, and perhaps even interdependent.

At the heart of the story of Narcissus and Echo, we have the picture of an attractive young man with whom, as Graves has it, "anyone might excusably have fallen in love". Having heartlessly rejected many suitors of both sexes, including the nymph Echo, Narcissus finally falls in love with someone he sees as he gazes into a still pool, apparently unaware, as we might imagine an infant might be, that he was looking at his own reflected image. In the end, Narcissus is consumed by his unrequited longing, distraught at his possessing and yet not possessing this beautiful boy who awakens in him a passion he cannot bear. Echo, who has been condemned by Hera to being unable to use her own voice except to repeat the words of others, can only watch and repeat his final cry of "Alas!, Alas!" as he plunges a dagger into his breast (Graves, 1955, pp. 286–288).

Surely in this myth we see Narcissus as *longing for* the other, not *wanting to be* the other. We might say that the mystery of the state of mind of Narcissus in this myth is like the mystery of the state of mind of Oedipus. Surely Oedipus must know—or does he, or should he—that this desirable woman whom he would marry is in fact his mother. And surely Narcissus must know that this beautiful young man for whom he longs is in fact his reflection.

We have some idea why Oedipus would not want to know what he appears not to know, as we understand the wish to deny the reality of the divide between the generations. At one level, the story of Oedipus is the drama of the little boy who wants to be his father's equal. Hating his smallness and inadequacy, his vulnerability and dependence, he unconsciously achieves his wish to be identical with his father. Unnoticed, apparently by him or anyone else, he takes his father's place. One uncomfortable aspect of the difference between the generations is that it marks the reality of procreation, that we are the *out-come* of our parents' intercourse, having entered the world helpless, life itself continuing to be precarious but for those on whom we depend *absolutely*.

This familiar story is complex enough, but, since the radical challenge to our assumption about the ground of our anxiety in the work of Wilfred Bion and Donald Meltzer, we must ask what it is about, for example, this dependence on those who give us life that makes it so emotionally intolerable. Through an almost incomprehensibly arduous reorienting of our framework of assumptions, Bion pointed us away from frustration and disappointment towards the difficulty of acknowledging emotional experience itself. Dependence can lead to either frustration or satisfaction, either of which defines an emotion that can be felt to be unbearable. We know that frustration is linked with mental pain, but it is only with difficulty that we have come to acknowledge Melanie Klein's insight that satisfaction can lead to the mental pain of envy. In Meltzer's *Apprehension of Beauty*, we are challenged to go even further and to consider that the aesthetic impact of the primal object on which we are dependent, the mother, is itself an overwhelming experience, as if the beauty were too painful to look at (Meltzer, 1988). In that book, Meltzer explores many clinical illustrations of what is meant by "wildly recoil from the impact of the aesthetic of the object".

If we were to approach the story of Narcissus in the spirit of Bion and Meltzer, what might we imagine him as wishing to deny? Why would he harbour an unconscious ambition to be the equal of the one for whom he longs, equal in the sense of "identical to"? Or would we say that he, unconsciously, wants this other to be a version of himself? It is interesting to consider whether we might be reading back into the myth the assumption of our popular notion of narcissism as a kind of infatuation with oneself. But if we suppose that a myth like this carries an unconscious wisdom in the very shape of the story and the images, then I think we must take seriously the picture of the *longing for the other* at the heart of the story.

Because the loved one in the Narcissus story turns out, of necessity, to be the same gender, it has been linked, as we shall see, with homo-sexuality. I think we need to be able to distinguish between specific questions of same-gender object choice and the larger question of the recognition of a fundamental difference of the other. Is it possible that the second great reality that we find so unbearable—the difference between the sexes—carries a universal meaning quite apart from questions of heterosexuality and homosexuality in a conventional sense? Is it possible that the difference between the sexes, like the difference between the generations, is a *locus* of both the unbearable beauty of, as well as the unbearable dependency on, an *other*? If so, these differences locate an emotional tension, an emotional experience, the reality of which must be attacked and undermined.

Compare this picture with the distinction about the "direction" of identification made by Laplanche and Pontalis in their discussion of this most critical of concepts in psychoanalysis:

> In everyday usage, identification in this last sense [identification of oneself with] overlaps a whole group of psychological concepts—

e.g. imitation, *Einfühlung* (empathy), sympathy, mental contagion, projection, etc.

It has been suggested for the sake of clarity that a distinction be drawn within this field, according to the direction in which identification operates, between an identification that is *heteropathic* (Scheler) and *centripetal* (Wallon), where the subject identifies his own self with the other, and an *idiopathic* and *centrifugal* variety in which the subject identifies the other with himself. Finally, in cases where both of these tendencies are present at once, we are said to be dealing with a more complex form of identification, one which is sometimes invoked to account for the constitution of a "we". [Laplanche & Pontalis, 1973, p. 206]

Echo presents us with an image of someone condemned to being able to give voice only to the words of others, while Narcissus offers us an image of someone who seems able to love only an other who is a reflection of himself. We could say that these two represent the "heteropathic" and "idiopathic" directions of identifying with an other. What I want to call attention to is the fact that these are pictures of "object-relating", albeit object-relating of a peculiar kind. This corresponds with Freud's first use of the term "narcissism" to account for homosexual object-choice:

[They] pass through a phase of very intense but short-lived fixation to a woman (usually their mother), and, after leaving this behind, they identify themselves with a woman and take *themselves* as their sexual object. That is to say, proceeding from a basis of narcissism, they look for a young man who resembles themselves and whom *they* may love as their mother loved *them*. [Freud, 1905d, p. 145 n.1, added 1910]

Note that in this picture Freud includes identifications in both directions in reference to the self–other link: on the one hand the object chosen resembles the self, while on the other hand the self in this relationship resembles the mother whose love the self seeks to recreate. Whatever one may make of this as a description of the unconscious dynamics in same-gender object choice, it is interesting to think about it as a description of narcissistic object choice. It retains the formal structure of a genuine object relationship, in that we have both lover and beloved. To put it into the form of a simple children's drama, it is as if I were to say to you:

"I'll teach you about true love. You be me and I'll be my mother. I will love you [playing me] as you [remember, that's really me played by you] should be loved, something I know about since I know how I should be loved. And you will love me [playing my mother] as I [of course, I mean my mother] should be loved, again something I know about since I loved my mother, and I am [playing] my mother and you are [playing] me."

As director, producer, scriptwriter, and one of the two actors in this scenario, mine is the only authentic voice, the only point of view. Constructed in this way, there is no need for an imaginative attempt to picture anyone else's experience or point of view. Creative imagination, in the sense of my needing to imagine someone else's point of view, is not necessary, because the only experience and point of view represented is mine, and that I can know, or believe I know, with absolute certainty.

When we encounter certainty in our patients, or indeed in ourselves, about the experience, feelings, beliefs, and points of view of the other, we need I think to consider the function of a need for certainty. The person who is subjectively so certain about something *apparently outside* himself or herself is, in one sense, right in that certainty—at least insofar as one can be certain what one feels, thinks, believes. The certainty itself is a mark of the absence of an other, either in the sense that for the moment the two have become one, or in the sense that the reality of the other is ignored, denied, or in some other way undermined.

The distinction that marks the relating to a genuine other is the moment, as Meltzer puts it so evocatively, "when an object can be given its freedom to come and go as it will" (Meltzer, 1978b, p. 468). In his brief but remarkably evocative paper, "A Note on Introjective Processes", Meltzer links this capacity for relinquishing the need for controlling one's objects with the process that results in a different kind of identification, introjective identification. I believe that this concept is at the heart of an understanding of what Melanie Klein called the depressive position and Ronald Britton elaborated as triangular space. It is a remarkable idea, and an even more remarkable experience when one discovers in one's patients, or more importantly in oneself, this capacity to allow the object "its freedom to come and go as it will". We will return in the final chapter to this way of thinking—a way, one might say, of thinking about the aim of the psychoanalytic process, when we consider criteria for the termination of therapy. But first I want to sketch a picture that is evolving of what contributes to the couples' *folie à deux*.

## Imitation and adhesive identification

As we have seen, to allow one's external objects their freedom, one must first have the experience of a relationship with one's internal objects in which their freedom is a genuine possibility. The anxieties attendant on that possibility lead to the narcissistic defensive structures that we have been exploring. I want to look more closely now at a form of narcissistic relating which makes use of clinging, imitative attachment. We have a vivid picture of just such a primitive struggle with separation anxieties in *The Cocktail Party*. Edward cries to Lavinia that he experiences her as engulfing him, as a "python", an "octopus": "Must I become after all what you would make me?" We have seen in the last three chapters the vivid picture that Eliot paints of "two becoming one [flesh]" as Edward protests of his wife that he "cannot live without her" because she has made him "incapable of having any existence of [his] own" (Eliot, 1950, p. 101, I.3.460–461; p. 112, II.155–156).

In their description of the phenomenology of a form of narcissistic identification characterized by imitation, Esther Bick and Donald Meltzer coined the term "adhesive identification". As I have noted in chapter three, Meltzer suggests that "intolerance to separation can be said to exist when there is present an absolute dependence on an external object in order to maintain integration". Note again that here is meant not just "separation" in the sense of the absence of the object, but in the presence of a genuinely separate other. This external object functions as virtually a *part of the self*, in this case as the containing *skin* that holds the self together. He gives a graphic description of this serious psychopathology in children:

> This can be seen in autistic and schizophrenic children in whom the need for physical contact, or constant attention, or to be held in contact by constant verbalisation, reveals the absence of the psychic equivalent of the skin. [Meltzer, 1967, p. 14]

Although I am not suggesting that Eliot literally intended to portray an "autistic" or "schizophrenic" character in Edward, we can talk about, as Tustin does, "pockets of autism" in otherwise less disturbed patients (Tustin, 1991). Edward gives voice to this sense of the other, not as a genuine other, but instead functioning as a "second skin". Without her he says he "began to dissolve", "to cease to exist". This form of identification plays a significant role in the disturbed relationships that we see in the couples who turn to us for therapy, in some ways as significant in different ways as the role played by the now more familiar (and certainly more discussed) process of projective identification. Little attention has been paid to this adhesive form of identification in the literature of psychoanalytic psychotherapy with couples, and yet it helps us to understand some of the dynamics that we see most often in our work with couples.

In Meltzer's description of the phenomenon of adhesive identification, he calls attention to a peculiar observation. Some children and adults seemed to lack a sense of internal space, instead evidencing what he characterizes as an impression of "two-dimensionality". Objects were related to primarily through contact or lack of contact. He further points out that such a "two-dimensional" self would, in the language of Bion, "have no means for distinguishing between an absent good-object and the presence of a persecuting absent-object" (Meltzer et al., 1975, p. 225).

We could also say that there would be a similar failure to distinguish between a present object "with a mind of its own", unwilling (or unable) to do what was wanted or needed by this self, and the "presence of a persecuting absent-object". Such a present *independent* object may feel particularly persecuting, although in desperation contact is more important than the quality of the contact.

Interestingly, in reference to these adhesive states Gaddini argues that the aim of imitation "seems to be that of re-establishing in a magical and omnipotent way the fusion of self with object" (Gaddini, 1969, p. 21). But it is important to note that this state of mind is linked with the obverse state. Not only are separation anxieties countered by being "stuck to" or "fused with" the object in unconscious phantasy, but there is correspondingly no door that can be closed against this fusion happening (Adams, 1997).

This can be seen more clearly when we consider what constitutes the capacity for internal space, for three-dimensionality. Meltzer suggests that the move from a two- to a three-dimensional structure of mental functioning is linked with not just an awareness of orifices but, more importantly, with the struggle to guard or close those orifices. This is experienced first in the encounter with an object that can protect itself against intrusion, closing its orifices against an intrusive attempt to penetrate. This experience can lead to a similar capacity subsequently in the self.

> The potentiality of a space, and thus the potentiality of a container, can only be realized once a sphincter-function has become effective.... His material [the child patient "Barry" under discussion] shows with particular clarity that the capacity of the object [Barry's therapist] to protect and thus to control its own orifices is a precondition for the self to make a move in that direction, of continence as well as of resistance to aggressive penetration. [Meltzer et al., 1975, p. 226]

It often happens in therapy with a couple that we find one or both partners in a state of mind that in some ways resembles that of these young patients so vividly described in *Explorations in Autism*, especially in this characteristic which I am suggesting can be understood as the obverse of imitation or mimicry. The obverse to a lack of a "skin" would be some door that can be closed, so that one does not feel defined by the other. And this is true both for the self and for the self's objects. If my object cannot preserve itself, its difference, in the face of my passion, how can I be myself without the other becoming my reflection? If I cannot preserve myself, my difference, in the face of the other's passion, how can I prevent my becoming a reflection of my object, or my object's desires?

One might be tempted to picture adhesive identification in terms of the defence against separation anxieties, a way of keeping "stuck to" the object that is threatening to disappear. But what we see in couples in therapy is, as I am suggesting, the obverse, a picture of what it is like "successfully" being "stuck to" the object or having the object "stuck to" oneself. In fact, this is one version of the sadomasochistic *folie-à-deux* relationship. This brief description of one couple I saw with a co-therapist is typical of such an "adhesive hell":

> Mr and Mrs M both protested desperately against the feeling that the other "defined" them. Although this is one of the most com-

mon complaints from couples in therapy, there was a special intensity in the way Mrs M would interrupt whenever Mr M described, from his point of view, something about her, what she had said, or done, or meant. Whenever I or my co-therapist would comment that of course he was speaking from "his point of view", we discovered through many painful exchanges that these words had no emotional meaning for her. Especially in moments of intense emotions, the notion of "a point of view" was a meaningless abstraction for her. It was if she were open and exposed, with no adequate protection from what he said.

At times she would literally put her hands over her ears as if to close those orifices to block out his words. And there was one particularly shocking time when she actually began to scream, pleading for him to stop talking, as if his words were painful missiles assaulting her through her ears. It was not an aggressive, hostile scream, but the scream of someone in the kind of intense pain caused by a high-pitched piercing sound.

It was also gradually possible to talk with her about her belief that my co-therapist and I were also as open and exposed to his omnipotent, defining words as was she. What he said at those moments seemed to her to have the capacity to define what was real for us. Clearly she could not entertain with any emotional conviction the possibility that we might be able to listen carefully and sympathetically to him, while thinking for ourselves and having our own point of view. His words simply were an "aggressive penetration", although "penetration" perhaps gives the wrong impression. It was not as if his words got inside her, but that they simply were her, as if she were as thin as a sheet of paper.

But I do not mean to give the impression that she was alone in this experience of having no idea of the concept of "a point of view". If her version of this relationship had an almost hysterical quality, an endless flow of words defining him to stop him from defining her, his version had an empty, passive quality. The only way he could keep her from defining him was to absent himself, either physically or emotionally. He was able in the session to act almost as if were a robot, puzzled about what it was that she wanted of him and trying to feel whatever it was that she was wanting him to feel.

If anything, it was even harder for him to entertain the possibility that he might listen to her without being defined by her. He never quite understood what was expected of him, only that nothing he did satisfied her. Yet it was so obvious to him that she must be right about all this "emotional stuff" that his only question was how not to ignite her touch paper. "Keep a low profile" was his motto, since he could not begin to understand "what she was on about". You can imagine that his capacity, as she put it, to "blank her", left her infuriated, while he stared at her uncomprehendingly when she erupted in desperation. Often at such moments he would catch the eye of my co-therapist or me, surreptitiously raising his eyebrows and tilting his head in a gesture of contempt. It never occurred to him that not only was his contempt not hidden, but his "blankness" conveyed his contempt in the most sadistic way imaginable.

When he did make an effort to listen and to accommodate her and her feelings—which he felt was most of the time—his role seemed to be to decipher what he was supposed to do, or say, or, insofar as he understood what it meant, to feel. He felt that when his attempt at compliance was successful, things went along reasonably well between them. This would last, he would tell us ruefully, until in a moment of forgetfulness he would say something from his own "point of view" and the explosive cycle would start all over again. For the most part, however, his watchful caution prevailed as he chose his words carefully, saying what he thought she wanted to hear.

It is interesting to compare this with the exchange between Edward and Lavinia in *The Cocktail Party* about his passivity to which she forms the perfect complement (pp. 92–93, I.3.279–298). I mention this scene in which Edward's repeated "fitting in" with his wife, his "giving in" to her, mirrored by her "giving in" to him, because this humorous and all-too-familiar exchange, repeated almost daily by couples in our consulting-rooms, reminds us of the ordinariness of these dynamics. When we talk about severe psychopathologies, pockets of autism, and narcissistic object-relating, we can forget how ordinary in one sense these dynamics are. Although we find that the scene with Edward and Lavinia makes us laugh, perhaps wryly, it is difficult, even impossible, to find anything humorous in the scene with Mr and Mrs M. Instead of humour, the presence of which might mark the possibility of some emotional distance, the room is at times electric with tension as his passivity sets off a fire-storm in her.

If these couples were to develop a sense of humour about their dilemma, they would have to be in a very different state of mind. We might hope that couples in therapy have opportunities for standing back and seeing themselves the way the audience can see Edward and Lavinia. However, to do that requires a sense of space, of internal space, which in turn requires a capacity to observe oneself and the theatre of one's internal world. When Edward says that he doesn't mind where they go on their honeymoon, and thinks he means it as a compliment, or when Mr M watches his words in a desperate attempt to say and be just what he thinks his wife wants, there seems to be no sense of space in either of them. For each there is only a relationship, or better a "connection", with an other to which he can more or less happily adapt and attach himself—or not!

In these couples where each partner has this kind of adhesive connection with the other, we might describe the resulting relationship as a kind of adhesive *folie à deux*. In fact, the most intractable couple dramas that we now more often see in our consulting-rooms are those in which there is a mixture of this two-dimensional adhesive *folie à deux* with aspects of more three-dimensional intrusive projections to form a sado-masochistic *folie à deux*.

## The claustrum of intrusive projections

We began our exploration of the intrusive projections that contribute to these intractable *folie-à-deux* couple relationships in chapter six in a brief retrospective on projective identification. In order to think more about the complex phenomena connected with the notion of projective identification, I want to turn now to some distinctions that Donald Meltzer has drawn in his examination of Bion's fundamentally important contributions to the subject. Bion's concept of *con-*

*tainer–contained* has so coloured our use of the notion of *projective identification* that it has become common to assume that this unconscious phantasy of splitting off parts of the self and projecting them has as its aim the wish to communicate. But here, as throughout our exploration of narcissistic relating, it matters whether there can be a tolerating of the anxieties linked with the acknowledgement of a genuine other.

There can be communication only if the person acting as a "container", in Bion's language, can bear to be the recipient of the disturbing projections and still sustain an ability to think about the experience. That may be an increasingly difficult state to achieve and maintain the more intrusive the projections, especially in what Meltzer calls their "projective" aspects as distinct from their "identificatory" aspects (Meltzer, 1992, p. 4).

The *identificatory* aspects concern the transformation in the self in the omnipotent phantasy of projective identification—such as grandiosity, psychotic depressive states, hypochondria, confusional states. The effect on the self of this splitting-off parts of the self has been the major focus in the, by now very large, literature in the Kleinian tradition on the psychopathologies of this primitive defence. The examination of what Meltzer calls the *projective* aspects has, I think, largely been his unique contribution to our understanding of the phenomenon of these intrusive processes. I am particularly interested in this distinction in this context because of its implications for the couple relationship in which these intrusive projections play a significant role.

The so-called projective aspects concern the nature of the phantasied experiences when *inside* that phantasy world into which one has intruded, the "claustrophobic" aspects. What is it like in there? What are the unconscious phantasies about the inside of the object into which one has intruded that result from this unconscious phantasy of intrusion? Questions such as these lead us from what I think are more familiar issues of the difficulty of being the recipient of intrusive projections associated with, for example, the grandiosity of the projections, to something even more disturbing. That is, these projective aspects of the intrusiveness mean that the recipient of the projections is in a position in which it is difficult—sometimes, I think, virtually impossible—to escape being drawn into what Meltzer describes as a "claustrum".

In publications over the past decade and a half, Meltzer has proposed a modification of our terminology, moving from a *quantitative* distinction in terms like "massive" projective identification to a *qualitative* distinction. Thus he proposes some definitions that are helpful to consider, although they have not entered the mainstream of psychoanalytic discourse:

*Projective identification*—the unconscious phantasy implementing the non-lexical aspects of language and behaviour, aimed at communication rather than action (Bion).

*Intrusive identification*—the unconscious omnipotent phantasy, mechanism of defence (Melanie Klein).

*Claustrum*—the inside of the object penetrated by intrusive identification.

*Container*—the inside of the object receptive of projective identification.

[Meltzer et al., 1986, p. 69]

In order to explore the significance of the notion of "claustrum" adequately, I would have to establish the link between intrusive projections into *external* objects and intrusive projections into *internal* objects. For our purposes here, I will simply assume that projections into external objects are dependent in some fundamental ways on projective processes that are going on internally with internal objects. Some readers may find this idea too condensed to be useful, and I can only apologize by saying that I have decided that the kind of exploration of this topic that I think needs to be done is simply beyond the boundaries of this book. Therefore, I will be alluding to Meltzer's seminal 1992 book, *The Claustrum: An Investigation of Claustrophobic Phenomena*, focusing on implications for the couple relationship.

The critical "arena" for our understanding of these intrusive projections is the *interior of internal objects*, specifically the internal mother. It is interesting that Meltzer uses the term "geography" to describe this "interior", emphasizing the spatial quality of experience in unconscious phantasy—that is, that the "internal world" and "internal objects" necessarily have a psychic reality which is "spatial". But it is also interesting, in passing, given the etymological meaning of *geo-graphy* as the charting of *Gaea*, the "deep-breasted earth" whom Hesiod described as the most primitive omnipotent source and mother of all life—mother of the universe, the gods, and the human race. This is confirmed in the Homeric hymn in which the poet says: "I shall sing of Gaea, universal mother, firmly founded, the oldest of divinities" (Larousse, 1959, pp. 87–89). Even this etymological sense of the "geography" suggests that it is in some fundamental way the "mapping" of inside of the *internal mother*.

Herbert Rosenfeld recognized phantasies of living in an unreal world that has qualities of a structure suggesting that it is a representation of the inside of an object, the mother (Rosenfeld, 1987, pp. 168–169). John Steiner also notes: "Sometimes it is possible to get information about deeper phantasies in which psychic retreats appear as spaces inside objects or part-objects. There may be phantasies of retreating to the mother's womb, anus, or breast, sometimes experienced as a desirable but forbidden place" (Steiner, 1993, p. 8). Steiner also reminds us of Rey's discussion of the "claustro–agoraphobic" dilemma and the "marsupial space" (Steiner, 1993, pp. 52–53).

The geography that is central, therefore, to the "phantasy geography" of the self is the geography of the internal regions, or, as Meltzer has it, the "compartments" of the internal mother. The view of the inside of the internal mother (and critically, the means by which this view is arrived at) forms a template for all relationships. Thus in his exploration of the "projective" aspects of projective identification, Meltzer is suggesting that the *mode* of entry *in phantasy* into the mother's body determines the quality of the experience of the phantasy of the nature of what is found *inside her body*. This stands in contrast with the respect for the mother as an other who is known *only* through imagination, not through omnipotent intrusion in phantasy.

This omnipotent "knowledge" of the internal mother—and consequently, because it is a "template" for important relationships, of the "interior" of the other in an intimate relationship—creates the sense of living, through intrusive identification, in what Meltzer calls a *claustrum*. He notes that, when the part of the personality ensconced in the claustrum gains control of consciousness, marked changes occur:

> The experience of the outside world becomes dominated by the claustrophobic atmosphere, meaning that the person, in whatever situation he finds himself, feels trapped. Job, marriage, holiday, on

trains, buses or lifts, in personal or casual relations, in restaurants or theatres—in every area there is a tangible atmosphere of catastrophe imminent and "No Exit" (Sartre). [Meltzer, 1992, p. 119]

The reference to Sartre's *No Exit* is of particular interest here in the light of our discussion of *The Cocktail Party* and what I am suggesting is Eliot's gloss on Sartre's notion that "hell is other people". When Edward cries out that "hell is oneself / the others merely projections", could we say that he is trapped in a *claustrum*? And what would that mean? How would describing Edward's dilemma in that way add anything to our understanding of him, or of the relationship between him and Lavinia, or, for that matter, between him and Celia? To put the question I am raising in a different form: what is the relationship between Meltzer's description of the experience of the outside world as dominated by a "claustrophobic atmosphere" and the hypothesis of a deeply unconscious process of intrusive identification?

Meltzer is suggesting a correlation between the latter and the former. As I discussed in chapter seven, we are often presented in sessions with couples with "enacted dreams" in the form of stories about their experiences together. This means that we are left to infer or re-create the unconscious phantasies from the way they experience each other and their shared world. I propose then that what we primarily observe are phenomena like the "claustrophobic atmosphere" of their shared world. We are left to imagine the unconscious intrusive identification that may underlie that claustrophobic atmosphere.

With a fictional character like Edward in *The Cocktail Party*, by definition we have no access to any unconscious phantasies, whether of intrusive identification or whatever. Similarly, we have no reliable access to Eliot's state of mind as he created this character and this dialogue. In this we are in the same situation as we are in with our couples in therapy. We are limited to what we observe, and we do well to let modesty rule our speculations about the underlying unconscious processes. It is the joy of literature, and what intrigues us most, that we are at liberty to let our imagination roam over the text (or the material that couples present to us), remembering that we are in the realm of *imagination*. When we choose to share some of our imaginings with our couples, it is with the aim of stimulating their own capacity for curiosity and imagination, which in turn can create a sense of space between them and their different versions of shared experiences.

Intrusive projections leave no space for the imagination. This helps us to understand, I think, the fundamental difference between a genuine intimacy with the other and a "pseudo-intimacy" which is actually a narcissistic form of relating. The former is based on the reality that the other is known *only* from the outside. The latter is based on the phantasy of getting *inside* the other. Meltzer invites us to consider the difference between the picture of the inside of the internal mother which results from the use of *imagination* and the one that results from the phantasy of omnipotent intrusion. Seen from the "outside"—that is, through the use of imagination—the primary quality of this region of the internal mother is "richness", having the nuances of "generosity, receptiveness, aesthetic reciprocity; under-standing and all possible knowledge; the locus of symbol formation, and thus of art, poetry, imagination" (Meltzer, 1992, p. 72). However, "experienced" from the inside influenced by the motives of intru-sion, Meltzer suggests a very different picture:

> Generosity becomes *quid pro quo*, receptiveness becomes inveigle-ment, reciprocity becomes collusion, understanding becomes penetration of secrets, knowledge becomes information, symbol formation becomes metonymy, art becomes fashion. [Meltzer, 1992, pp. 72–73]

The imaginative *knowing* of the other, inspired by an imaginative *knowing* of the internal mother, is constructed necessarily out of ele-ments of experience of the external world, respecting the privacy of the interior of the mother. It is characterized by an attitude that Bion has brought into our vocabulary from his reading of the letters of the poet John Keats. Keats described this attitude of mind, of which he believed Shakespeare was the prime exemplar, as *negative capability*: "that is, when [one] is capable of being in uncertainties, mysteries, doubts, without any irritable reaching after fact and reason" (Bion, 1970, p. 125). No matter how intimate the "knowledge" of the other, it is always characterized by uncertainties, mysteries, and doubts.

We know, however, that in many of the couples whom we see, there is a sense of *certainty* in the so-called knowledge of the other, a "certainty" often characterized by boredom and complacency, or persecution and tyranny, depending on what is omnisciently "known". This certainty, resulting as it does from a phantasy of omnipotent intrusion, is characterized by what Meltzer elsewhere called "the delusion of clarity of insight" (Meltzer, 1976). We have all seen it many times in couples in therapy, and it is closely related to the complaint of intrusive attack on the privacy and integrity one partner makes against the other. Ultimately, it is also the basis for the physical as well as psychological violence seen in many of these couples.

These are couples with whom it feels almost impossible for us to think for ourselves because we feel drawn into and trapped in their claustrum world with them. As therapists, we are not only the "recipients" of this intrusive projective identification, we are also *in the presence* of their intrusive identification with their internal objects which is so profoundly powerful that we often feel no option but to be drawn into acting as claustrum dwellers with them in the nightmare worlds in which they are trapped.

In such a nightmare world, our countertransference experiences are sometimes almost too much to bear. And if what we might call this *claustrum transference* results in such a difficult countertransference experience (although I recognize that this idea involves some reformulation of the understanding of transference), what must this claustrum transference lead to in the couple relationship? It leads, I suggest, to something that Donald Meltzer has described as *"mutual projective identification in action"*, and what I am talking about as interlocking complementary intrusive projections.

## Complementary intrusive projections

In a recent interview, Meltzer suggested that *"mutual projective identification in action"* is an important couple phenomenon distinct from the schizoid mechanism that Melanie Klein described (Meltzer, 1995, p. 111). I quote him at length here again, because the implications require us to re-examine some of our fundamental assumptions about primitive processes of projection and identification in the couple relationship. Meltzer observes:

> I think . . . there is also a phenomenon that has a strong resemblance to [projective identification] that is really mutual projective

identification in action, and it seems to give rise to what we call a *folie-à-deux* relationship. In the case of couples, it can give rise to sadomasochism, which is probably its most frequent phenomenology.... This form of fusion by projective identification seems to be different from the schizoid mechanism that Mrs Klein was talking about. It seems to be really a rather sophisticated mechanism and much more closely connected with hysterical and obsessional phenomena than with schizoid mechanisms, as far as I can tell. [Meltzer, 1995, pp. 110–111]

Without taking up in detail Meltzer's suggestion that this *folie-à-deux* relationship seems connected with hysterical and obsessional phenomena, I just want to note that we see in couples like Mr and Mrs M that each tries futilely to control the other, although Mr M's emotional withdrawal seems more closely linked with an overt obsessionality. What seems like Mrs M's hysterical response to his blankness may, I think, be related to what I discussed in chapter two when we considered the phenomenon of the "impenetrable other". There I noted that either the infant, faced with an object that cannot take in its desperate projections, makes increasingly violent attempts to get through to this impenetrable object, or it withdraws to the blankness of a hopeless situation that it cannot face. Mr and Mrs M seem to represent both poles of that dynamic.

At this point in my attempt to give more content to the idea of a *folie à deux* that takes us beyond the basic psychiatric definition of a shared paranoid disorder, I want to direct our attention to the question of the experience of being the recipient of intrusive projections. We are by now accustomed to thinking of projections as having the potential for unconscious communication, at least projections that are intimately linked with a process of identification—how I identify myself and how I identify the other. And yet, in Melanie Klein's original description in 1946 of the phenomenon that she wanted to bring to the attention of the psychoanalytic world, it would have been hard for the ordinary analyst to see how there could be any potential for communication

Consider again Melanie Klein's observations that the kind of projection she wanted to describe were projections, in unconscious phantasy, of "excrements and bad parts of the self" which were meant, in that unconscious phantasy, "not only to injure but also to control and to take possession of the object" (Klein, 1946, p. 8). It is intuitively obvious why one might want to get rid of parts of the self, whether substances or emotions felt to be poisonous and dangerous, but why does one want to "control and take possession" of the object into which these substances or emotions are projected?

As we saw in chapter two, projective identification is a dynamic of the pleasure-ego, to use Freud's language, which has the unconscious aim to "gerrymander" the boundaries of self and other. As Melanie Klein put it in reference to the phantasy of projecting these bad "excrements and bad parts of the self": "In so far as the mother comes to contain the bad parts of the self, she is *not felt to be a separate individual* but is felt to be *the bad self*" (Klein, 1946, p. 8, emphasis added). The anal quality of this dynamic is clear. It is as if we hear a "superego-ish" parent saying "control yourself", your anger or whatever, and the child responds, "it wasn't me, it was him/her"— "and I'm doing my best to control him/her".

What is it like to be on the other end of that kind of projection, a projection in which someone peremptorily defines both himself or herself *and me* without so much as a by-your-leave? We have seen that Bion's introduction of the concept of the container–contained relationship gives us a way of thinking about these intrusive projections which allows for the possibility that they can function as a primitive form of communication. But again that is true *only if* the person who is the recipient of these projections can act as a "container" in Bion's sense can bear to be the recipient of the disturbing projections in the sense of sustaining a capacity for thinking. In the words of Betty Joseph, projective identification "*can* act as a communication whatever its motivation"—that is, "whether it is 'aimed' at communicating a state of mind or at entering and controlling and attacking the recipient" (Joseph, 1989, p. 175).

In his exposition of Bion's clinical thinking, Donald Meltzer captures some of the flavour of what it is like to be on the other end of intrusive and unwelcome projective identification. We might schematize his comments as a three-part experience for a therapist: (1) "the experience of having been manipulated to play a role in someone else's phantasy"; (2) "the realisation of [it] which is accompanied by *anxiety* and *humiliation* leading to *retaliatory* impulse"; and (3) *not* acting on that impulse while remaining able to think about what is happening to me and how I am feeling (Meltzer, 1978a, *III*, p. 14).

This "retaining a balanced outlook", to use Bion's language we discussed earlier, *not acting out* these retaliatory impulses, is a central part of our responsibility to be an adequate emotional *container* for our patients, no matter how intrusive the projections. In a couple relationship, we sometimes see not only a lack of this capacity to acknowledge the truth of the other's experience without retaliation, but a counterprojective process as part of the unconscious retaliation. If the truth of the other, so to speak, is disowned and intrusively projected into me, it is perhaps not so surprising that it can feel as if I were being manipulated to play a role in the other's phantasy. The anxiety and humiliation that that may tend to induce in the recipient of the projection means, it might be imagined, that the impulse to retaliate may correspondingly be very strong.

Recognizing this impulse to retaliate when it feels difficult or even impossible to tolerate intrusive projections still leaves the question as to the form of the retaliation. One option, as we have already seen, is found in Michael Feldman's notion of an "impenetrable" object— that is, one form of retaliation can simply be to reject the intrusive projection (Feldman, 1989; Fisher, 1993). Although its aim—consciously, at least, may not be retaliation, it can produce an intense desperation escalating into more and more violent projections. The aim of the impenetrable barrier may be to fend off the intrusive projections, but my experience with couples would lead me to think that its unconscious aggression suggests retaliation. The partner of an impenetrable other certainly seems to me to experience this "blanking off" as retaliatory.

But sometimes the response to intrusive projections goes beyond this being impenetrable. The dynamic can be even more insidious. When we talk about responses to intrusive projections or projective identification, we are in effect talking about *countertransference*. For help conceptually with an analysis of countertransference, I want to turn here to the complex exposition by Heinrich Racker of two kinds of responses to a transference experience, what he called the "concordant" and the "complementary" countertransference. In the former, the analyst identifies, using Freud's terminology, "his ego with the patient's ego". He goes on to suggest that in this *concordant* countertransference, the analyst identifies "each part of his personality with the corresponding part in the patient's personality—his id with the patient's id, his ego with the ego, his superego with the superego". In *complementary* (a term that Racker credits to Helene Deutsch) countertransference, "there exist also highly important identifications of the analyst's ego with the patient's internal objects, for example, with the superego" (Racker, 1968, p. 134).

It should be noted that here Racker uses the term "complementary" in a very specific technical sense: the analyst's identification with an internal object of the patient. "The complementary identifications", he suggests, "are produced by the fact that the patient treats the analyst as an internal (projected) object, and in consequence the analyst feels treated as such; that is, he identifies with this object" (Racker, 1968, p. 135). He goes on to make an interesting point regarding what he sees as the relationship between the concordant and the complementary identifications:

> The complementary identifications are closely connected with the destiny of the concordant identifications: it seems that to the degree to which the analyst fails in the concordant identifications and rejects them certain complementary identifications become intensified. It is clear that rejection of a part or tendency in the analyst himself,—his aggressiveness, for instance—may lead to a rejection of the patient's aggressiveness (whereby this concordant identification fails) and that such a situation leads to a greater complementary identification with the patient's rejecting object, towards which this aggressive impulse is directed. [Racker, 1968, p. 135]

Racker's analysis of the dynamics of these two kinds of countertransference implies that intrusive projections or projective identification tend to find objects that are both unconsciously receptive and, at the same time, rejecting. That is, when one splits off a part of the self that I have described as a "subjective" aspect of the self—say, "feeling aggressive", to use Racker's example—the recipient of the projection tends to resonate with the projection. Some people call it the "hook" on which the projection is hung. The recipient of the projection, we might say, identifies with the projection. That is one sense in which it is a "projective identification".

We might also think of this in terms of an unconscious "wisdom" that recognizes in a couple the unconscious wish to be the same, their unconscious desire to avoid separation and separateness. This works well when the subjective aspect of the self is, say, a feeling loving. It would be the counterpart of Edward and Lavinia's shared belief that one could never love and the other could never be loved. In the falling-in-love, both the "loving" and the "loveable" aspects of the self can be projected and accepted in an escalating illusion of oneness.

But when in analysis what is projected by the patient is a feeling of aggressiveness, then the analyst who is not feeling aggressive, as Racker points out, may be disinclined to identify with the patient. In his language, the "concordant identification" fails. The patient does not feel understood. What is worse is that not only is the analyst an "impenetrable" object, but unconsciously, Racker suggests, the analyst becomes identified with the patient's rejecting object against whom the aggressive feelings had been directed. The failure of one kind of identification, the concordant, leads to the unwanted success of another unconscious identification, the complementary.

This is a complex dynamic, and I do not want to belabour the point. I think that the reader will soon enough recognize it in his or her own clinical experience. The point I want to emphasize is just how insidious as well as complex such a dynamic is when there is no one to turn to for help in tolerating intrusive projections without retaliating in this most damaging of ways. One has somehow to find a way to "step aside" from this dynamic emotionally, and sometimes that requires finding an actual "third" to facilitate that creation of mental space. Even those whose professional discipline has meant an extensive experience of personal analysis can find that the emotions of the moment flood the couple relationship, destroying, at least for that moment, the "triangular space" essential for one—in Bion's language—to retain a balanced outlook and not (unconsciously) retaliate. A psychoanalytic training does not mean that we escape falling into these retaliatory patterns. The question is only how well we can recover from them.

## Interlocking intrusive and adhesive dynamics in the folie à deux

What I want to do in conclusion is bring together the dynamics that we have explored in reference to both adhesive identification and intrusive projective identification. It may be objected that, as the one can be characterized as two-dimensional and the other as three-dimensional, I am mixing two incompatible clinical pictures. My experience with couples suggests to me that there can be what I would describe as interlocking adhesive and intrusive dynamics that function in a particularly sado-masochistic way. This sado-masochism, I think, is inherent in the narcissistic "solution" to the anxieties of separateness in the context of a wish for intimate closeness with the loved other.

We will see in the final chapter that the ability to give the object its freedom without losing the passion for the object is a mark—perhaps the most important mark—of emotional maturity. It is also the mark of a capacity for "marriage" as I have been describing it in this book.

The *folie à deux* is, I think, a particularly insidious shared defensive pattern in couples motivated by an intolerance of both separation and closeness. The latter may seem strange, as the context is a desire for intimacy with the other. But an intimacy premised on the reality of separateness exposes the couple to the separation anxieties that are unbearable. But if the narcissistic "solution" is premised on a oneness, as we have seen, the fusion soon becomes intolerable when there are complex, contradictory feelings. At times, the couple can join forces to project these negative feelings and hostile internal objects into some object outside the couple relationship in a shared paranoid defence. Indeed, some couples can do this to a remarkable extent, in a more or less effective "us-and-them" strategy.

However, to the extent that the couple cannot join in a shared projection, the negative feelings ricochet in an escalating fashion, as Racker described in his analysis of countertransference experiences. As a result, one might say that the adhesive dynamics exacerbate masochistic tendencies and the intrusive dynamics exacerbate sadistic tendencies, mutually reinforcing each other in the couple relationship as each partner feels increasingly locked into intensifying spirals of retaliation. The couple's *folie à deux* offers no way out. As Edward said: "There was a door / And I could not open it; I could not touch the handle." Some couples do not even see that there is a door out of their "hell", their "claustrum". Even when they finally manage to find their way to therapy, the first step, before they can touch the handle, is to find a way to believe that there is a door out of their hell.

I experienced one of the most dramatic illustrations of this dynamic with a couple who sought help in a state of turmoil and desperation because of their inability to separate and to end their relationship. They both claimed that they wanted and, worse yet, needed to separate. However, in spite of numerous attempts, using different devices to help each of them as if they were literally addicted to the relationship, they had always come back together in unbearable panic. They simply could not understand this, and they described their experience vividly as being emotionally like "siamese twins", as though joined physically. When they separated, it was as if it left an open wound, as if the skin had been ripped open. It was more than just the unbearable pain. It was as if part of the self was torn away and it was impossible to survive alone, as what felt like being an incomplete self. They were "claustrophobic" *in* the relationship but "agoraphobic" when contemplating being *out* of the relationship.

I am presenting them not because the specifics of their version of narcissistic relating are so common, but because it is one picture of a *folie à deux*.

Mr A described their relationship as a perversion of Proust, the kind of relationship that has no beginning and can have no ending, only a middle. It began, so to speak, when he lost his accommodation and found himself staying with Ms Z. Why not, she said. From the beginning, they were "soulmates" and could be together for hours on end without speaking, as each knew what the other was thinking. In this they reminded me of a cross-cultural couple who had an idyllic relationship at first when neither spoke the language of the other, not needing to communicate. When that couple began to speak each other's language, they could not believe, nor could they tolerate how different they were.

And Mr A and Ms Z both agreed that really it was never a genuine relationship. They spent session after session recounting and arguing over all the ways each was not what the other wanted, ironically betraying their unconscious assumption that the other ought to conform to exactly what they had expected of each other. Both described how each was drawn in by the other in a way that each felt defined by the other, the other holding an essential part of the self which could not be recovered. Ending the relationship, therefore, was felt to be tantamount to disaster.

Both had been in therapy, as they described it, "forever", and both continued in individual therapy throughout the time they were seen as a couple. Their individual therapists both said that they were pleased for the two of them to be seen as a couple, and one could imagine the frustration of these therapists because the couple's exchanges were full of psychological jargon. In the sessions with them, there was a feeling that what passed for understanding was just another way of becoming entangled in a meaningless but endless enmeshment with the other. Either of them could talk for a whole session, and they filled the sessions with words, although most of the time there was no sense that either speaker or listener understood what was being said or what was going on. This felt particularly shocking as both were talented and intelligent and held jobs doing creative work. Nevertheless, it required considerable presence of mind for me not to become lost with them in a caricature of therapy.

In the face of this chaotic, tense environment, I found myself becoming increasingly forceful and bold with them, much different I thought than was my usual style. It felt that if were I not asserting myself like this, we all might be overwhelmed in a whirlpool of confusion. It became essential to focus on what was happening in the session rather than on the content of what they talked about, although the content often seemed on the face of it rich with potential, if confused, meaning.

In my notes at the time I wrote: "This couple functions on a more primitive level than almost any couple I have seen in therapy." I would not say that now, although this couple does still stand out in my mind. In working with such a disturbed couple, I think what I said was much less important than the fact that I was there relating to them as a couple and to each of them as separate individuals, something that the reader will easily imagine was not easy. And yet they (especially he, since she is so compliant as to almost never be able to hold on to her view) cared desperately that I get it right in what I did say. There was hell to pay when I got it wrong, almost as if words were things and misspeaking was actually a mishandling (of the baby).

The test for this couple was whether they could define and separate themselves from each other, maintaining a relationship with me that might allow them to, as they put it, "tear themselves away". The difficulty was for them to feel that they could do this in a way that felt emotionally genuine without having to enact it literally by at the same time walking out of the therapy. For them it felt an intolerable paradox, and we were always on the cusp of this impossible possibility. Each at different times would gather the strength to make a move to feel like a separate person, while finding the emotional reserves and the psychic space to allow them to remain together in therapy until the separating could become something other than annihilation for both.

These two people could, at times, get enough psychic distance to describe their experience in what we might call "as-if" language, although those moments felt tenuous. In the heat of the moment, there was a psychotic-like state of mind, sufficient to immobilize this couple in their desperation. She would become blank, sometimes unable to remember what she was saying either to him or to me. He often became correspondingly aggressive, insisting that she understand his complex and convoluted theories about their relationship, sometimes reaching such a pitch of excited agitation that he was shouting.

This *claustro/agora-phobic* dilemma represents the alternating poles of their narcissistic "solution". On the one hand, the claustrophobic feelings represented the intense and unbearable anxieties of the narcissistic fusion as the couple tried to be "one". On the other hand, the agoraphobic feelings represented the experience of their attempts to separate which both felt as an abandonment inevitably leading to annihilation. It is a dynamic that echoes through the familiar *folie à deux* of another couple struggling with these issues, a story that I want to recount and explore in the final chapter, as we consider the apotheosis of the narcissistic "solution" in the relationship between Othello and Desdemona.

# CHAPTER TWELVE

# Termination and Othello's version of Eliot's "two ways"

"Let's begin with a tale, a tale of hateful jealousy and suspicion, as well as, one might say, a tale of remarriage." With that invitation which opened chapter one we began this exploration of the developmental achievement I am conceptualizing as the emergence from narcissism towards marriage, or re-marriage, and its links with the psychoanalytic process in therapy with couples. The reader will be aware by now that in a similar way I am proposing to end with a tale, also a tale of hateful jealousy and suspicion. It is true that Shakespeare's play *Othello* is not, in any obvious way, a tale of remarriage. And yet in setting the discussion of this disturbing play as a counterpoint to *The Winter's Tale* I mean to focus attention on the intimate link between endings and beginnings, separation and union, and, one might say, an idea of marriage.

In a word, I want to end our exploration of the psychoanalytic process with couples by thinking about endings in therapy in the context of the emergence from narcissism. Discussion of the process of and the criteria for termination inevitably takes us back to the most fundamental questions. My aim in this final chapter is to revisit the way of thinking I have been developing about the nature both of the psychoanalytic process and of marriage in order to consider how this might help us to think about the termination process itself. To do this, I want to return to *The Cocktail Party*, to the endings that T. S. Eliot proposes for his characters, his "two ways". This will lead us directly into the images of Shakespeare's *Othello* considered in relationship to *The Winter's Tale*.

Stanley Cavell is the person who brought to my attention the pairing of these two plays, making the interesting suggestion that each can be considered a commentary on the other. Each play turns on an accusation of adultery, an accusation that, as Cavell points out, is "known by every outsider, everyone but the accuser, to be insanely false" (Cavell, 1987, p. 125). As I said in the first chapter, plausibly we might have begun with *Othello* and ended with *The Winter's Tale*. It would make a difference, I think, how one imagines the mood of this "happy ending" as Leontes invites Paulina to lead them to somewhere where they may each "answer to his part". Will this be a celebration of reunion and restoration? And, if so, how will it include a grieving for the dead child Mamillius? One can hardly imagine a greater contrast when we turn to the ending of *Othello*, however, even if one pictures grief to be at the heart of that concluding scene of *The Winter's Tale*. Readers will share with me a sense of apprehension when anticipating the end of the story of Desdemona and Othello, an apprehension of, to use that word with such unnerving associations, a *termination*.

In a way, it might seem strange, therefore, to end this book with an exploration of a play in which, as Cavell suggests, "not a marriage but an idea of marriage, or let us say an imagination of marriage, is worked out" (Cavell, 1987, p. 131). One might think that it is the working out of an *idea*, almost in the literal sense of a "picture", of marriage, but an "idea" that makes marriage in any ordinary sense impossible. As we shall see, it is an idea of a "perfect oneness", intolerant of differences. At least this is a thought I want to explore. Couples often seek out therapy in a state that seems to contain such a view of marriage, a view that makes marriage, their marriage at any rate, impossible.

In juxtaposing narcissism and marriage, I have intended to portray the capacity for an intimate adult relationship as a developmental process in which one emerges, so to speak, from the state in which the other is felt to be *perfectly* attuned and responsive. Since we have been considering couples whose marriages are marked by narcissistic forms of relating, I hope by this point that it will have become clearer why I speak in terms of "re-marriage". In one sense, the fundamental human tension I am picturing as "*narcissism ↔ marriage*" is never finally resolved, and thus every "successful" marriage is a continuing process of remarriage, of emerging from narcissism towards marriage.

Each discrete developmental move resonates with that first emerging from the mother–infant—or should we say, the pregnant-woman–foetus—union. And yet in another sense the endings and separations that mark these developmental processes are also markers of our mortality, our finitude. We encounter the shape of this reality in the form of the difference between the generations, the separating from and leaving the generation that gave us birth in order to give birth to the next, and finally the leaving everything to the succeeding generations.

This linking of birth and death, the beginning and the ending, is a theme that haunted T. S. Eliot, especially in his early poetry and throughout the plays which stretch from his little-known, unfinished poetic drama *Sweeney Agonistes* to *The Elder Statesman*. In *Sweeney* Eliot sings the dynamic of the generations in the rhythms of the black ragtime resonant of life in the St. Louis of his birth (Sigg, 1994, pp. 20–24):

> Birth, and copulation and death.
> That's all, that's all, that's all, that's all,
> Birth, and copulation and death.
> . . .
> Birth, and copulation and death.
> That's all the facts when you come to brass tacks:
> Birth, and copulation and death.
> I've been born, and once is enough.
> You don't remember, but I remember,
> Once is enough.
> . . .
> Life is death.
>
> [Eliot, 1963, pp. 131, 133]

Although it may seem strange to think of the story of *Othello* in these terms, Stanley Cavell has sketched out a view of the play which resonates with this "life is death" theme. For example, he suggests that we hear echoes of it in Othello's poignant "It is the cause" soliloquy as the Moor comes into Desdemona's bedchamber for the last time, speaking as she sleeps: ". . . when I have pluck'd the rose, / I cannot give it vital growth again, / It must needs wither . . ." (V.ii.13–15). At one level, it is obvious that Othello is speaking here of his intention to take the life of his bride. He knows that "to put out the light" is to extinguish what he cannot restore should he repent. The light, the lamp, that he carries can be lit again, should he repent. But he cannot restore that "light" he is about to put out.

In one of his most haunting, yet I think quite plausible, observations on the workings of Othello's mind, Cavell proposes the idea that this scene is also a picture of the unseen scene that opens the play, the wedding night—the "plucking the rose" picturing both the feared intercourse with the virginal bride, intercourse which leads potentially to birth and new life, *and* the taking of life. Is it possible that there is an idea of marriage which makes intercourse tantamount to death? What is that idea? In this chapter, I want to explore this play, again not as literary criticism but, as I have done with *The Winter's Tale*, to consider its portrayal of states of mind that cannot tolerate the emotional experiences that mark a relationship to a genuine other.

We will come back later to another of Eliot's early poems that echoes the beat of *Sweeney Agonistes* to see how it takes us into the mind of the poet as he struggles to create for himself and his listeners the rhythm of marriage, as he seeks to image marriage. Meanwhile, in the context of my announced intention to explore *termination*, the reader may be wondering why I am introducing these uncomfortable associations with life and death. I too have wondered as I have reflected on the choice to conclude this book with Shakespeare's *Othello*, linking it with Eliot's "two ways" epitomized in *The Cocktail Party* by Edward and Lavinia's "making the best of a bad job" and Celia's martyrdom "crucified very near an ant-hill".

It seems unavoidable that, in company with all those audiences acquainted with the play, we enter Shakespeare's theatre to encounter Othello and Desdemona, and Iago, in the shadow of the ending that we all anticipate. Whether or not it is true for the reader, I know that for myself in the writing of this book I have felt the shadow of Othello, consciously at least since the images of this play began to colour my picture of the developmental dynamics in which narcissism and marriage are linked. The shadow has only deepened in my subsequent discovery of the young T. S. Eliot's disturbing portrayal of what goes on in the mind of an "Othello" in his very early, and until very recently unpublished, poem, *The Love Song of St. Sebastian*.

But why should the image of Othello cast a shadow over our story of the struggles to emerge from narcissism towards marriage? Surely there is some hope that a couple seeking and sustaining an engagement in the psychoanalytic process can move towards a greater capacity as a couple to tolerate the anxieties and agonies, as well as the joys, of a genuine relationship. And yet as we approach the end of this process there is, I think, a sense of unease. In focusing our attention on the question of termination and the related themes that I want to explore in this chapter, it is this sense of apprehension that I most want to try to understand.

## Till death unite them and they part no more!

I want to take us back to where we left Edward and Lavinia Chamberlayne, as their brief encounter with their Uninvited Guest and "therapist", Sir Henry Harcourt-Reilly, was nearing its end. Eliot chose to close the play, after much struggle with various alternatives, with a third act which mirrors the original cocktail party with another cocktail party two years later, given this time by the couple together. It has been much criticized on dramatic grounds, including by Eliot himself, because, so to speak, "nothing new happens" (Eliot, 1951). One might say that this final act is a retrospective, creating a mood familiar to therapists when termination is on the horizon.

Before this party can begin, unexpectedly the same few guests whom we met at the first party arrive early. All of them, that is, except Celia, the young woman who had been having an affair with Edward and is portrayed as choosing the "other way". In choosing that other way she seemed unable to accept what faced Edward and Lavinia, the "making the best of a bad job". How could anyone give up the vision of love she holds and settle for that? Never mind that Reilly says that, in a world of lunacy, violence, stupidity, and greed, it is a good life. Alternatively, might we be tempted to think that

Celia is expressing a romantic's attack on the "good-enough" couple with their "good-enough" life. It would seem that Celia believed that the vision of love that haunted her made any ordinary relationship impossible.

What is the kind of love that belongs to ordinary life? When we left Celia, she had come to Reilly to try to understand a kind of longing for an experience ". . . remembered like a dream / In which one is exalted by intensity of loving." It is "A state one does not know / When awake". She knows that she cannot accept what Edward and Lavinia seem to want to be able to accept. And yet she is unsure whether this longing, although remembered like a dream, is for something to which she can aspire, or whether it is a kind of illness. Indeed, she says, ". . . if all that is meaningless, I want to be cured / Of craving for something I cannot find / And the shame of never finding it" (Eliot, 1950, p. 136, II.626, 633–635).

If there is one theme that runs through all the stories that couples have shared with me as they sought help in therapy, it would be a variation of the agony to which Eliot gives voice in Celia Coplestone. It is not an agony limited to or uniquely characteristic of Western culture with its image of romantic marriage with its falling in love. The falling in love that haunts all intense intimate relationships is a being in love remembered like a dream. Those Westerners who know little of the experience of what we tend to call "arranged marriages", or who fail to recognize the arrangedness of their own spontaneous falling in love, forget, I think, that this original dream of being in love with that first love object was an archetypal "arranged marriage". That the infant was not consulted as to its first love object, or that the mother was the recipient of the gift of a particular child whom, no matter what attempts at genetic engineering, she did not choose, is a fact of life. Perhaps we should add it to Money-Kyrle's three central facts of life (Money-Kyrle, 1971). Falling in love with that first loved object was in the context of an "arranged marriage". Gift or curse, or both, falling in love and being in love are never simply choices.

But that is not the question before us, nor the question with which Eliot is struggling. What he wants to know concerns the link between the love characteristic of what we might call the ordinary, good-enough marriage, his "making the best of a bad job", and this inner intensity of loving. Are they two ways, one forever haunting the other, but never brought together? Consider one answer posed by Sir Henry Harcourt-Reilly, the song-loving "One-Eyed Riley".

Eliot was fond of including humorous, and often obscure, allusions in his dramatic work, giving him some satisfaction when none of his critics appeared to notice and comment on them (Eliot, 1959, pp. 102–104). Near the end of the dramatically difficult Act III, after some humorous but trivial exchanges, suddenly the mood changes as Alex discloses Celia's fate in some distant place among the natives. Lavinia has noticed that Reilly, unlike the others, does not seem shocked. Indeed, he seems almost satisfied. She wants him to reveal his view of Celia's disturbing end, and he responds to Lavinia: "Do you mind if I quote poetry, Mrs Chamberlayne?" Doubtless most audiences hearing these lines would be unaware of the poet's intention to seek in *The Cocktail Party* a contemporary form for poetic drama:

> What I should hope might be achieved ... is that the audience should find, at the moment of awareness that it is hearing poetry, that it is saying to itself: "*I* could talk in poetry too!" Then we should not be transported into an artificial world; on the contrary, our own sordid, dreary daily world would be suddenly illuminated and transfigured. [Eliot, 1951, p. 141]

> [But] I laid down for myself the ascetic rule to avoid poetry which could not stand the test of strict dramatic utility, with such success, indeed, that it is perhaps an open question whether there is any poetry in the play at all. [p. 144]

And earlier:

> But if our verse is to have so wide a range that it can say anything that has to be said, it follows that it will not be "poetry" all the time. It will be "poetry" when the dramatic situation has reached such a point of intensity that poetry becomes the natural utterance, because *then it is the only language in which the emotions can be expressed at all*. [p. 134, emphasis added]

So when Reilly asks Lavinia if he may quote poetry, we are, I think, meant to smile, wondering whether or not we have been listening to poetry all along. Or is Eliot indulging himself in some self-deprecating humour as he has Reilly quote Shelley's *Prometheus Unbound*, where Prometheus is being spoken to by his mother, Earth:

Ere Babylon was dust
The magus Zoroaster, my dead child,
Met his own image walking in the garden.
That apparition, sole of men, he saw.
For know there are two worlds of life and death:
One that which thou beholdest; but the other
Is underneath the grave, where do inhabit
The shadows of all forms that think and live
Till death unite them and they part no more!

[Shelley, 1820, Act I]

What does Eliot have in mind with the introduction of this sombre poem portraying the uncanny experience of meeting one's double, one's own image. Shelley's poem is followed by, what is for *The Cocktail Party*, a long speech in which Reilly discusses Celia Coplestone as a woman under the sentence of death. The guests at this cocktail party, the party we could call the "double" of the cocktail party with which the play opens, have just heard that in the intervening two years Celia had joined a nursing order and had been sent to a remote, primitive country troubled by insurrection and where half the natives were dying of pestilence. We are given quite gruesome details. Three nursing sisters had refused to leave their station. One died in the jungle and the other "will never be fit for normal life again". When the rescuers arrived, they found Celia's body, "or at least, they found traces of it". And then we hear that she must, it seems, have been crucified "very near an ant-hill" (p. 169, III.330–333).

Early audiences, like many of the critics, responded with puzzlement and hostility to this dramatic change in mood in this final act. One minute we are enjoying comic banter about monkeys, and then suddenly we are hearing details of the bizarre and violent death of the young woman who in some ways becomes—despite, or indeed because of, her departure from centre stage—the most important character in the play (Eliot, 1959, p. 103). Originally, we are told, Eliot had determined to leave Celia's fate vague. Then in response to pressure from Martin Browne, his director, friend, and guide into the world of the theatre, Eliot revised the script. He has her *crucified very near an anthill* (Browne, 1966, p. 22).

But the story of the early drafts of *The Cocktail Party* has an even more startling twist. In one of Eliot's early re-draftings, he had added that she had been "smeared with a juice that is attractive to ants". Browne recalls that the horror-effect upset many people, and Eliot was persuaded to leave out that additional gruesome detail. Linked with the introduction of Shelley's *Prometheus Unbound* we are offered two views, a dichotomy of two worlds, the world of the ordinary and the world of the dream-like passion. But does Eliot suggest that this dichotomy is permanent, or do the two exist as separate only "Till death unite them and they part no more". In Shelley's version, this other world contains the

> Dreams and the light imaginings of men,
> And all that faith creates or love desires,
> Terrible, strange, sublime and beauteous shapes.
>
> [Shelley, 1820, Act I]

Here Eliot takes a risk in the context of a cocktail party, the epitome of, at least what he sees as, the ordinariness of everyday life, to introduce the most terrible, strange, and sublime, the impact, might we say, of the aesthetic object. If we imagine with Bion the minus grid, the minus-L, minus-H, and minus-K, might we also not imagine the "minus-aesthetic-object"? And what would that look like? A beautiful young nurse crucified very near an anthill, smeared with a juice attractive to ants? If it is a shockingly coarse image, what else might we expect if Eliot is trying to image the negative of that "beauteous shape"? If one balks at Eliot's image, we can perhaps appreciate why Bion, who was no poet, chose his abstract mathematical "poetry" of minus L, H, and K.

We can either accept what seems to be the case in *The Cocktail Party*—that is, that Eliot in the end could see only two mutually exclusive ways—or we can wonder whether this play was part of his life-long struggle to discover whether, and how, these two worlds can come together this side of death. Traditionally, Eliot has been seen as counterposing the love of God with the love of one human being for another. And Eliot himself seems to reinforce this view. When his friend, mentor, and employer, Sir Geoffrey Faber, in describing the play as a masterpiece, ventured one minor objection concerning Reilly's view of marriage, Eliot wrote back defending Reilly's understanding of marriage:

> It is a question of the universe of discourse in which one is moving. There are undoubtedly degrees of understanding—but in the uni-

verse of discourse in which Reilly is moving during that speech, there are two primary propositions: (1) nobody understands you but God; (2) all real love is ultimately the love of God. [letter dated 29 August 1949, quoted in Coghill, 1974, p. 192]

Ringing in my ears are the words from the husband, "she has never understood me, all I wanted is for her to understand me". In a different way, his wife says something basically similar, he was never really there for me. What would it mean to believe that nobody understands you but God, that all real love is ultimately the love of God? Is this what is meant by a love "remembered like a dream / In which one is exalted by intensity of loving". Is it "A state one does not know / When awake"? Is every couple, after the ecstasy of the all-too-fleeting "falling in love", condemned in the subsequent marriage to "make the best of a bad job"?

It is a familiar experience, one I think not only couple therapists experience again and again, that at the end of a "successful" therapy the patients—individual or couple—say that nothing in their lives has changed except their capacity to deal with what before had felt unbearable and unacceptable. We do, quite rightly, I think, agree with these patients that this is an outcome not to be disparaged. To have a capacity for suffering instead of avoiding and evading the reality of our experience is itself a developmental achievement.

But does that mean that the heights of ecstasy in which one is "exalted by intensity of loving" is, as some suggest, a desired and to be valued aspect of the paranoid–schizoid dimension of our complex existence? What would it mean to accept that no human being can ever really understand me? If, instead of reading Melanie Klein's view of the paranoid–schizoid position as chronologically prior to the depressive position, we considered that the earliest experience was the aesthetic impact of the primal object, we might take a different view of this "falling in love". If the experience of what Shelley described as the "terrible, strange, sublime and beauteous shapes" is the unbearable experience of the aesthetic object, then Eliot's question remains for us whether and how we might aspire to it in the ordinariness of our intimate relationships.

It is with these questions posed by Eliot in The Cocktail Party in our minds that I want to turn to Shakespeare's Othello. As we considered The Winter's Tale in terms of separation and marriage, I want to think

about another picture of chilling narcissistic rage. What has this
newly wed husband discovered about his wife that makes him curse
marriage?

> O curse of marriage
> That we can call these delicate creatures ours,
> And not their appetites!
>
> [*Othello*, III.iii.272–274]

What stirs Othello's rage here? Does he any less than Narcissus in his
dream-like passion want to possess that beautiful creature opposite
him? In this play, I suggest that we have, among its many and complex portraits of human emotion, a picture of the dynamic that I have
been noting as *narcissism ↔ marriage*.

And can it be accidental that here, as in *The Winter's Tale*, we begin
with the intergenerational tension between a father and his child, a
father who cannot accept the separateness of a daughter who has a
mind of her own. We seem never far in our exploration of these
dramas, as we are in the explorations in our consulting-rooms, from
that triangular drama we call Oedipal. It is interesting, however, that
*Othello* opens with, not, as in *The Winter's Tale*, a father struggling to
acknowledge that his child is in fact his child, but rather a father,
Desdemona's father Brabantio, struggling with the curse of his child,
the "curse" that "we can call these delicate creatures ours / And not
their appetites!"


## Even now an old black ram is tupping
## your white ewe

*Othello* opens with a scene that can be thought about primarily, if not
exclusively, in terms of its theatrical function, introducing all of the
central characters and quickly engaging us in a fast-moving story
line. It is characteristic of Shakespeare's dramatic writing, however,
that sometimes one comes across an idea, an observation, a way of
staging or acting a scene that takes hold of our sense of what is
important in that scene. It can sometimes then become impossible to
shake off this way of seeing it. Stanley Cavell, in his brief essay on
*Othello*, has done that to my picture of the opening scene, although

my use of some of Cavell's ideas may be far from what he had in mind (Cavell, 1987, pp. 125–142). In effect, Cavell asks us to think about our field of attention in this scene, which in itself can affect our capacity for observation. In the consulting-room, this is one of our primary tasks, to observe what our patients find too frightening or painful to see. What do we see in this opening scene, or perhaps ought we, with Reilly, take note of what we do not see?

We are introduced to Iago, Othello's "ancient" [ensign], now third in command to the Moor, passed over as Michael Cassio has just been appointed lieutenant. And we hear in some detail Iago's complaint that his rival lacks comparable experience in the field, but, he moans, it is the "curse of service". "Preferment goes by letter and affection, / Not by the old gradation, where each second / Stood heir to the first" (I.i.36–38). Iago asks rhetorically whether in justice he is bound (affin'd) to *love* the Moor? "Love" is not quite the word on our minds when Iago declares of his loyalty to Othello: "Were I the Moor, I would not be Iago: / In following him, I follow but myself" (I.i.57–58).

This animated exchange allows the poet to convey to his audience what we need to know to make some sense of the central characters and story line at the outset. But what of the setting? What draws our attention, unconsciously as well as consciously? Iago and Roderigo are on a street late at night outside the house of a Venetian Senator, Brabantio, a member of the city–state government that, as we learn in the next scene, is about to commission the noble Moor to lead a military force to counter the attack of the Turks in Cyprus. Soon these two conspirators are shouting, making noise, and rousing Brabantio's household with shouts of "thieves, thieves, thieves!" Why? Iago shouts up to the old man:

> Zounds, sir, you are robb'd, for shame put on your gown,
> Your heart is burst, you have lost half your soul;
> Even now, just now, an old black ram
> Is tupping your white ewe; arise, arise,
> Awake the snorting citizens with the bell,
> Or else the devil will make a grandsire of you,
> Arise I say.
>
> [I.i.86–92]

From the beginning we puzzle over the character and motivation of

Iago. What leads this man to devote himself, not to the service of the Moor, but to his destruction, not "for love and duty" but for his own peculiar, private end. It does not look a happy marriage between the Moor and his Ancient. What are we to make of Shakespeare's juxta-posing Iago's bitter disappointment and cynical hatred of his posi-tion of service with the alarming and intrusive revelation to Brabantio, the father of Desdemona, that his beautiful young daugh-ter has eloped with the black general who not only Venice as a whole, but he personally, has admired, honoured, and relied upon? Mischief making certainly. What business of Iago's is it?

There is a rising intensity which could almost sound and look like the intrusive finger-pointing excitement of a little boy at a wedding reception. As the bride and groom go upstairs to their bridal cham-ber, it is as if he shouts, they're doing it, they're doing it right now! Doing what? Iago shouts to Brabantio: "Your daughter, and the Moor, are now making the beast with two backs." And there is some-thing particularly shocking about racial slurs to suggest a kind of miscegenation, "the devil will make a grandsire of you".

> You'll have your daughter cover'd with a Barbary horse; you'll
> have your nephews [grandsons] neigh to you; you'll have
> coursers for cousins, and gennets for germans [blood rela-
> tions].
>
> [I.i.110–113]

Differences could hardly be portrayed more dramatically: the Moor, the thick-lipped, sooty-black, experienced man of war and the gentle young Desdemona with skin "whiter than snow", described by her father as more likely to be afraid of him than to fall in love with him. It is "against all rules of nature". This play seems to offer an image of marriage, true marriage, as the coming together of that which is unlike, the overcoming of separation and difference so that the "two become one". Brabantio precedes Othello in succumbing to the in-sidious suggestion, voiced by Iago, that separateness is betrayal, that to be other is to deceive.

Again, I want to emphasize that I am not arguing for a particular interpretation of this complex play. My aim is to explore a particular picture of the tensions between a state of mind we call narcissistic and a state of mind in which intercourse and the intimacy of mar-riage become possible.

The opening scene looked at this way suggests an interest, perhaps more unconscious than conscious, in what we do not see: the
wedding night. What would this interest be, what would we want to
see in this most private of the intimate coming together of two people, this most mysterious moment of potentially generative intimacy.
There seems to be a persistent question running through the play,
"are you fast married?", a question echoed in our growing unease
as each "wedding night" is interrupted—is the marriage consummated? On that first night, there is the command to set sail for
Cyprus "tonight, this night", Othello and Desdemona then sailing
(strangely?) in separate ships—and whose decision was that, and
why. Then, on the night of the arrival in Cyprus when the lovers are
reunited in a mood of anticipated ecstasy, the Turkish fleet sunk, we
see Othello and Desdemona appear in their nightclothes, their night
together disturbed by the fight between Cassio and Montano.

Consider the idea that only on what turns out to be the last night
do we see, with our own eyes, "ocular proof" of what happens between bride and groom in the bedchamber. I am assuming that this
thought becomes more disturbing the more one thinks about it, and
the more one senses the many images, the scenes and lines of *Othello*
being reshaped by it. Is this a nightmare picture in the mind of the
little child of what it fears is going on from the sounds it hears from
the parental bedroom? Or, more disturbingly, is it a picture, someone's picture, of the simultaneous loss and magical restoration of
perfection, the wedding night as beginning and ending, or is it ending and beginning? The "ruin of loveliness". The mood of apprehension is almost palpable.

But before we consider these disturbing thoughts prompted by
Cavell's comments on this play, I want to turn back to the father,
Brabantio, and his dismay: "Who would be a father?"

## She has deceiv'd her father, may do thee

There is, I think, a very straightforward sense in which Brabantio,
this father of fair Desdemona has cause to feel aggrieved—a feeling
that any parent might share. He has indeed been deceived. His

daughter, for whatever reason, and it is easy enough to imagine it, did not feel that she could talk to her father about her wish, her intention, to marry the black general who had so often been an honoured guest in their home. Now he hears from outsiders that, at that moment, their marriage is said to be being consummated.

But when Brabantio enters the Council chamber later that same night, the Duke having assembled his consuls to an emergency meeting to deal with the threat of the Turkish fleet, he speaks with such urgency that the Duke turns away from the affairs of state to find out what disturbs him. "My daughter, O my daughter!", he cries, to such effect that the Duke assumes her dead. She is dead to him, Brabantio insists, "abus'd, stol'n . . . and corrupted" (I.iii.60). Shakespeare provokes our imagination as he has Iago shout to this father that he has been robbed: "You have lost half your soul" (I.i.87).

Allowing for Iago's alarming hyperbole designed to undermine this distraught father's capacity to think about what has happened, we still must wonder at this picture of what is lost, or threatened to be lost. "Half his soul"! It brings to mind many initial couple sessions where one or the other partner is in a similar state of alarm, unable to think, in terror at the possible loss of their "other half". We hear echoes of Edward's anguish at the disappearance of his wife Lavinia as he feels himself begin to dissolve, to cease to exist (Eliot, 1950, p. 112, II.151–156).

As in The Winter's Tale, Shakespeare offers us yet another variant on that endlessly complex relationship at the core of human experience, what we call the "Oedipal" triangle. Had Freud, however, focused his attention at a different point in variations of the triangular dynamic, we might be speaking of it as "Leontean", or now perhaps even "Desdemonan". Note that in the version of this triangular dynamic in Othello there is only one passing reference made to Brabantio's wife, Desdemona's mother. We do not miss the mother in this story. Why? She might be necessary were we to focus in some pedestrian fashion on the biological, but she is redundant to the psychological, the emotional, mathematics. Desdemona outlines her Oedipal development as a shift of loyalty from one man, her father, to another, her husband. When pressed by her father before the Duke and his Council, and before her chosen, Othello, she describes this transition as if it were indeed clear and unproblematic:

My noble father,
I do perceive here a divided duty:
To you I am bound for life and education,
My life and education both do learn me
How to respect you, you are lord of all my duty,
I am hitherto your daughter: but here's my husband:
And so much duty as my mother show'd
To you, preferring you before her father,
So much I challenge, that I may profess,
Due to the Moor my lord.

[I.iii.180–189]

But Brabantio feels himself a father scorned. Bitterly he gives Othello what he already has, and what he would keep from him. Having lost his only child, he is bitter: "I had rather to adopt a child than get it." If our modern gender bias inclines us to think primarily, or perhaps only, of a bond between mother and child that can make separation feel like a physical wound, Shakespeare reminds us that a father too knows something of that experience—both a "Brabantion", as well as a "Leontean" father. Are these two not mirror images of each other, neither able to tolerate a paternal intimacy premised on separateness?

If we imagine *Othello* to open with our unconscious background attention drawn to the unseen bridal bedroom with its potential *beginning*, we have in the foreground of our attention the *ending*, at least in Brabantio's view, the ending of the relationship of which the other is a beginning—the parent–child relationship. Are the lovers in their bridal chamber, these two who could hardly be more other, as different as black and white, *getting a child*? Who will stop this endless train of betrayals, if every coming-together is a betrayal of another having-been-together? The Duke, in an expansive mood trying to paper over the differences between one of his Senators and his leading General, appeals to Brabantio: "If virtue no delighted beauty lack, / Your son-in-law is far more fair than black" (I.iii.289–290). But this offended father will have none of it. He growls to Othello, almost under his breath, the lines that set the stage for the rest of the play:

Look to her, Moor, have a quick eye to see:
She has deceiv'd her father, may do thee.

[I.iii.292–293]

These lines also set the stage for Iago, "honest Iago" as Othello insists in the very next line. As to the father's warning about his treacherous daughter, this new husband stakes his "life upon her faith" and entrusts her to his Ancient, Iago, to see her separately to Cyprus. But first he says to her: "Come, Desdemona, I have but an hour / Of love, of worldly matters, and direction, / To spend with thee; we must obey the time" (I.iii.298–300).

## O curse of marriage

Shakespeare's *Othello* is endlessly fascinating, and we could easily lose ourselves wandering among the surprises in every scene, in speech after speech. But my aim here is to explore the tension that overshadows almost every scene. There is sense of dread linked with the picture, the idea, the imagining of marriage implicit in this play in which the beginning is ominously felt to be an ending. Surely our hope is to discover whether, and in what way, there might be an ending that could be, or become, a beginning.

We find Othello very quickly taking up the despair bequeathed him by his father-in-law, as Iago gives voice to an unease in his relationship with the "delicate creature" he has made his wife. The mood of the play moves rapidly from the moment of the passionate reunion of the two lovers on Cyprus intensified by their anxious apprehension because of the storms through which they have separately sailed. In fact, the question of time in this play is both interesting and important.

M. R. Ridley, in his Introduction to the Arden edition of *Othello*, discusses A. N. Wilson's "double time scheme", pointing out that it is as if the movement of the play's action moves on the one hand as if by a "short time" clock and on the other by a "long time" clock. Except for the indefinite sailing time, there is the wedding night and then a mere thirty-three hours from the time the principals meet again on Cyprus (Ridley, 1958, pp. lxvii–lxx). And, it is vital to note, Shakespeare has Othello sail in one ship, Cassio in another, and Desdemona, Iago, and Emilia in a third. The significance of that is that there is literally no time in which the adultery of Desdemona with Cassio insinuated by Iago could have taken place. It brings to mind Stanley Cavell's unsettling idea that Othello is disturbed by his own deflowering of his virgin bride. On the other hand, there are numerous remarks that suggest that the play describes a situation extending over a long period of time, almost as if the betrayal is not something that happened at a moment in time, but that betrayal is inherent in the structure of the relating, and not simply located within its chronology.

As I said, the mood shifts rapidly from the passion of re-union to the moment we find a tormented Othello crying "O curse of marriage". And what is this curse, this curse that tormented the father of Desdemona and now her husband: "That we can call these delicate creatures ours, / And not their appetites!" (III.iii.272–274). What is Othello discovering as he appears more and more wounded by the insinuating observations from the "honest Iago"? What is he becoming aware of as he listens to his "internal Iago", this new husband who cannot bear doubts, this husband who has committed himself to the highest stakes: "My life upon her faith"? (I.iii.294). The stakes could not be higher for this man: ". . . when I love thee not / Chaos is come again" (III.iii.91–92). But what disturbs him?

There are, in fact, two marriages at the heart of this play, and I do not refer here to the relationship between Iago and Emilia his wife, interesting and important though that marriage is in articulating a cynical counterpoint to the theme of the idealized romantic secret courtship and elopement of the two principals. Iago takes a view that might please a Schopenhauer, the philosopher of will. He insists "that we are thus, and thus . . . lies in our wills". Without our capacity to reason, we would be at the mercy of our passions, our emotions would overwhelm us.

We can hear the terror in this speech, the terror of emotion, a terror that we find typically in the men in the couples in therapy. These men would endorse Iago's idea that without our rationality to balance our "sensuality", "the blood and baseness of our natures would conduct us to most preposterous conclusions". Love, he tells the protesting Roderigo, is but an offshoot of "our raging motions, our carnal stings, our unbitted lusts". Love is "merely a lust of the blood, and a permission of the will" (I.iii.319–336). And Emilia, as one might expect of the wife of a man with such beliefs, suggests a complementary view of men to Desdemona. A woman finds behind

this façade of rationality just the kind of passion Iago has described.
A woman soon finds what a man is:

> They are all but stomachs, and we all but food;
> They eat us hungerly, and when they are full
> They belch us.
>
> [III.iv.101–103]

This is almost as crude as Eliot's "crucified very near an ant-hill".
Here, instead of a *minus*–"beauteous-shape", we have a caricature of
the wish to devour the loved object. Devour indeed! And then belch
out what is no longer beautiful! It is a way of possessing the loved
other which makes a mockery of an intimate relationship.

But when I refer to a second marriage, or, more properly, to a
second image or idea of marriage, in fact I have in mind the one
portrayed in the growing relationship between Othello and Iago cul-
minating in *their* betrothal scene. But before we consider that picture
of what we might call a "narcissistic marriage", if we are prepared
to allow such an idea or image of marriage, I want to consider the
apparent transformation of Othello from a loving, trusting husband,
who can hardly believe his good fortune, into a tortured, enraged
cuckold. When Othello first begins to have doubts typical of one
newly married, he seems solid and sensible about the realities, both
of Desdemona's attractiveness and of his own weaknesses:

> To say my wife is fair, feeds well, loves company,
> Is free of speech, sings, plays, and dances well;
> Where virtue is, these are more virtuous:
> Nor from mine own weak merits will I draw
> The smallest fear, or doubt of her revolt,
> For she had eyes, and chose me.
>
> [III.iii.188–193]

Indeed she did choose him, although we have already seen that her
father's original view was that Othello must have used some magic
potion to bewitch and steal his daughter. We know that marriage, at
least in the view of marriage which I have trying to describe in this
book, is not a single momentary choice, but a lifetime of continual
choosing. It is a relationship shaped by choosing between alternatives, a relationship whose basic shape is triangular. The choosing of

the one means the exclusion of the other, a dynamic the experience of which can be painful for both those in the couple and for the one excluded, as Ronald Britton detailed in his lucid exposition of these dynamics (Britton, 1989).

It is clear that these triangular dynamics are premised on choice. If it were not a matter of someone *choosing* someone else, whether my mother choosing my father over me, or my lover choosing my rival, or whatever the couple from which I am excluded, it would not be the painful experience it is. The alternative, as Desdemona's father Brabantio at first believed, must be something involuntary, that Othello must have used a magic potion to bewitch her. She could not have *betrayed* him. That would be, and was, unbearable.

Othello's version of his betrayal borders on something similar. He believes that fidelity is possible only with the aid of something like magic. When the choice of betrayal is possible, it must be inevitable. It is a logic, an unconscious if not a conscious logic, in most of the couples I have seen in therapy. This husband believes that the "magic" that makes marriage possible—possible for him at least—lies in something he has inherited from his mother, a handkerchief.

It is interesting, just as an aside, that here we have another version of the conventional view that it is the woman who holds whatever it is that makes enduring intimate relationships possible, in this case a handkerchief passed from mother to son *to give to his wife* that she might keep it safe. Is this remarkably resilient prejudice perhaps based in the child's belief (based, of course, on its experience) that the primary couple is mother and child rather than the parental couple? One might imagine that, if unchallenged, this belief, grounded as it is in what seems such an undeniable experience and only challenged by learning what is painful to accept, might become a core unconscious phantasy.

It may be that this belief remains unchallenged in part because the father wants to abdicate all responsibility in this inherently painful situation. Surely facing the reality that the primary couple *is the parental couple*, with whose intercourse the conception of the mother-baby couple lies, is a developmental achievement—a developmental achievement of no little difficulty or significance.

But what does this handkerchief handed down from mother to daughter-in-law mean for Othello and his picture of faithfulness in marriage?

> That handkerchief
> Did an Egyptian to my mother give
> She was a charmer, and could almost read
> The thoughts of people; she told her, while she kept it
> 'Twould make her amiable, and subdue my father
> Entirely to her love: but if she lost it,
> Or made a gift of it, my father's eye
> Should hold her loathly, and his spirit should hunt
> After new fancies: she dying, gave it me,
> And bid me, when my fate would have me wive,
> To give it her; I did so, and take heed on 't,
> Make it a darling, like your precious eye,
> To lose it, or give 't away, were such perdition
> As nothing else could match.

[III.iv.53–66]

What holds two people together in the intimacy of marriage is a mystery to Othello. His version of events is structurally very similar to Brabantio's: my mother must have used a magic potion to bewitch my father, and in fact she told me so. Is this, then, an expression of the inverse Oedipus complex, the son's longing that *he* might be father's fancy, when, without the magic of the handkerchief, father would hold mother "loathly"? Or is this an expression of the panic in Othello—not that Desdemona's eye might roam without this magic handkerchief, but that his might? Does he doubt his own capacity for fidelity?

Desdemona, who has now lost the handkerchief, cannot, or rather does not want to, believe that it can mean more than her word to him. But why can he not trust her? Here he is, with the not unusual doubts of a newly married husband: how is it that this precious creature should love me ... *and only me*? He is desperate that what he has inherited from his mother, whatever it is that held the parental couple together, is kept safe. Since these doubts erode the confidence in his own feelings for Desdemona, she must be the custodian of this mysterious thing. As the scene comes to a conclusion, Desdemona is in a state of shock as Othello shouts with increasing volume "the handkerchief, ... the handkerchief ... the handkerchief!" (III.iv.90–93).

The curse of marriage in Othello's tortured mind is that there is the possible third. It is an idea of marriage as a curse shared by most, if not all, of the couples I have seen in therapy, and an idea, I suggest, shared by all couples throughout the relationship in one way or another. It is an expression of the narcissism from which we all struggle continuously to emerge. And I think that the idea Stanley Cavell introduces that the deflowering of the bride, the wedding night itself, is already a betrayal, suggests that Othello is the picture of one who can bear neither being the excluded third nor being part of an excluding couple, again a familiar picture. What is betrayed? Some idea of a perfect union, a dyad that is perfectly one without the intrusion of any awareness of an other, any contamination of a difference or separateness.

In a fascinating way, Shakespeare creates just such a picture of a "perfect union", but here between Othello and Iago. It culminates in a ceremony, call it an exchange of vows, as the drama of *Othello* reaches a point from which it feels impossible to turn back. Our sense of dread becomes almost unbearable as Iago responds to Othello's pledge, "In due reverence of a sacred vow", with his own pledge, "I am your own forever" (III.iii.468).

## In the due reverence of a sacred vow, I am your own forever

What emerges between Iago and Othello is a perverse version or image of marriage, complete with a "sacred vow". If we can picture a minus—beauteous-object, this, I submit, is a minus-marriage, a narcissistic "marriage" if you please. But before we expose ourselves to "ocular proof" of this version of the fantasy of perfect union, let us first go back to an earlier scene in which Othello's doubts are giving him a headache. Desdemona tries to comfort him but finds that her handkerchief, the talisman meant by Othello's mother to preserve her son's marriage, is too small to bind his suffering head. She drops it. And he says, "let it alone". Why if it is so important does he tell her to leave it, and why does she comply? In terms of the dramatic construction of the play, of course, it makes possible Emilia's finding of the handkerchief and giving it to Iago to seal Othello's suspicion of his bride.

I am glad I have found this napkin;
This was her first remembrance from the Moor,
My wayward husband hath a hundred times
Woo'd me to steal it, but she so love the token,
For he conjur'd her she should ever keep it,
That she reserves it evermore about her,
To kiss, and talk to; I'll ha' the work ta'en out,
And give't Iago: what he'll do with it
Heaven knows, not I,
I know nothing, but for his fantasy.

[III.iii.294–324]

This expression "ha' the work ta'en out" is an interesting one. It is clear in the context of the three times that Shakespeare uses it in this play that it means "copied", that is, copy out the pattern of the handkerchief. Not only does Emilia plan to copy this pattern in the handkerchief, "spotted with strawberries" as we learned from Iago's description, but Cassio also has demanded that his mistress Bianca do the same for him. It is as if Shakespeare were playing with the idea that not only is there a magic talisman that keeps one faithful in love, but that there is something that can be copied, imitated. We have entered a world in which there is little comprehension of emotions, no capacity to think about emotional experience, where love and faithfulness can at most be copied or imitated.

We find in Shakespeare's *Othello* a remarkable picture of what I want to characterize as a perverse version of the idea of marriage in which the "two become one". It is a caricature of the ecstasy of the shared experience of falling-in-love, a state we might describe as a "falling-in-hate", hate being an emotion that can be shared unambiguously. I sometimes wonder with some couples I have seen who share such a profound hatred, such coming together in revenge, whether they may be seeking just that state of oneness they have sought in vain.

I discussed the idealized fantasy of two being or becoming one at the beginning of chapter eleven. Eliot articulates this illusion so eloquently when writing quite openly of his own experience of the falling in love late in his life with the woman who became his second wife: "The breathing in unison / Of lovers / *Who think the same thoughts without need of speech / And babble the same speech without need of meaning*" (Eliot, 1969, p. 7, emphasis added). But the reality is that this illusion cannot be sustained. One couple symbolized this experi-ence for me. They came for therapy complaining of a complete in-ability to understand each other, at odds over everything. Neither was born in this country; they had met here at university, each com-ing from non–English speaking countries and neither originally speaking the language of the other. They had come here to learn English, so when they met they did not share that language either.

But that was no problem! They fell in love with each other in-stantly and felt no need for words. They understood each other per-fectly, and on this point they were agreed. It was bliss. Having never felt understood at home by their respective families, they had at last found someone with whom they could share everything. Eliot's lines amazingly were literally true for them. As one might expect, the problems began as they began to share a language, escalating through the birth of two children, until they found themselves, as I said, at odds over almost literally everything and in despair as they had both cut themselves off from their families and did not know where to turn.

This couple, like the couple we have been discussing, the older black General married to the fair young daughter of a Venetian Sena-tor, epitomized difference. But there is, as I suggested, another cou-ple whose exchange of vows we witness. I want to describe this kind of couple relationship, this image or idea of marriage, as *homophilic*, a term suggested to me by the husband in a couple therapy session. I do not know how widely used this word is, but I think it is apt for the "love of sameness".

Many commentators on *Othello* suggest an unconscious homo-sexual relationship between Iago and Othello, and those who have seen Ian McKellan's portrayal of Iago will appreciate the subtle ways in which he heightens the feelings that support that interpretation. But I am not interested in the question of homosexuality here. In fact, I think that the issue of homosexuality can be misleading since the same-gender object choice does not tell us much, if anything, about the quality of the relating. In my experience of therapy with the few gay couples I have seen, they shared similar struggles with the tri-angular Oedipal dynamics I have been describing in heterosexual couples. The emphasis, I suggest, should be on the "homo" not on the "sexual", on the idea of "same"—for that is what "homo" means, "hetero" meaning "other".

What is striking about the coming together of Iago and Othello, their "falling-in-hate", their marriage of vengeance, is not a sexual passion for someone of the same gender. It is the quality of what they share, what brings them together in the exchange of vows, the hatred and revenge. Only in such a couple might one imagine no ambivalence, entertain no difference, a relationship in which one can *own the other* and *own the other's appetites*!

The ceremony begins as Othello is at last one with Iago in his insinuations against Desdemona, or, one might say, Othello is consciously at one with his internal gang, his "internal Iago":

> Now do I see 'tis true; look here, Iago,
> All my fond love thus do I blow to heaven, . . .
> 'Tis gone.
> Arise, black vengeance, from they hollow cell,
> Yield up, O love, thy crown, and hearted throne,
> To tyrannous hate
>
> [III.iii.451–456]

Love has been dethroned by tyrannous hate. And lest we be in any doubt that the ceremony of the exchange of vows has begun, the stage directions here are for Othello to kneel. With a poetic speech that Swinburne called "one of the most precious jewels that ever the prodigal afterthought of a great poet bestowed upon the rapture of his readers" (cited in Ridley, 1958, p. 121n), Othello vows his single-minded devotion. Iago, like an officiating priest, poses the question that Othello may perhaps change his mind:

> Never, Iago. Like to the Pontic sea,
> Whose icy current, and compulsive course,
> Ne'er feels retiring ebb, but keeps due on
> To the Propontic, and the Hellespont:
> Even so my bloody thoughts, with violent pace
> Shall ne'er look back, ne'er ebb to humble love,
> Till that a capable and wide revenge
> Swallow them up.
>
> [III.iii.460–467]

We have good reason to suspect that Shakespeare offers here an explicit caricature of wedding vows. Othello ends this pledge never to look back, never to give way to "humble love", with a religious oath: "Now by yond marble heaven, / In the due reverence of a sacred vow, / I here engage my words." The adjective "marble" brings to mind the way Othello hardens his heart: ". . . my heart is turn'd to stone; / I strike it, and it hurts my hand" (IV.i.178). And he protests that this is what Desdemona has done:

> O perjur'd woman, thou dost stone they heart
> And makest me call what I intend to do
> A murder, which I thought a sacrifice.
>
> [V.ii.64–66]

His image of Desdemona's "alabaster" skin, whiter than snow, in his "It is the cause" soliloquy, also echoes the image of Hermione turned to stone for sixteen years, as both she and her husband are hardened by hatred and revenge.

The notes in the Arden edition of *Othello*, quote Dr Brooks' suggestion that Othello's reference to marble is appropriate as being "no less unrelenting in its hardness and purity (and demand for purity) than Othello and his vow themselves" (Ridley, 1958, p. 122n). It is the purity of the denial of difference. Purity may have been what Othello sought in his fair and gentle bride, but, disappointed in her flawed reality, he turns against her. As Cavell puts it: "He cannot forgive Desdemona for existing, for being separate from him, outside, beyond command, commanding, her captain's captain" (Cavell, 1987, p. 136). But Othello now finds in his bitter disappointment and rage a "purity" that cannot not fail him. It is the purity of the hatred and revenge that he can now share, perfectly, with his new partner Iago.

At the conclusion of Othello's vow, the stage directions then indicate that Iago should join him in kneeling. He responds with a vow of his own, which continues what seems even more now a caricature of a wedding vow.

> Do not rise yet.
> Witness, you ever-burning lights above,
> You elements that clip us round about,
> Witness that here Iago doth give up
> The excellency of his wit, hand, heart,
> To wrong'd Othello's service: let him command
> And to obey shall be in me remorse,
> What bloody work so ever.
>
> [III.iii.469–476]

The witnesses are called upon to observe Iago's vow, one might say, to love, honour, and obey. And lest anyone protest that there is no pledge of love, Othello responds: "I greet thy love; / Not with vain thanks, but with acceptance bounteous." But what are we to make of this mockery of what we might imagine to have been the vows exchanged but a very short time ago by Othello and Desdemona?

Following the picture we have seen developing, it is as though here we have a "marriage" that can indeed be consummated. Here, the question "are you fast married" will be answered not by the blood-stained sheets of the bridal bed, but by the blood of Cassio. Iago's vow has been to kill him as Othello has demanded. But not Desdemona's blood! Othello vows her death but he will "not shed her blood" (V.ii.3). Would to do so bring too close in his mind the identification of intercourse and murder? It is a question that arises if we can, for a moment, entertain Cavell's disturbing idea which has reverberated throughout our exploration of this play: "The whole scene of murder is built on the concept of sexual intercourse or orgasm as a dying" (Cavell, 1987, p. 134).

Shakespeare paints a remarkable picture of what I am suggesting is a perverse, one might say narcissistic, idea of marriage. This version of a perfect union is a version, as I say, of a marriage that *can* be consummated. That is, it can be consummated in hatred and revenge because in these there can be an unambiguous union. The narcissistic wish for sameness, for perfect purity of oneness, cannot be consummated in the passion and ecstasy of love. That is what Narcissus discovered. And it is worth remembering that that story too ended in death, the perfect union.

There is, however, another way one can imagine to preserve the fantasy of perfection, an unspoiled union. And there is no more eloquent portrayal of it than that of Keats in his "Ode on a Grecian Urn", where we encounter that "still unravish'd bride of quietness".

> Bold Lover, never, never canst thou kiss,
> Though winning near the goal—yet, do not grieve;
> She cannot fade, though thou hast not thy bliss,
> For ever wilt thou love, and she be fair!
>
> [Keats, 1820]

Keats reflects on the figures on an urn, especially the "still unravish'd bride of quietness" captured by the artist frozen in time.

No consummation threatens to spoil the perfection of the moment. To the bridegroom, the poet can say: "For ever wilt thou love, and she be fair!" That is Othello's dilemma. A genuine relationship, with all the ambivalences that mark ordinary intercourse, threatens the purity and perfection for which he longs. Must a perfect union in love be unconsummated? Othello's own solution in the end is, I think, not that of Iago's. And yet in its way it is perhaps even more shocking and disturbing.

Iago's image of marriage turns on a unity of hate and revenge. There can indeed be a unity of destructive feelings, leading to shared destructive action with a kind of perverse purity. However, as Shakespeare demonstrates so acutely, even that unity is unstable, not because it is impossible to sustain a perverse unity of hatred and revenge, but because the object of that hatred and revenge can shift. The contempt that Iago has for Othello, displayed openly in that scene after the successful murder of Desdemona by the latter and the botched murder of Cassio by the former, is matched by the hatred that Othello has for Iago.

Couples, too, seem sometimes almost to share unconsciously Iago's version, or caricature, of marriage, and they can even have a temporary stability in a perversion of their relationship into a "marriage of hatred and revenge", as long, and only as long, as they join in an attack on an object external to the couple. All too often, however, the object of hatred becomes the partner in that "marriage", the hatred and revenge shared only in directing at the other.

But in the end I think that Othello's solution has less to do with Iago's perverse narcissism and more to do with a state of mind that became clearer to me after discovering a striking articulation of what I can now imagine to be Othello's state of mind in Desdemona's bedchamber in that final act.

## Young Eliot's portrait of an Othello

Instead of looking at the conclusion of *Othello*, the scene in which the man "who loved not wisely, but too well" murders the one he loves, I want to turn to an early poem of T. S. Eliot. This poem, *The Love Song of St Sebastian*, remained unpublished until Eliot's second wife,

Mrs Valerie Eliot, and the Eliot Trust gave permission to Christopher Ricks to publish a critical edition, *Inventions of the March Hare* (Eliot, 1996), of the previous unpublished poems from 1909–1917.

This surprisingly shocking early poem of Eliot was written while he was still a graduate student at Harvard. It stands, I think, not only as an articulation of the kind of state of mind one can imagine characteristic of Othello, but also as a shocking antiphonal to a very similar state of mind imaged in John Keats' *Ode on a Grecian Urn*. With a chill we realize that Eliot is imagining achieving a love similarly unspoiled, but here by ensuring that his love was no longer beautiful to anyone but him in a violence echoing Othello.

I cannot quote the entire poem here, but urge the reader to set this poem alongside *Othello*. It begins with the image of a lamp in the night and ends

> I think that at last you would understand.
> There would be nothing more to say.
> You would love me because I should have strangled you
> And because of my infamy;
> And I should love you the more because I had mangled you
> And because you were no longer beautiful
> To anyone but me.
>
> [Eliot, 1914]

## Allowing the object its freedom: the capacity for mourning

I want now to try to use Eliot's disturbingly intimate picture of the mind of "an Othello" to take us back to the question of termination in psychoanalytic therapy with couples. Consider where the line of thought I have been following is leading us. If there is one concept, one experience linked with the termination process in therapy, a process often thought about in terms of the experience of weaning, it is *mourning*.

It will be obvious that I do not intend a systematic exploration of termination in psychoanalytic therapy with couples. Readers who want a more detailed examination of the process in a number of different kinds of ending of therapy may want to consult David and

Jill Scharff's careful analysis (1991, pp. 121, 263–290). My interest here is to understand how an appreciation of the importance of the capacity for mourning helps to make sense not only of the ending of therapy, but also of the beginning of an emergence from narcissism towards marriage. There is undoubtedly a kind of paradox here, but it is only an apparent paradox. It is, in fact, a core conviction of contemporary psychoanalysis that it is a capacity for mourning that allows one to relinquish omnipotent control of the object on the threshold of the depressive position, and to move hopefully towards genuine object relating—a process that we recognize as never finally coming to a permanent resolution.

In one sense, it would seem to be obvious that giving up omnipotent control of the object must involve a process something like mourning. And yet the more one thinks about it, the more one might puzzle. Those familiar with Freud's discussion of mourning in his seminal paper "Mourning and Melancholia", for example, might find it surprising to want to link the process of mourning with an idea of marriage as a capacity for intimacy with someone felt to be genuinely other.

In this 1917 paper, Freud describes how successful mourning is a gradual process of withdrawal of libido from all attachments to the lost loved object in response to the reality that the loved object no longer exists. It is a painful process which cannot take place at once but is carried out, bit by bit, "at great expense of time and cathectic energy":

> Each single one of the memories and expectations in which the libido is bound to the object is brought up and hypercathected, and detachment of the libido is accomplished in respect of it. . . . It is remarkable that this painful unpleasure is taken as a matter of course by us. The fact is, however, that when the work of mourning is completed the ego becomes free and uninhibited again. [Freud, 1917e, p. 253]

How could such a process have anything to do with the intimacy of marriage? In the first place, the loved object is alive, not dead. And in the second place, would not the withdrawal of libidinal attachment mark the end of an important reason for the existence of the marriage?

We might think of mourning in the context of a relationship as a mourning for the omnipotent control of the object, that what is lost is not the object but the control of the object, just as Othello bemoans the ". . . curse of marriage / That we can call these delicate creatures ours, / And not their appetites!" Weaning, for example, is a loss not of the object altogether, but of a particular kind of relationship to the object. Or it is a loss of a "part-object", the breast, and access to it as the source of nourishment.

But there is another way in which we can think about a process similar to what Freud has described, but with important differences. Consider, for example, John Steiner's very clear summary of the view that we might think of a process of mourning connected with the central role of projective identification in pathological object relations. That is, he suggests, we think

> more in terms of detachment of parts of the self from the object rather than in terms of detachment of libido. . . . If mourning can be worked through, the individual becomes more clearly aware of a separateness of self and object and recognizes more clearly what belongs to self and what belongs to the object. When such separateness is achieved it has immense consequences, because with it go other aspects of mental function which we associate with the depressive position, including the development of thinking and symbol formation. [Steiner, 1993, p. 61]

How is it that the process of withdrawing projections, establishing clearer boundaries between oneself and the other person, can leave one feeling uneasy as if one were in the shadow of death? It is almost as if we cannot imagine loss and mourning—even if it is the loss of illusions and projections of parts of the self—without this apprehension of something unbearable.

Of all those who have attempted to describe this process, the person I have found most helpful has been Donald Meltzer. He helps us to make sense of a dimension in the dynamics of mourning to which I think both *Othello* and Eliot's voicing of the agony of an "Othello" point. There is more to this experience than can be captured in our pedestrian language of separation and loss, and concern for the other. I agree with Meltzer that what the poets describe is not to be understood simply as romantic agony:

The aesthetic conflict is different from the romantic agony in this respect: that its central experience of pain resides in uncertainty, tending towards distrust, verging on suspicion. The lover is naked as Othello to the whisperings of Iago, but is rescued by the quest for knowledge, the K-link, the desire to know rather than to possess the object of desire. The K-link points to the value of the desire as itself the stimulus to knowledge, not merely as a yearning for gratification and control over the object. *Desire makes it possible, even essential, to give the object its freedom.* [Meltzer & Williams, 1988, p. 27]

In a little-known paper, Meltzer describes something of the essential nature of this process. Although originally presented to and published internally by the British Psycho-Analytical Society twenty years ago, "A Note on Introjective Processes" only became generally available recently (Meltzer, 1978b, pp. 458–468). I want to explore some of the central ideas in that paper to consider their relevance to the question at hand: termination, mourning, and the idea of marriage I am describing under the picture of *"narcissism ↔ marriage"*.

In this paper, Meltzer juxtaposes a dream of a patient in the termination phase of analysis and John Keats' poem "Ode on a Grecian Urn" in order to cast, as he quotes from Bion, a "beam of darkness" on that most mysterious of processes, the process of taking something inside where it is then reliably available to us, what we call *internalization* or *introjection*. Meltzer describes introjection as "the most important and mysterious concept in psychoanalysis" (Meltzer, 1978b1994, p. 459). He concludes that this process of having something inside available, even essential, for our emotional well-being, call it a good internal object, is itself dependent paradoxically on the capacity that we have good reason to think must be consequent on having such a good internal object—that is, the capacity to let the object go. And yet that is precisely what he says:

> When an object can be given its freedom to come and go as it will, the moment of experience of relationship with that object can be introjected. [Meltzer, 1978b, p. 468]

To make sense of this apparent paradox we must ask what is involved in giving the object its freedom—and, conversely, to be given one's freedom. We can be gripped by these questions only, I think, when we see the importance of the process of introjection.

Meltzer describes a patient's termination dream that provides an image for this experience which he proposes as the experience that makes possible the process of introjection. The dream, which preceded a weekend of country sports, concerned Mr A's experience of a female figure on a broomstick, an "apparition moving at speed", and two women who were heard to say, "Look up quick, or you will miss Mr A" (pp. 460–461). For this man, his interest in hunting and shooting provided an image of relating to the object from which he was clearly moving away, leaving the safety-catch on, forgetting to load his gun, and here in the dream leaving his gun with friends. One has to imagine here a magical attempt to arrest, so to speak, the object, ideally a moving object. It was clear from the material discussed in the paper that there was an increasing concern for the object, no doubt an important aspect of the sense of moving towards termination. From the aim of a "trophy", mounted and displayed, there seems increasingly a wish to preserve the object, given that even a careful shot risks damaging what would then become unappealing as a trophy. A scatter-gun approach spoils the aim of the exercise.

Meltzer offers the image of a "perfect shot" as "the moment when the bullet has left the gun but not yet struck the deer". Mr A is contemplating taking up photography as an alternative hobby, and one can see this as a way to preserve the object, even the moment of contact with the object, without risking the damage shooting with a gun can cause—well, without that risk unless one counts the effect on the critical moment of an experience as the obsessional photographer fiddles to get "the right shot"! What is most striking in Meltzer's discussion is a "dream" in his mind prompted by the dream in his patient's mind:

> Now imagine that you are a baby who sees your mother enter the room, your eyes riveted to the sight of the slight bulge of her nipple in her blouse, and she moves towards you only to seem to rush past and out of sight. Now change what one woman in the booth says to the other from: "Look up quick, or you'll miss Mr A" to a slightly teasing breast, saying: "Look up quick or you'll miss, Mr A". [Meltzer, 1978b, p. 462]

One could think here of what has been described by other writers in terms of "object constancy", the capacity to hold in mind the absent object. But we are being invited to focus on the moment of desire for the object that can be lost, near but just outside the ability of the one who desires it to control it. He suggests this moment as the prototype of the emotional experience seen in terms of the capacity to accept "the object 'coming from afar' and relinquishing it to disappear once again" (p. 466). Against this accepting and letting go is the desperate wish to hold on to that elusive object, that elusive experience.

But the reality is that the desperate wish to "hold on" leads to a crushing, damaging, even destroying of just what is so desperately wanted and needed. The object, and the moment of experience of the object, Meltzer suggests, "satisfies only insofar as the object can be allowed its freedom" (Meltzer, 1978b, p. 466). This way of thinking about the process of introjection, of continuing to have alive inside oneself just what is so fleeting and elusive, is an elaboration, as Meltzer makes clear, of Bion's contribution to our understanding of the development of the mind. And this takes us back to our discussions in chapter two, but now we can see that the facing of emotional reality, ours and the others', involves a capacity to let go.

Think for a moment about what we mean by "mourning". Freud's emphasis on the relinquishing of the loved object involves bringing up each aspect in which the libido is bound to the object. What happens then, in his view, is that the object is "hypercathected", the attachment is intensified, and then the detachment of the libido is accomplished in respect of that aspect. It is a process that goes on until the ego is free of all those libidinal attachments, free to move on to new ones presumably. But is it quite like that? I think that my experience of mourning is slightly different.

Is this "detachment", this "letting go", a giving up of the "libidinal" attachment, to use Freud's language? Or is it more like "giving the object its freedom". When we think about the role of mourning in terms of the withdrawal of projections that Steiner and others describe, that seems more a kind of allowing the object freedom, the freedom to be itself, not filled with my projections. When we think of the painful dynamics of the Oedipal triangle, we might say that what is required is that one tolerate the feelings of being excluded from a couple, giving the couple its freedom, "freedom to be without me"—or to tolerate the uncomfortable feelings of being part of a couple and allowing the third its freedom, freedom perhaps to be unhappy, even aggrieved at being excluded.

Freud seems to have in mind a kind of serial attachment, detaching from one object in order to be free to make a new attachment. There is a certain plausibility to that view, although I must say it has rather the feel of the "either/or", paranoid–schizoid world that we encounter particularly in couples who feel that there is no emotional space in their relationship. Any attachment to an other feels like a betrayal, even when that other is an apparently longed-for child.

Mourning is doubtless a complex set of emotions rather than some simple emotion, but structurally might we not think of it as including a painful letting go, not in the serial sense Freud seems to believe, but in the Oedipal sense? That is, might it involve those painful feelings of an attachment which must make room for the other's other attachments? In a sense, death is the ultimate experience of being excluded, and it can be pictured in Oedipal (or "Leontean") terms. If we think about mourning in this way, it might be seen to have more in common with the process of learning to experience and think about the difficult emotions of the earliest coming to terms with the presence of the third.

Linked with this is the fact that we think of mourning in terms of the emotions of both the loss of the object and the loss of the love of the object. One of the things I have learned most powerfully in my experience of therapy with couples is that even more painful and perplexing than the loss of the object, in the sense of the object's love for me, is the loss of the love of the object in the sense of my loss of *my* love for the object. This was what most disturbed Edward in *The Cocktail Party*, discovering himself as a man who only thought that he was in love, having to face his inability to love. It fit with Lavinia's loss of the love of the young man that she knew all along in her heart of hearts did not love her, because, as she believed, no man could ever love her.

But this brings us to Bion's major contribution to our thinking about emotional reality. We might think, and I imagine that it is a widespread assumption, that in order for an infant to hold in mind the absent object in a non-persecuting way, or for one to be able to tolerate the complex feelings of letting the loved object out of sight, there would have to be a "good-enough experience" with a "good-enough mother". Bion has introduced us to the possibility of considering that it is the *emotional experience* itself that is the basis for the growth of the mind. Meltzer builds his analysis of the process of introjection on this assumption:

> Now this would lead to a very different idea of satisfaction. . . . An experience is "satisfying", by this definition, insofar as it produces an "emotional experience" that can be utilized for thinking. And I am suggesting that this satisfaction, of having something to think about, whether pleasurable or painful, is the essential precondition for introjection. . . . It is clear from the history of our patients that they have often been broken in their development by bad, painful experiences—weaning, birth of the next sibling, the primal scene, death of a loved object. But it is equally apparent from the histories of great men—Keats, for example—that they have been "made" by the acceptance and assimilation of these same events. Equally, we see patients who have been "broken" by good experiences, where they have inflamed megalomania, or conversely, stirred intolerable feelings of gratitude and indebtedness. Freud's "character types met within analysis" could be seen to fall into this category. [Meltzer, 1978b, pp. 466–467]

This takes us to a new understanding of the aim of psychoanalysis and of the criteria for termination, to what Bion characterized abstractly as the presence of the K-link. Let me put it in terms of a question. What or whom was Othello strangling? Or the St Sebastian of T. S. Eliot—what or whom was he strangling? "You would love me because I should have strangled [whom or what?]." "And I should love you the more because I had mangled [whom or what?]." Is it "my emotions"? Is this Othello attempting to regain some peace of mind, strangling his bride in a vain attempt to quieten his intolerable emotions? Are these the painful arrows piercing this St Sebastian, the picture of unimaginable agony in the mind of the young Eliot? Is it his emotional life that is mangled?

The result is seldom the murder portrayed by these poets. Rather, it is more likely to be, as we so often see in our consulting-rooms, a person turned to stone. With couples, it is often one partner hysterically wishing to make some emotional contact with the other partner whose heart turns more and more to stone. It was said of Eliot that he was unconscionably cold in his not visiting Vivienne during all the years in the mental home, the woman said to have a "banshee voice" as she fought to hold on to her disappearing husband. On the cover of Ackroyd's biography of Eliot, A. N. Wilson is quoted commending this "convincing portrait of a subject who was so elusive that he hardly existed" (Ackroyd, 1984). There are many variations, both in the individuals we see and in the couples whose narcissistic relating adds the poignancy that we have seen in the stories we have explored. But what they share in common is an attack on their emotions, the strangling of an acknowledgement and ability to think about them.

The termination process with couples, in my experience, is more varied and, in some ways more difficult, than that with individual patients, largely due to the intersection of the couple and the individual needs. But one way of thinking about the psychoanalytic enterprise with both individuals and couples has at its heart a process, shall we call it "mourning", in which the painful emotions of relating with an *other* who is outside one's omnipotent control can be experienced and thought about. This way of thinking about the analytic process helps give us also a way to think about termination. One could almost describe psychoanalytic therapy as "termination therapy", with its almost continual emphasis on the experience of separations large and small, the dynamics of both being part of a couple that excludes an other, as well as being that excluded third.

Ideally, we might think that when a couple come to a point when they can think together about their emotional experience instead of trying to control the other through intrusive projections or emotional abandonment, they are also ready to be free of the therapy. The couple hopefully have come to a point at which they are able in the dynamics of their relationship to allow the other the kind of emotional freedom that either makes the continued loving presence of the other a gift, or allows the other to leave to form a new relationship. It is sometimes as clear as that—sometimes, but not often.

The hardest situation to judge, in my experience, is when two people are at different stages in this process of giving the other his or her freedom. This is especially critical when one partner is less ready, much less ready, to leave the therapy. Shakespeare's portrait of the despair of these emotions of not being able to bear separation in the figure of Othello is, in my experience, painfully accurate. It means that, when it comes to endings, I would now err on the side of caution.

## A gracious couple, begetting wonder: it has begun

To end in the mood of Eliot's St Sebastian or Shakespeare's Othello might represent some of the painful reality of therapy with couples, as every couple therapist would, I think, acknowledge. But is it possible to find a link with the end of The Winter's Tale, the story with which we began, which makes plausible a picture of a genuine emergence from narcissism towards marriage? One way to consider that question is to return to the final act of The Cocktail Party.

In my reading of Eliot's play, I have for a long time felt myself agreeing with most critics—including the poet himself and most of his strongest supporters—that the ending was, for the most part, a dramatic failure. The emotional distance is dramatically implausible, the distance between this couple, Edward and Lavinia, two years after their brief "therapeutic" encounter with Sir Henry Harcourt-Reilly, Spender's "eminence grise of the psycho-analytical world", and young Celia, reported to have been "crucified very near an ant-hill". It is the distance between the all-too-ordinary and the something almost other-worldly. For example, we find Edward and Lavinia preparing for another cocktail party. Then we are told, it is their destiny. But now, as we look more closely at this ending, I am not so sure.

At the conclusion of Act II, Reilly and Julia are discussing the outcome of their interventions with the couple, Edward and Lavinia, and with Celia. Having just finished that intense session with Celia, Reilly says: "And when I say to one like her / 'Work out your salvation with diligence', I do not understand / What I myself am saying." Julia responds like the good supervisor she seems to be: "You must accept your limitations." Reilly petulantly protests at her supervisor's role: "When I express confidence in anything / You always raise doubts; when I am apprehensive / Then you see no reason for anything but confidence" (Eliot, 1950, pp. 144–145, II.781–783, 777–779). I am not sure what my supervisees would say, but I know that termination is as a difficult time for the supervisor as it is for the therapist. Nevertheless, we must move to the ending.

After two years, the couple seem to have changed. Reilly had actually been more worried about them than about Celia, perhaps because in his own life Eliot could see himself more in the role of the martyr than in the kind of domestic life that Reilly foresees for Edward and Lavinia. They are the ones, he tells Julia, that he worries about sending back to their life together. These are his termination anxieties:

> To send them back: what have they to go back to?
> To the stale food mouldering in the larder,
> The stale thoughts mouldering in their minds.
> Each unable to disguise his own meanness
> From himself, because it is known to the other.
> It's not the knowledge of the mutual treachery
> But the knowledge that the other understands the motive—
> Mirror to mirror, reflecting vanity.
> I have taken a great risk.
>
> [pp. 142–143, II.742–750]

But the couple have chosen, as Celia has chosen. Reilly concludes: "They accept their destiny." And what is that destiny?

In correspondence about the final act with Martin Browne the director, Eliot makes clear that he is willing to rewrite the ending so that the final scene takes place after all the cocktail party guests had left, except, of course for the key figures. But he adds that he timed it as the unexpected arrival of these key figures before the party begins: "It seems to me to add to the point of the scene for the audience to have in mind that my people have got to go on with the party in spite of everything" (letter dated 15 March 1949, quoted in Coghill, 1974, p. 196).

That is their destiny, but how have they changed? They each now seem more able to make emotional space for the other in a way that would have seemed impossible before, Edward in the presence of his wife to speak of his feeling responsible for what happened to Celia, and Lavinia able to acknowledge her husband's feelings and even feel regret over having been unkind to Celia. There are, in addition, two specific changes. One change is noted right at the beginning as Edward and Lavinia relax before the guests arrive. Edward has joked about Lavinia ringing him earlier, to reassure him "That you hadn't run away?", he quips, in a way that makes clear how much emotional freedom they now have with each other. And then Edward, clearly unprompted by Lavinia, tells her that he likes the dress she is wearing. She responds, surprised and pleased—it is the first time he has paid her a compliment *before a party*, and that, she says, is when one needs them! (pp. 149–150, III.20–24).

The other change is more subtle and, in fact, may go unnoticed by most audiences. Eliot was perhaps unsure of making a big point of it, or perhaps he just liked the idea that only some would see the interpretation he alluded to. If I am not mistaken, the 1986 London production of *The Cocktail Party* took Eliot's hints and played this last scene with Lavinia subtly, but clearly, pregnant. Some have based this interpretation on Edward's responding to her worrying that he was tired by saying: "It's you who should be tired." A very slim clue indeed.

Having learned so much about the workings of Eliot's mind from the recent publication of the correspondence from 1898–1922 (Eliot, 1988), we can anticipate that we will learn much more when the subsequent volumes are published. But we are fortunate that Nevill Coghill was given permission to publish some of the Eliot correspondence to do with *The Cocktail Party* (Coghill, 1974). He quotes, for example, from a letter from Sir Geoffrey Faber, to which I have already referred, in which Sir Geoffrey objects to a view of marriage which was "an over-simplification which came near to being a falsification". This, he imagines, is because it concentrates "upon a marital relationship which doesn't seem even to contain the idea of children". Eliot replied on 29 August 1949:

> Oh, and as for Lavinia, I thought it was obvious, from one line at the end of Act III [which became Act Two] and one line in the opening dialogue of Act IV [which became Act Three], that Lavinia was going to have a baby. At her age, I fear it will be an only child. . . . [quoted in Coghill, 1974, p. 192]

The second line to which Eliot refers is surely the one I have already quoted about Lavinia needing to rest. The first, I think, is in Julia's lines in the "libation" scene at the end of Act Two: "May the holy ones watch over the roof, / May the Moon herself influence the bed" (II.796–797). It is not surprising to me that Eliot pictures Lavinia as expecting a baby. I have already noted at the end of chapter eight the language in which he describes the conception, gestation, and delivery of this play with the image of a newborn child. Even more striking is his response to Sir Geoffrey's praise: "I think the play a masterpiece, and as a sexagenarian I am now qualified to express my admiration—not to say sheer envy—of your power of making new growth."

I am specially gratified by what you say of "power of making new growth". This meant a lot to me, because I had always believed a Nobel Prize to be a sort of advance death certificate, and I was putting everything I had into this play in the effort to keep alive. [letter dated 15 March 1949, quoted in Coghill, 1974, p. 190]

The point, I suggest, about new life, a new beginning, for Lavinia and Edward, is not whether this couple actually has a child or not, but whether, as Sir Geoffrey said, they have a marital relationship that contains the *idea* of a child. That is, it is a question of whether their idea of marriage is an imaging of intercourse, creative intercourse, or a sterile insistence on identification, a being the same. Ronald Britton puts the point eloquently:

"Marriage", whether celebrated or uncelebrated, socially contracted or uncontracted, or simply conspicuous by its absence, remains at the centre of "family life". I think it does so because the idea of a couple coming together to produce a child is central in our psychic life, whether we aspire to it, object to it, realize we are produced by it, deny it, relish it, or hate it. [Britton, 1995, p. xi]

One can read Eliot's *The Cocktail Party* as insisting that in the end there are two mutually exclusive ways. One is linked with, to return to Shelley's images, "Dreams and the light imaginings of men, / And all that faith creates or love desires, / Terrible, strange, sublime and beauteous shapes". It is described by Meltzer in his apt phrase, the "apprehension of beauty". The other seems a poor alternative indeed, this "making the best of a bad job". It sounds less like the realism of the depressive position than a hollow, life-defeating dichotomy.

The temptation is to read *The Cocktail Party* as an either/or, as if it were biography describing the reality of these exclusive options for its central characters. I think one could also say of Shelley's *Prometheus Unbound* or Keats' *Ode on a Grecian Urn* that both seem to be juxtaposing the beautiful as unattainable with the ordinary, the mundane, which is all too attainable. That might be to read these poems as expressions of a romantic agony. But might we also think that, when these poets portray this dichotomy as one that can be brought together only after death, they are creating for us an image of what may feel beyond us, but something to which we can aspire. Aspire, that is, in the sense of allowing some kind of intercourse between them. And we can have this aspiration because we can at least have an image of it thanks to our poets.

Eliot concludes *The Cocktail Party* with the special guests, Alex and Julia and Peter, and the *"Uninvited Guest"* Reilly, all taking their leave. Reilly says that it is right that the Chamberlaynes should be giving a party. Lavinia is glad that Alex told them about Celia, but now she is uncertain how to face their guests. Edward thinks that he understands something:

> Oh, it isn't much
> That I understand yet! But Sir Henry has been saying,
> I think, that every moment is a fresh beginning;
> And Julia, that life is only keeping on;
> And somehow, the two ideas seem to fit together.
>
> [p. 179, III.535–539]

Lavinia still doesn't want to see these people who are about to arrive, but Reilly responds: "It is your appointed burden." Edward and Lavinia are left alone to face the party. I will leave the penultimate word to Eliot and to those two creatures of his imagination, the husband and his pregnant wife, and the image of a marriage:

> Edward, how am I looking?
> I might almost say, your best. But you always look your best.
> Oh, Edward, that spoils it. No woman can believe
> That she always looks her best. You're rather transparent,
> You know, when you're trying to cheer me up.
> To say I always look my best can only mean the worst.
> I never shall learn how to pay a compliment.
> What you should have done was to admire my dress.
> But I've already told you how much I like it.
> But so much has happened since then. And besides,
> One sometimes likes to hear the same compliment twice.
> And now for the party.
>             Now for the party.
> It will soon be over.
>             I wish it would begin.
> There's the doorbell.
>             Oh, I'm glad. It has begun.
>
> [pp. 180–181, III. 548–561]

*It has begun.* Were we to take this as a picture of a marriage renewed, an emergence out of narcissism towards marriage, we must, I think, return to the question that we have been exploring throughout this book. What allows for the possibility of re-marriage here? Returning, in our imagination, to Leontes and *The Winter's Tale*, do we not find here a similar theme of remorse for attacks on the reality of internal objects as well as external objects? We have seen that, in effect, this attack on the reality of the other becomes a destructive attack on an internal couple, an inability to give that couple its freedom. And, in a further stretch of imagination, might we picture Edward joining Leontes both in his remorse and in his speech of wonder? Would Edward, this father-to-be, with his unexpectedly pregnant wife Lavinia, have had a dream of loss and remorse? And might this suggest that this beginning for Edward and Lavinia, or should we say this beginning again, is grounded in an unconscious acknowledgement of the gracious internal couple?

> O, alas!
> I lost a couple, that 'twixt heaven and earth
> Might thus have stood, begetting wonder, as
> You, gracious couple, do.
>
> [*The Winter's Tale*, V.i.130–133]

# REFERENCES

Ackerman, N. W. (1958). *The Psychodynamics of Family Life*. New York: Basic Books.

Ackroyd, P. (1984). *T. S. Eliot*. London: Hamish Hamilton. [Reprinted Penguin Books, 1993.]

Adams, M. (1997). The understudy: a case of adhesive identification. *Journal of the British Association of Psychotherapists*, 33 (2, Part 2): 53–71.

Adams, M. (1999). Turning a blind eye: misrepresentation and the denial of life events. In: S. Ruszczynski & S. Johnson (Eds.), *Contemporary Psychoanalytic Psychotherapy in the Kleinian Tradition*. London: Karnac Books.

Adelman, J. (1992). *Suffocating Mothers: Fantasies of Maternal Origin in Shakespeare's Plays, Hamlet to The Tempest*. London: Routledge.

Barker, P. (1993). *The Eye in the Door*. Harmondsworth, Middlesex: Penguin Books.

Bion, W. R. (1967). *Second Thoughts*. London: Heinemann. [Reprinted London: Karnac Books, 1987.]

Bion, W. R. (1970). *Attention and Interpretation*. London: Tavistock. [Reprinted London: Karnac Books, 1984.]

Britton, R. (1989). The missing link: parental sexuality in the Oedipus complex. In: J. Steiner (Ed.), *The Oedipus Complex Today: Clinical Implications* (pp. 83–101). London: Karnac Books.

Britton, R. (1995). Preface. In: S. Ruszczynski & J. Fisher (Eds.), *Intrusiveness and Intimacy in the Couple* (pp. xi–xiii). London: Karnac Books.

Browne, E. M. (1966). *The Making of a Play: T. S. Eliot's "The Cocktail Party"*. Cambridge: Cambridge University Press.

Burne, G. S. (Tr. & Ed.) (1966). *Selected Writings of Remy de Gourmont*. Ann Arbor, MI: University of Michigan Press.

Bush, R. (1984). *T. S. Eliot: A Study in Character and Style*. Oxford: Oxford University Press.

Campbell, D. (1998). *Ideas Which Divide the Tavistock: What Are They Really About?* Scientific meeting audiotape, Tavistock Clinic Library, 12 January.

Caper, R. (1992). Does psychoanalysis heal? A contribution to the theory of psychoanalytic technique. *International Journal of Psycho-Analysis, 73*: 283–292.

Casement, P. (1985). *On Learning from the Patient*. London: Tavistock Publications.

Cavell, S. (1987). *Disowning Knowledge: In Six Plays of Shakespeare*. Cambridge: Cambridge University Press.

Coghill, N. (1974). Commentary. In: T. S. Eliot, *The Cocktail Party*, edited by N. Coghill. London: Faber & Faber.

Colman, W. (1993). Marriage as a psychological container. In: S. Ruszczynski (Ed.), *Psychotherapy with Couples: Theory and Practice at the Tavistock Institute of Marital Studies* (pp. 70–96). London: Karnac Books.

Colman, W. (1995). Gesture and recognition: an alternative model to projective identification as a basis for couple relationships. In: S. Ruszczynski & J. Fisher (Eds.), *Intrusiveness and Intimacy in the Couple* (pp. 50–59). London: Karnac Books.

Deutsch, H. (1942). Some forms of emotional disturbances and their relationship to schizophrenia. *Psychoanalytic Quarterly, 11*: 301–321. [Also in: *Neurosis and Character Types: Clinical Psychoanalytic Studies*, New York: International Universities Press, 1965.]

Dicks, H. V. (1953). Experiences with marital tension seen in the psychological clinic. *British Journal of Medical Psychology, 26*: 181–96.

Dicks, H. V. (1967). *Marital Tensions: Clinical Studies towards a Psychological Theory of Interaction*. London: Routledge & Kegan Paul [Reprinted London: Karnac Books, 1993.]

Dutton, D., Saunders, K., Starzomski, A., & Bartholomew, K. (1994). Intimacy-anger and insecure attachment as precursors of abuse in intimate relationships. *Journal of Applied Social Psychology*, 24 (15): 1367–1386.

Eliot, T. S. (1914). *The Love Song of St Sebastian*. In: *Inventions of the March Hare: Poems 1909–1917*, edited by C. Ricks. London: Faber & Faber, 1996.

Eliot, T. S. (1919). *Hamlet*. In: *Selected Prose of T. S. Eliot* (pp. 45–49), edited by F. Kermode. London: Faber & Faber, 1975.

Eliot, T. S. (1920). *The Sacred Wood*. London: Faber & Faber.

Eliot, T. S. (1922). *The Waste Land*. In: *Collected Poems 1909–1962*. London: Faber & Faber, 1963.

Eliot, T. S. (1925). *The Hollow Men*. In: *Collected Poems 1909–1962*. London: Faber & Faber, 1963.

Eliot, T. S. (1926/32). *Sweeney Agonistes*. In: *Collected Poems 1909–1962*. London: Faber & Faber, 1963.

Eliot, T. S. (1933). *The Use of Poetry and the Use of Criticism*. London: Faber & Faber.

Eliot, T. S. (1935a). *Burnt Norton*. In: *Collected Poems 1909–1962*. London: Faber & Faber, 1963.

Eliot, T. S. (1935b). *Murder in the Cathedral*. London: Faber & Faber.

Eliot, T. S. (1939). *The Family Reunion*. London: Faber & Faber.

Eliot, T. S. (1950). *The Cocktail Party*. London: Faber & Faber.

Eliot, T. S. (1951). Poetry and drama. In: *Selected Prose of T. S. Eliot* (pp. 132–147), edited by F. Kermode. Faber & Faber, 1975.

Eliot, T. S. (1953). Lecture: three voices of poetry. In: *Selected Prose of T. S. Eliot*, edited by F. Kermode. London: Faber & Faber, 1975.

Eliot, T. S. (1954). *The Confidential Clerk*. London: Faber & Faber.

Eliot, T. S. (1959). Interview with Donald Hall. *The Paris Review*, 21 (Spring/Summer). [Also in: G. Plimpton (Ed.), *Writers at Work: The Paris Review Interviews* (second series, pp. 89–110). Harmondsworth, Middlesex: Penguin Books, 1963.]

Eliot, T. S. (1963). *Collected Poems 1909–1962*. London: Faber & Faber.

Eliot, T. S. (1969). *The Elder Statesman*. London: Faber & Faber.

Eliot, T. S. (1988). *The Letters of T. S. Eliot, Vol. 1: 1898–1922*, edited by V. Eliot. London: Faber & Faber.

Eliot, T. S. (1996). *Inventions of the March Hare: Poems 1909–1917*, edited by C. Ricks. London: Faber & Faber.

Euripides (n.d.). *Alcestis*. In: D. Greene & R. Lattimore (Eds.), *The Complete Greek Tragedies*. Chicago, IL: University of Chicago Press, 1955.

Feldman, M. (1989). The Oedipus complex: manifestations in the inner world and the therapeutic situation. In: J. Steiner (Ed.), *The Oedipus Complex Today: Clinical Implications* (pp. 103–128). London: Karnac Books.

Fisher, J. (1993). The impenetrable other: ambivalence and the oedipal conflict in work with couples. In: S. Ruszczynski (Ed.), *Psychotherapy with Couples: Theory and Practice at the Tavistock Institute of Marital Studies* (pp. 142–166). London: Karnac Books.

Fisher, J. (1996). *The Domain of the Self*. Scientific meeting audiotape, Tavistock Clinic Library, 13 May.

Freud, A. (1936). Identification with the aggressor. In: *The Ego and the Mechanisms of Defense* (pp. 109–121). London: Hogarth Press, 1979.

Freud, S. (1905d). *Three Essays on the Theory of Sexuality*. S.E. 7.

Freud, S. (1909c). Family romances. S.E. 9.

Freud, S. (1910h). A special type of choice of object made by men. S.E. 11.

Freud, S. (1915c). *Instincts and their Vicissitudes*. S.E. 14.

Freud, S. (1917e). Mourning and melancholia. S.E. 14.

Freud, S. (1925h). Negation. S.E. 19.

Gaddini, E. (1969). On imitation. In: A. Limentani (Ed.), *A Psychoanalytic Theory of Infantile Experience: Conceptual and Clinical Reflections* (pp. 18–34). London: Routledge, 1992.

Gordon, L. (1977). *Eliot's Early Years*. Oxford: Oxford University Press.

Gordon, L. (1988). *Eliot's New Life*. Oxford: Oxford University Press.

Graves, R. (1955). *The Greek Myths* (combined vol.). London: Penguin Books, 1992.

Greene, R. (1588). *Pandosto*. In: *The Winter's Tale* (Appendix IV, pp. 181–225), edited by J. H. P. Pafford. *The Arden Edition of the Works of William Shakespeare*. London: Routledge, 1996.

Gribinski, M. (1994). The stranger in the house. *International Journal of Psycho-Analysis, 75*: 1011–1021.

Grotjahn, M. (1965). Family interviews as an aid to psychoanalytic therapy. In: *Forest Hospital Publications, 3*: 34–40.

Henry, O. (1906). *The Gift of the Magi*. New York: Dover Publications, 1992.

Hess, N. (1987). King Lear and some anxieties of old age. *British Journal of Medical Psychology, 60*: 209–215.

Hinshelwood, R. (1991). *The Dictionary of Kleinian Thought*. London: Free Association Books.

Hobson, P. (1993). *Autism and the Development of Mind*. Hove: Lawrence Erlbaum Associates.

Jones, D. E. (1960). *The Plays of T.S. Eliot*. London: Routledge & Kegan Paul.

Joseph, B. (1971). A clinical contribution to the analysis of perversion. In: E. Bott Spillius & M. Feldman (Eds.), *Psychic Equilibrium and Psychic*

*Change: Selected Papers of Betty Joseph* (pp. 51–56). London: Tavistock/ Routledge, 1989.

Joseph, B. (1975). The patient who is difficult to reach. In: E. Bott Spillius & M. Feldman (Eds.), *Psychic Equilibrium and Psychic Change: Selected Papers of Betty Joseph* (pp. 75–87). London: Tavistock/Routledge, 1989.

Joseph, B. (1983). On understanding and not understanding: some technical issues. In: E. Bott Spillius & M. Feldman (Eds.), *Psychic Equilibrium and Psychic Change: Selected Papers of Betty Joseph* (pp. 139–150). London: Tavistock/Routledge, 1989.

Joseph, B. (1989). *Psychic Equilibrium and Psychic Change: Selected Papers of Betty Joseph*, edited by E. Bott Spillius & M. Feldman. London: Tavistock/Routledge.

Kafka, F. (1933). *Metamorphosis and Other Stories*, transl. by W. Muir & E. Muir. New York: Schocken Books. [Reprinted London: Penguin Books, 1961.]

Keats, J. (1820). *Poems, Selections: Oxford Poetry Library*, edited by E. Cook. Oxford: Oxford University Press, 1994.

Kenner, H. (1959). *The Invisible Poet: T. S. Eliot*. London: Methuen.

Klein, M. (1926). The psychological principles of early analysis. In: *Love, Guilt and Reparation and Other Works 1921–1945. The Writings of Melanie Klein, Vol. 1* (pp. 128–138). London: Hogarth Press, 1975. [Reprinted London: Karnac Books, 1992.]

Klein, M. (1927). Symposium on child analysis. In: *Love, Guilt and Reparation and Other Works 1921–1945. The Writings of Melanie Klein, Vol. 1* (pp. 139–169). London: Hogarth Press, 1975. [Reprinted London: Karnac Books, 1992.]

Klein, M. (1930). The importance of symbol-formation in the development of the ego. In: *Love, Guilt and Reparation and Other Works 1921–1945. The Writings of Melanie Klein, Vol. 1* (pp. 219–232). London: Hogarth Press, 1975. [Reprinted London: Karnac Books, 1992.]

Klein, M. (1945). The Oedipus complex in the light of early anxieties. In: *Love, Guilt and Reparation and Other Works 1921–1945. The Writings of Melanie Klein, Vol. 1* (pp. 370–419). London: Hogarth Press, 1975. [Reprinted London: Karnac Books, 1992. Also in: J. Steiner (Ed.), *The Oedipus Complex Today: Clinical Implications* (pp. 11–82). London: Karnac Books, 1989.]

Klein, M. (1946). Notes on some schizoid mechanisms. In: *Envy and Gratitude and Other Works. The Writings of Melanie Klein, Vol. 3* (pp. 1–24). London: Hogarth Press, 1975. [Reprinted London: Karnac Books, 1993.]

Laing, R. D., Phillipson, H., & Lee, A. R. (1966). *Interpersonal Perception: A Theory and a Method of Research*. London: Tavistock Publications.

Laplanche, J., & Pontalis, J.-B. (1973). *The Language of Psycho-Analysis*. London: Hogarth Press. [Reprinted London: Karnac Books, 1988.]

Larousse (1959). *The New Larousse Encyclopedia of Mythology*. London: Hamlyn.

Lattimore, R. (1955). Introduction. In: D. Greene & R. Lattimore (Eds.), *Euripides—I: Alcestis, The Media, The Heracleidae, Hippolytus* (pp. 2–5). Chicago, IL: University of Chicago Press.

Meltzer, D. (1966). The relation of anal masturbation to projective identification. *International Journal of Psycho-Analysis, 47*: 335–342. [Also in: E. Bott Spillius (Ed.), *Melanie Klein Today: Developments in Theory and Practice, Vol. 1* (pp. 102–116). London: Routledge, 1988.

Meltzer, D. (1967). *The Psycho-Analytical Process*. Perthshire: Clunie Press.

Meltzer, D. (1976). The delusion of clarity of insight. *International Journal of Psycho-Analysis, 57*: 141–146. [Also in: *The Claustrum: An Investigation of Claustrophobic Phenomena* (pp. 74–85). Perthshire: Clunie Press, 1992.

Meltzer, D. (1978a). *The Kleinian Development*. Perthshire: Clunie Press. [Reprinted London: Karnac Books, 1998.]

Meltzer, D. (1978b). A note on introjective processes. In: *Sincerity and Other Works: Collected Papers of Donald Meltzer* (pp. 458–468), edited by A. Hahn. London: Karnac Books, 1994.]

Meltzer, D. (1981). The Kleinian expansion of Freudian meta-psychology. *International Journal of Psycho-Analysis, 62*: 177–185.

Meltzer, D. (1983). *Dream-Life: A Re-examination of the Psycho-Analytical Theory and Technique*. Perthshire: Clunie Press.

Meltzer, D. (1986). The psychoanalytic process: twenty years on, the setting of the analytic encounter and the gathering of the transference. In: *Sincerity and Other Works: Collected Papers of Donald Meltzer* (pp. 551–556), edited by A. Hahn. London: Karnac Books, 1994.

Meltzer, D. (1992). *The Claustrum: An Investigation of Claustrophobic Phenomena*. Perthshire: Clunie Press.

Meltzer, D. (1994). *Sincerity and Other Works: Collected Papers of Donald Meltzer*, edited by A. Hahn. London: Karnac Books.

Meltzer, D. (1995). Donald Meltzer in discussion with James Fisher. In: S. Ruszczynski & J. Fisher (Eds.), *Intrusiveness and Intimacy in the Couple*. London: Karnac Books.

Meltzer, D., et al. (1975). *Explorations in Autism: A Psycho-Analytic Study*. Perthshire: Clunie Press.

Meltzer, D., et al. (1986). *Studies in Extended Metapsychology: Clinical Applications of Bion's Ideas*. Perthshire: Clunie Press.

Meltzer, D., & Williams, M. H. (1988). *The Apprehension of Beauty*. Perthshire: Clunie Press.

Money-Kyrle, R. E. (1971). The aim of psychoanalysis, *International Journal of Psycho-Analysis*, 52: 103–106. [Also in: *The Collected Papers of Roger Money-Kyrle* (pp. 442–449). Perthshire: Clunie Press, 1978.]

Morgan, M. (1995). The projective gridlock: a form of projective identification in couple relationships. In: S. Ruszczynski & J. Fisher (Eds.), *Intrusiveness and Intimacy in the Couple* (pp. 33–48). London: Karnac Books.

Neely, C. (1978). Women and issue in "The Winter's Tale". *Philological Quarterly*, 57: 182–183. [Also in: C. Neely, *Broken Nuptials in Shakespeare's Plays* (pp. 193–194). New Haven, CT: Yale University Press, 1985.]

O'Shaughnessy, E. (1989). The invisible Oedipus complex. In: J. Steiner (Ed.), *The Oedipus Complex Today: Clinical Implications* (pp. 129–150). London: Karnac Books.

Pincus, L. (Ed.) (1960). *Marriage: Studies in Emotional Conflict and Growth*. London: Tavistock Marital Studies Institute.

Pinkney, T. (1984). *Women in the Poetry of T. S. Eliot*. London: Macmillan.

Plimpton, G. (Ed.) (1963). *Writers at Work: The Paris Review Interviews* (second series). London: Penguin Books.

Racker, H. (1968). *Transference and Countertransference*. London: Hogarth Press.

Rascovsky, E., & Rascovsky, M. (1972). The prohibition of incest, filicide and the sociocultural process. *International Journal of Psycho-Analysis*, 53: 271–276.

Rey, J. H. (1988). That which patients bring to analysis. *International Journal of Psycho-Analysis*, 69: 457–470. [Also in: J. H. Rey, *Universals of Psychoanalysis in the Treatment of Psychotic and Borderline States*, edited by J. Magagna (pp. 229–248). London: Free Association Books, 1994.]

Ridley, M. R. (Ed.) (1958). *Othello. The Arden Edition of the Works of William Shakespeare*. London: Methuen, 1986.

Riviere, J. (1936). A contribution to the analysis of the negative therapeutic reaction. *International Journal of Psycho-Analysis*, 17: 304–320. [Also in: A. Hughes (Ed.), *The Inner World of Joan Riviere: Collected Papers 1920–1958* (pp. 134–153). London: Karnac Books, 1991.]

Robertson, J., & Robertson, J. (1953). *A Two-Year-Old Goes to Hospital*. Ipswich: Concord Films Council.

Rosenfeld, H. (1947). Analysis of a schizophrenic state with depersonalization. *International Journal of Psycho-Analysis, 28*: 130–139. [Also in: *Psychotic States* (pp. 13–33). London: Hogarth Press, 1965; reprinted London: Karnac Books, 1985.]

Rosenfeld, H. (1965). *Psychotic States.* London: Hogarth Press. [Reprinted London: Karnac Books, 1985.]

Rosenfeld, H. (1987). *Impasse and Interpretation.* London: Tavistock Publications.

Rothstein, A. (1992). Observations on the utility of couples therapy conducted by a psychoanalyst—transference and countertransference in resistance to analysis. *Psychoanalytic Quarterly, 59*: 519–541.

Ruszczynski, S. (Ed.) (1993). *Psychotherapy with Couples: Theory and Practice at the Tavistock Institute of Marital Studies.* London: Karnac Books.

Ruszczynski, S., & Fisher, J. (Eds.) (1995). *Intrusiveness and Intimacy in the Couple.* London: Karnac Books.

Sanders, K. (1978). Shakespeare's *The Winter's Tale*—and some notes on the analysis of a present-day Leontes. *International Review of Psycho-Analysis, 5*: 175–177.

Scharff, D., & Scharff, J. S. (1991). *Object Relations Couple Therapy.* New York: Jason Aronson.

Segal, H. (1955). Notes on symbol formation. *International Journal of Psycho-Analysis, 38*: 391–397. [Also in: *Melanie Klein Today: Developments in Theory and Practice, Vol. 1: Mainly Theory* (pp. 160–177). London: Routledge.]

Sencourt, R. (1971). *T. S. Eliot: A Memoir*, edited by D. Adamson. London: Garnstone Press.

Shelley, P. B. (1820). *Prometheus Unbound.* In: *Shelley: Complete Poetical Works* (pp. 204–270). London: Oxford University Press, 1971.

Sigg, E. (1994). Eliot as a product of America. In: A. D. Moody (Ed.), *The Cambridge Companion to T. S. Eliot* (pp. 14–30). Cambridge: Cambridge University Press.

Spender, S. (1975). *Eliot.* Fontana Modern Masters. London: Fontana Press.

Steiner, J. (1989). The aim of psychoanalysis. *Psychoanalytic Psychotherapy, 4*: 109–120.

Steiner, J. (1993). *Psychic Retreats: Pathological Organizations in Psychotic, Neurotic and Borderline Patients.* London: Routledge.

Stokoe, P. (1995). *Can Working with a Couple Ever Be Described as Psychoanalysis?* Unpublished paper, Society of Psychoanalytical Marital Psychotherapists.

Teruel, G. (1966). Considerations for a diagnosis in marital psychotherapy. *British Journal of Medical Psychology, 39*: 231–236.

Trosman, H. (1974). T. S. Eliot and *The Waste Land*. *Archive of General Psychiatry*, *30*: 709–717.

Tustin, F. (1991). Revised understandings of psychogenic autism. *International Journal of Psycho-Analysis*, *72*: 585–592.

Vendler, H. (1980). T. S. Eliot. In: *Part of Nature, Part of Us: Modern American Poets* (pp. 77–85). Cambridge, MA: Harvard University Press.

Welldon, E. (1988). *Mother, Madonna, Whore: The Idealization and Denigration of Motherhood*. London: Free Association Books.

Williams, R. (1968). *Culture and Society: 1780 – 1950*. New York: Columbia University Press, 1983.

Williams, M. H., & Waddell, M. (1991). *The Chamber of Maiden Thought: Literary Origins of the Psychoanalytic Model of the Mind*. London: Routledge.

Winnicott, D. W. (1965). Ego distortion in terms of true and false self. In: *The Maturational Process and the Facilitating Environment* (pp. 140–152). London: Hogarth Press.

# INDEX